Safety Regulation in International Aviation Law

This book analyses the complex regulations and standards governing aviation safety on a global scale. Combining theoretical analysis with practical insights, it offers a comprehensive exploration of the normative foundations and real-world applications of international aviation law in ensuring air travel safety.

From the foundational principles established by the Chicago Convention to the evolving challenges posed by technological advancements and geopolitical shifts, this book provides a nuanced understanding of the complex legal landscape shaping aviation safety. Through in-depth critical analysis, the book examines the role of key stakeholders – including states, international and regional organizations, and regulatory bodies – in promoting and enforcing safety standards. By exploring the intersection of legal theory and practice, this book sheds light on the practical implications of normative principles in addressing contemporary safety concerns, such as the COVID-19 pandemic. It encourages the regional institutionalization of civil aviation in order to improve local and regional aviation safety.

The book will be of interest to researchers, practitioners, and policymakers seeking to navigate the legal frameworks and ethical considerations underpinning aviation safety law.

Grzegorz K. Zając holds a PhD in social sciences, specializing in aviation law, aviation safety, and international relations. He has published over 50 academic works in Polish and English and serves on the editorial boards of the *Journal of International Trade, Logistics and Law* and the *International Journal of Commerce and Finance*. A member of the Polish Association for European Law, he participates in and organizes numerous international conferences. With extensive leadership experience, he has held positions such as Director of the Institute of International Relations and Head of International Cooperation at various universities.

Routledge Research in Air and Space Law

International Aviation Labour Law
Andrea Trimarchi

The Law and Regulation of Airspace Liberalisation in Brazil
What is the Way Forward?
Delphine Defossez
Aviation Law and Governance

Navigating Global Challenges and Conflicts
Jędrzej Górski and Yun Zhao

Safety Regulation in International Aviation Law
Normative Aspects of Safety
Grzegorz K. Zając

For more information about this series, please visit:
www.routledge.com/Routledge-Research-in-Air-and-Space-Law/book-series/SPACELAW

Safety Regulation in International Aviation Law

Normative Aspects of Safety

Grzegorz K. Zając

Routledge
Taylor & Francis Group
LONDON AND NEW YORK

First published 2025
by Routledge
4 Park Square, Milton Park, Abingdon, Oxon OX14 4RN

and by Routledge
605 Third Avenue, New York, NY 10158

Routledge is an imprint of the Taylor & Francis Group, an informa business

British Library Cataloguing-in-Publication Data
A catalogue record for this book is available from the British Library

ISBN: 978-1-032-89016-6 (hbk)
ISBN: 978-1-032-90413-9 (pbk)
ISBN: 978-1-003-55787-6 (ebk)

DOI: 10.4324/9781003557876

Typeset in Times New Roman
by Deanta Global Publishing Services, Chennai, India

Contents

	Figures	*vi*
	Tables	*vii*
	Acknowledgements	*viii*
	Introduction	1
1	Theoretical and normative issues of aviation safety	10
2	The global institutional and legal system for aviation safety	41
3	The regional institutional and legal system for aviation safety	99
4	Impact of the COVID-19 pandemic on air transport safety regulations	165
	Conclusion	*189*
	Literature	*192*
	Index	*206*

Figures

1.1 Hierarchical structure of aviation law. 37
3.1 AST implementation status in AFCAC countries, as of 2021. 124

Tables

2.1 List of annexes to the Chicago Convention and the date of their adoption. 59
2.2 RSOO with division into regions of the world. 89
3.1 Overview of EU bilateral agreements with third countries in the field of aviation safety. 106
3.2 Comparison of accidents per million operations in the European region with the number in the world between 2011 and 2023. 116
3.3 AST objective 1 Achievement rate: reducing the accident rate in Africa from 8.6 to 2.5 per million departures by the end of 2023. 125
3.4 Comparison of the number of accidents in the Latin American region with the number in the world between 2008 and 2023. 137
3.5 Comparison of accidents per million operations in Asia Pacific with worldwide between 2009 and 2023. 148
3.6 Comparison of the number of accidents per million operations in the Middle East region with the number in the world between 2009 and 2023. 163
4.1 Summary of data on the impact of the COVID-19 pandemic on international air traffic globally in 2020. 179
4.2 Summary of data on the impact of the COVID-19 pandemic on domestic air traffic of countries with the largest share of the domestic market in 2020. 180
4.3 Summary of data on the impact of the COVID-19 pandemic on international air traffic globally in 2021. 180
4.4 Summary of data on the impact of the COVID-19 pandemic on domestic air traffic of countries with the largest share of the domestic market in 2021. 181
4.5 Summary of data on the impact of the COVID-19 pandemic on international air traffic globally in 2022. 181
4.6 Summary of data on the impact of the COVID-19 pandemic on domestic air traffic of countries with the largest share of the domestic market in 2022. 182

Acknowledgements

I am deeply grateful to Melwin Ignatius, Project Manager at Deanta, for his unwavering support and insightful guidance throughout this project. My sincere thanks go to the Routledge team—especially Diksha Bhugra, Nicola Sharpe, and Guy Loft—of the Taylor & Francis Group, for their exceptional professionalism, encouragement, and expertise. I would also like to express my deepest gratitude to my children, Justyna, Marcin, and Ewelina: your constant support and unfailing belief in me have been my greatest inspiration. Lastly, I extend my heartfelt appreciation to my parents for their enduring love and wisdom, which have guided me every step of the way. I also wish to thank my academic professors, colleagues, and everyone else who generously shared their time, expertise, and encouragement.

Introduction

Legal regulations in the field of air transport safety are the cornerstone for ensuring its safe functioning and development. The increasing number of passengers using the services of air operators and growing air traffic are leading to what if often described as "congestion in the sky", which is becoming a challenge for states and international organizations involved in civil aviation. Considering these factors, it is essential to recognize that without prioritizing the fundamental element of safety, the ambitious objectives for air transport cannot be achieved. Despite the air transport restrictions imposed during the 2020–2022 period due to the SARS-COV-2 coronavirus pandemic and the spread of COVID-19, projections remain robust.[1] According to the International Civil Aviation Organization (ICAO), air traffic is projected to reach 18.1 billion passengers in 2040, under a realistic (average) scenario.[2] Estimates by the Airports Council International (ACI) suggest that passenger air traffic could hit 19.3 billion passengers in 2041.[3] Many other non-governmental organizations (NGOs) indicate similar growth trends in aviation, although not as high as estimated before the COVID-19 pandemic in 2019. The International Council of Clean Transportation predicts that air traffic will grow by an average of 3.6% between 2018 and 2040, down from the 4.2% forecast before the pandemic to 15.9 billion passengers.[4] The two largest aircraft manufacturers,

1 Dube K., Nhamo G., Chikodzi D., *COVID-19 pandemic and prospects for recovery of the global aviation industry*, Journal of Air Transport Management, Vol. 92, 2021, ISSN 0969-6997, https://doi.org/10.1016/j.jairtraman.2021.102022; Rothengatter W., Zhang J., Hayashi Y., Nosach A., Wang K., Hoon Oum T., *Pandemic waves and the time after Covid-19 – Consequences for the transport sector*, Transport Policy, Vol. 110, 2021, ISSN 0967-070X, pp. 225–237, https://doi.org/10.1016/j.tranpol.2021.06.003; Zając G., *Kryzys lotniczy w związku z Coronawirusem [tr: Aviation crisis in connection with Coronavirus]*, in: Przegląd Komunikacyjneny, 11/2020, Wyd. Stowarzyszenie Inżynierów i Techników Komunikacji RP, Warsaw 2020, pp. 13–18.

2 ICCT, *Polishing my crystal ball: Airline traffic in 2050*, https://theicct.org/global-aviation-airline-traffic-jan22/, accessed 28.02.2024.

3 ACI, What to expect: Latest air travel outlook reveals short- and long-term demand, 22.02.2023, https://aci.aero/2023/02/22/what-to-expect-latest-air-travel-outlook-reveals-short-and-long-term-demand/, accessed 28.02.2024.

4 ICCT, *Polishing* ..., op. cit.

DOI: 10.4324/9781003557876-1

Airbus and Boeing, estimate that air traffic in 2040 will grow by an average of 3.9% and 4%, reaching 20 billion and 19.2 billion passengers, respectively.[5]

These aforementioned trends in the growth of air traffic indicate that the demand for air services will rise despite various restrictions or difficulties, such as the COVID-19 pandemic or the CORSIA mechanism adopted by the ICAO, imposing higher fees on air transport related to climate change. The rise in air traffic requires that the issues of civil aviation development safety be taken into account by states and international aviation organizations. This encompasses various aspects of the functioning of aviation, such as air traffic management, operational safety management at airports, safety oversight of air service providers, and many others. The responsibility of states and international institutions to ensure aviation safety is a priority issue in light of the challenges and threats faced by air transport.

International regulations on civil aviation safety cover various aspects of aviation activities. In this monograph, the primary research problem will concern the normative dimensions of safety in international aviation law, through a detailed analysis of the existing safety requirements within the area of the functioning of individual entities. The essence of the research problem centers on legal issues formulated at both the international and regional levels and on the practical application of the adopted legal norms. Significant attention is also focused on the process of institutionalizing aviation safety. This includes an in-depth discussion of the international system for the safe conduct of air operations within the ICAO, and analysis on the role and regulatory scope of the regional institutions and organizations engaged in aviation safety. The international nature of aviation requires harmonization of rules and standards of conduct in diverse circumstances in order to ensure the highest level of air transport safety.

This monograph provides an analysis of a research area that is of interest in many fields of science. Civil aviation, and in particular ensuring safety in this domain, is an interdisciplinary approach, combining the issues of legal sciences, international relations, economy, and management sciences. The complexity of the research problem requires in-depth analysis with regard to the legal regulation of safety issues in various aspects of the functioning of civil aviation. The process of institutionalization of aviation safety plays a key role in explaining the research issues discussed. The consolidation and the strengthening of aviation safety are carried out within the framework of functions performed by international institutions. According to Kukułka, there are three functions of institutionalization: stabilization, legitimation, and integration.[6] The stabilization function involves safeguarding the interests of all participants in a given international or regional institution. It also serves to affirm the equality of rights and partnership of all its members. The legitimation function pertains to regulating significant issues in international civil aviation. Through this function, important initiatives for the community can be highlighted, and legally regulated. Finally, the integration

5 *Ibidem.*
6 Kukułka J., *Teoria stosunków międzynarodowych*, Warsaw 2000, p. 211.

function is geared towards consolidating a particular community and developing its own interests. It mobilizes its members to greater activity and strengthens their mutual interactions.[7] Aviation safety, therefore, is a platform that integrates various states and organizations worldwide, both at the international and regional levels. Consequently, the main research problem will be examined in the context of these three functions of institutionalizing aviation safety.

Understanding the legal foundations in examining aviation safety is essential for the proper course of research considerations. The author intends to delineate international aviation law, with its central axis being the system of the International Civil Aviation Organization (ICAO), while also highlighting individual regional institutions acting in the field of aviation safety by emphasizing their regulatory function.

The issue of safety issues represents an extremely wide field of research. To narrow the focus, the author emphasizes the process of codifying international aviation law and the process of institutionalization. This monograph characterizes the structures and functions of various international and regional institutions affecting the solution of aviation safety problems and challenges. The author's intention was also to incorporate the broader context of international law governing civil aviation safety because, without knowledge of certain fundamental legal frameworks, it would not be possible to evaluate the current systems of aviation law and fully understand their functioning.

The research presented in this monograph is the result of scientific inquiry into the normative regulation of civil aviation safety. A discussion limited solely to international regulations without an accompanying theoretical analysis would be incomplete. Likewise, examining the process of institutionalization in the field of aviation safety offers a comprehensive perspective on the issues at hand. The codification of aviation law and institutionalization are closely linked. Therefore, the regulatory function of individual international and regional institutions in the area of safety will be expounded. Furthermore, the study will critically analyze the regulations in force during the COVID-19 pandemic in the period 2020–2022/2023, which significantly affected aviation safety, will also be analyzed. This synthetic approach addresses a complex research issue in a holistic manner.

The aim of the research is to elucidate the normative aspects of safety in international aviation law, both in the context of theoretical considerations regarding the theory of aviation safety and the practical application of the adopted legal regulations. So far, this topic has rarely been discussed in scholarly studies research. Therefore, the author decided to fill this gap by presenting a coherent and comprehensive analysis of the subject. It is also necessary to clarify and systematize in detail the process of institutionalization and codification of aviation law, as this will have an impact on aviation safety in global terms.

The applied research methods facilitated the verification of two hypotheses. The first hypothesis posits that the process of codification of aviation law contributes

7 *Ibidem.*

to the coherence of regulations and plays a crucial role in enhancing safety. The second hypothesis assumes that the process of regional institutionalization is advanced, deepens its scope of influence in terms of subjects and norm-formation, and fosters enhanced cooperation among states and other stakeholders.

To achieve the research goal and verify the hypotheses, a methodological holism, which is appropriate for the social sciences (including legal sciences), was adopted, and suitable research methods were applied, such as the dogmatic-legal method, the method of analysis and criticism of literature, the theoretical-legal method, the comparative method, and the observation method.

In order to analyze the research issues, the dogmatic-legal method was employed. The choice of this method was essential for the interpretation of legal provisions and the analysis of aviation law standards. The applied method of examining documents is one of the basic research methods used to analyze the purpose of the work and the hypotheses made. When discussing the research problem, reference should have been made to normative acts, documents and reference materials developed by international and regional institutions in the field of aviation safety. This method facilitated the analysis individual legal provisions in these documents, which are a valuable source of information in the discussed subject of research. In international aviation law, there are numerous legal documents regulating safety issues that should have been discussed, and their main assumptions and consequences presented.

The dogmatic-legal method is complemented by the use of analysis and criticism of literature. Through this approach, the views of the doctrine on aviation safety issues in a broad sense were presented, as well as the interpretation of existing regulations by eminent researchers worldwide. This method proved useful in demonstrating the originality of the research problem, a topic that has not been extensively developed in the scientific literature. It was recognized that, thanks to this method, the existing state of knowledge will be appropriately deepened and that it can have a significant practical value for the needs of state authorities and aviation institutions in terms of raising safety standards and implementing effective solutions for the development of civil aviation in a safe and coherent manner. By employing this method, the relevant selection and systematization of information were carried out, and then critical analysis was completed to determine the essence, purpose, and conditions of actual regulatory activity in the area of aviation safety of states and international institutions (including regional ones) indicated in the subject of the research process.

It should also be pointed out that the research employs the comparative method. This approach was used to compare existing legal and institutional arrangements in different legal systems around the world on civil aviation safety issues. Specifically, it compared current regulations and functioning of institutions in individual regional systems of the world in relation to the system of international aviation law.

The paper also employs a theoretical and legal methods, to present the author's original theoretical views, that are not further developed in the existing literature. They constitute an original approach to the subject of research. A creative analysis of considerations regarding the aviation safety paradigm at the international level in a realistic, liberal, or constructivist approach was made. This method allows for a synthetic approach to existing solutions as examples of the practical application of theoretical constructions. The literature lacks of comprehensive examination of theoretical issues in international aviation law, which constitutes a significant value in the creation of legal regulations. Therefore, the method used in this study may be valuable for the creation of aviation policy and strategy by states and international aviation organizations.

Finally, the observation method was employed as an auxiliary and complementary method to the analyzed research problem. Observations were made of the existing legal systems in the world regarding aviation safety, i.e. the international system constituting the foundation of other bottom-up regulations and the regional system. The observation covered facts concerning the practical implementation of the regulatory function of states and existing regional institutions. Thanks to this method, it was possible to compare the theoretical knowledge contained in source documents, including legislative ones, with the practical action and to indicate emerging inaccuracies or discrepancies.

In order to clarify the research problem and justify the hypotheses put forward, the structure of this monograph has been organized into four substantive chapters, supplemented by an introduction and a conclusion.

Chapter 1 is a theoretical consideration to explain later in the work the normative aspects of safety in international aviation law. Therefore, the category of safety in the interpretation of numerous researchers will be discussed extensively. The subject of consideration will also be the analysis at the international level of the aviation safety paradigm in a realistic, liberal, and constructivist approach. This chapter will present normative issues related to the definition of safety. Although not explicitly defined in international law, it is discussed in international aviation law, for example, in the provisions of Annex 19 to the Convention on International Civil Aviation (Chicago Convention). Worth stressing is that in addition to safety, the chapter also explores the related concept of security. Furthermore, this part will examine theoretical assumptions of aviation safety. Four detailed theories in aviation safety will also be subject to theoretical analysis: the system theory, the human factors theory, the safety culture theory, and the risk management theory. In order to discuss the normative aspects of aviation safety, an analysis of the international nature of air relations and aviation law has been carried out. It will explain the essence and characteristics of international aviation law, which is the legal basis on which the functioning of international aviation relations is based. Finally, the chapter traces the origin of the codification of international aviation law, hierarchy, and the development of harmonization of aviation regulations in the context of safety regulations.

Chapter 2 focuses on normative solutions concerning the safety of international aviation law in the context of presenting the global institutional and legal system. This is the part of the monograph that analyzes international civil aviation safety regulations. This chapter is devoted to normative aspects of safety at the level of international legal regulations. It presents the process of codification of aviation safety in the multilateral regime, by discussing the Chicago system, the Tokyo-Hague-Montreal-Beijing system, the Warsaw-Montreal system, and the compensation system. The legal scope and significance of the Global Aviation Safety Plan will also be explored in this chapter, focusing on its practical implementation in various regions of the world. Importantly, the chapter also covers the legal nature and importance of regional aviation safety groups, as well as the normative regulation of aviation safety and supervision. In the final part, the safety regulations existing in bilateral international agreements are analyzed.

The third chapter is dedicated to examining the functioning of the institutional and legal system of aviation safety in individual regions of the world. The subject of research is the application in practice of normative regulations on civil aviation safety at the regional level. Much attention is focused on the study of institutions functioning in different regions and the legislation on aviation safety implemented by these entities. This chapter presents the normative aspects of safety in practice by discussing the process of institutionalization and codification in the regions of Latin and North America, Africa, Asia, the Pacific region, and the Middle East and North Africa. The assessment focuses on safety levels in these regions based on an analysis of reports issued by regional safety oversight institutions.

In the last chapter, the subject of research will be current considerations of the impact of regulations related to the existence of the SARS-COV-2 coronavirus pandemic and COVID-19 disease on civil aviation safety. An analysis is made on the application of global and regional legal instruments implemented during the COVID-19 pandemic in the period 2020–2022/2023 to air transport safety. This chapter discusses regulations in Europe and the US. A lot of attention will be directed to the discussion of legal instruments regarding state aid for the aviation industry affected by the coronavirus pandemic. The discussion focuses on the legal consequences of norms and procedures related to the COVID-19 pandemic for air transport.

This monograph represents an advanced, comprehensive analysis of the normative approach to safety in international aviation law, based on an original presentation of theoretical considerations in the context of aviation safety theory, as well as a practical examination of regulations implemented at the regional level. The analysis of legal safety regulations is set within the multifaceted context of the process of institutionalization and codification in across individual regions of the world. Various research methods are discussed in detail. The usefulness of these methods is assessed through the prism of their effectiveness and the innovative nature of the study to achieve the intended research goals.

The novelty of this work lies in its integration of a thorough analysis of theoretical assumptions underlying aviation safety with the process of codification of international aviation law in this area. It is worth emphasizing that an innovative approach was made, consisting of the development of aviation safety theories, which are a key element in the process of the explanation of institutionalization processes on an international and regional scale and the harmonization of regulations aimed at strengthening safety in three dimensions: local, regional, and global. Until now, such a comprehensive perspective has been absent in the scientific literature. Understanding the fundamental methodological assumptions underlying the development of a normative approach to safety will contribute to the development of effective standards in the context of evolving the integration and legal coherence of regulations.

The multifaceted subject of research necessitated the use of numerous scientific methods typical of social sciences. In individual chapters of the monograph, descriptive, analytical, comparative, institutional, and legal methods are used. The latter two methods are used most extensively as they are consistent with the research area of law, in particular international law and international relations. All methods are based on the principle of correlation, defining the interconnections of international institutions with regional institutions as well as between the theoretical assumptions of safety theory and the safety paradigms in the formulation and implementation of international rules, norms, and standards.

The explanation of norms in this research process is anchored in Hans Kelsen's scientific reflections on the "pure theory of law".[8] According to Kelsen, there are three conceptuals of the system: static, mixed, and dynamic. All these systems are united by the highest norm, which is the one to which we assign the highest value. Kelsen points out that there are inherent hierarchical relations between norms, which means that the content of the lower norm can be derived from the content of the direct higher norm and that the direct superior norm constitutes the formal basis for the validity of the lower norm.[9] By utilizing Kelsen's ideas, this work demonstrates the hierarchy of aviation law, and underscores that international aviation law norms form the foundation for regional and national legislative norms, and each of these norms must comply with the norms of higher level, which are international regulations.

In the course of the research work, various scientific publications were used. In connection with the analysis of the normative approach to safety in international aviation law, as well as the latest activities and phenomena of regulations related to the COVID-19 pandemic, which are not widely reflected in the literature, this study is based on foreign-language literature, mainly scientific publications, source materials, and legal acts, mostly in English. First of all, when considering normative aspects, numerous legal acts of individual international and regional organizations as well as guidelines in the form of opinions and recommendations on civil aviation safety, were analyzed. The results of the research were based on statistical data on aviation safety on both global and regional scales, which were used to assess the practical application of the adopted legal solutions to different entities of international aviation law.

8 *The Pure Theory of Law*, Stanford Encyclopedia of Philosophy, 2002, https://plato.stanford.edu/entries/lawphil-theory/, accessed 15.03.2024.

9 Zalewska M., *The Metaphorical Aspect of Hans Kelsen's Pure Theory of Law*, Prinicipia, No 65/2018. S. 185–206.

This monograph outlines the functions of individual institutions in relation to the organization of the safety system, which reflects the applicable international and regional regulations in this field.

In the English-language literature, there are relatively few interdisciplinary studies dedicated to normative aspects of safety and security in civil aviation. Typically, existing publications are exclusively legal in nature, and address only a narrow segment of aviation law regulation, without considering the wider international context, including political, and economic dimensions. In addition, there are practically no studies on international aviation relations in the literature, and this monograph aims to fill this gap by examining the issues within the framework of normative conditions. Therefore, the research presented herein offers a rarely discussed political and legal approach, which has not been the subject of extensive studies so far. In the theoretical section on safety, books and scholarly papers by researchers such as among others: Jerzy Gryz (*Współczesny paradygmat bezpieczeństwa międzynarodowego* [tr: Contemporary paradigm of international security], Rocznik Bezpieczeństwa Międzynarodowego 2019), Jack Milligan (*Bet on the field: why field preemption should apply to the federal aviation act*, Journal of Air Law and Commerce, Vol. 85, No. 3, 2020), James Reason (*Human error*, Cambridge University Press 1990; *Achieving a safe culture: theory and practice*, Work and Stress 1998, Vol. 12, No. 3, 1998; *Safety paradoxes and safety culture*, Injury Control & Safety Promotion, Vol. 7, No. 1, 2000), Don Harris and Neville A. Stanton (*Aviation as a system of systems: Preface to the special issue of human factors in aviation*, Ergonomics, Vol. 53, No. 2, 2010), Pablo Mendes De Leon, Niall Buissing (*Behind and Beyond the Chicago Convention: The Evolution of Aerial Sovereignty*, Wolters Kluwer, 2019), and David Moriarty, (*Error management and standard operating procedures for organizations*, Practical Human Factors for Pilots, Academic Press, 2015). The normative section of this study is based on scientific papers and publications developed by academics, in particular such as: Izabela Kraśnicka (*Standardy żeglugi powietrznej w działalności Organizacji Międzynarodowego Lotnictwa Cywilnego* (*ICAO*) [tr. Air navigation standards in the activities of the International Civil Aviation Organization (ICAO)], Wyd. CH Beck, 2019), S. Z. Feller (*Comment on Criminal Jurisdiction Over Aircraft Hijacking*, Israel Law Review, Vol. 7, 2015), Peter P. C. Haanappel (*The law and policy of air space and outer space: a comparative approach*, Wolters Kluwer, 2003; *Bilateral Air Transport Agreements – 1913–1980*, The International Trade Law Journal, Vol. 5, 1980), and Marek Zylicz (*Prawo lotnicze międzynarodowe, europejskie i krajowe* [International, European and National Aviation Law, Warsaw, 2002).

This monograph may prove valuable for all those seeking to deepen their knowledge of the legal regulations governing aviation safety. By discussing the subject of normative aspects of safety in a dynamically developing sector of the economy, the book can be used in all regions of the world because it is available in English - the universal language of contemporary international relations. It will be particularly useful for students in education in the field of international aviation law, as well as international relations and air transport safety management.

Furthermore, the legal and safety issues discussed may also complement the knowledge of students from other faculties, in particular, homeland security. This publication is also a practical resource for representatives of state services dealing with aviation safety, such as border guards, air marshals, airport security services, and other related services, as well as for state regulatory bodies such as ministries of air transportation or civil aviation authorities. The study is also a valuable source of information for non-governmental entities, i.e. industry aviation organizations, air carriers, airport management authorities, and the entire aviation community. The monograph can be an inspiration for all people to explore and understand normative regulations, in this dynamically developing sector. It provides a comprehensive overview of international aviation law that is useful for a broader range of readers.

The author hopes that this publication, which is an and interdisciplinary analysis of the normative aspects of safety in international aviation law, will be used not only for the purpose of developing theoretical scientific considerations within the field, but will also serve as a basis for the practical application of the presented solutions in state institutions, international organizations, and other entities dedicated to ensuring safety in civil aviation.

1 Theoretical and normative issues of aviation safety

International aviation relations and international aviation law

Safety is a central component of international civil aviation and is an integral part of the strategic objective of the International Civil Aviation Organization (ICAO). All member states have a statutory obligation to ensure and improve aviation safety by creating a legal framework, applying measures to implement it, and establishing appropriate bodies. Aviation safety oversight is a key means of ensuring civil aviation safety through the effective implementation of international safety standards and recommended practices (SARPs) and relevant provisions of international aviation law. Independent civil aviation authorities are essential in this area to monitor the state of aviation safety in a given country, as well as to take effective action against all entities operating in its legal jurisdiction for failure to implement or violate safety regulations. Additionally, coordination and cooperation among the various institutions in the country in the field of aviation safety and aviation security against acts of unlawful interference is necessary.

The fundamental issue of scientific considerations is to show the theoretical aspects of the studied area of interest. Theory is a key element of the scientific process. In this chapter, by presenting the theoretical layer of aviation safety and its legal regulations, a comprehensive set of principles, rules, and recommendations that describe and explain phenomena related to the functioning of international civil aviation is provided. Thanks to the theoretical approach, further understanding and analysis of research issues become clearer. It becomes possible to identify individual phenomena and processes in a holistic way, as well as to discuss their consequences for various entities or the environment.

Theory in civil aviation is built on the basis of observations, experiments, data analysis, and scientific conclusions. This chapter will present theoretical considerations concerning the essence and theory of safety, taking into account its importance in civil aviation. An analysis of the paradigms of international and aviation safety will be carried out, which is extremely helpful in analyzing the issue of research. Within this broad category, the concept of aviation safety, which has a significant impact on the overall understanding of safety, will also be explained. Normative regulations on safety in air transport will also be examined. Definitions contained in international, regional, or national regulations are important when considering individual aspects such as state responsibility in the field of supervision, compensation systems related to aviation accidents and incidents, or passenger rights. The subject of consideration of this chapter will also be an

DOI: 10.4324/9781003557876-2

attempt to explain and discuss the essence of international aviation relations and the legitimacy of codifying international aviation law. From the very beginning of the creation of legal standards in the field of civil aviation, they have had an international character. Therefore, in the context of safety, it was justified to unify these norms and standards in the world. A specific hierarchy of legal standards in aviation is of fundamental importance for the specificity of this field of science as well as economic development.

1.1 Definitions and paradigms of aviation safety

Safety issues are widely discussed in various fields of science due to their diversity of perception and definition. This term is the subject of in-depth research due to its complexity, various conditions, or multiple directions of impact. The following presentation will provide definitions in the field of international law and international relations. There are many interpretations in the literature, which often also refer to threats. Koziej defines the safety of a given entity as its activity, the content of which is to ensure its survival and freedom to pursue its own interests in a dangerous environment and to oppose various threats.[1] Czupryński distinguishes between positive and negative aspects of safety. According to him, a positive approach is associated with describing the subject of interest and indicating the directions of development, and in negative terms, it is shown as the opposite of risks.[2] Threats are an inherent feature of safety, as the two terms are interrelated and interpenetrate. In addition, Zdrodowski argues with Evans and Newnham that safety is the absence of threats, protection against threats, as well as effective actions to prevent or remove them.[3] Grzywna *et al.* believe that in order to feel safe, you should diagnose the risks as much as possible because they affect the state of safety.[4] Safety can also be treated as a system of values to be sought and nurtured.[5] Rosicki emphasizes that in the aspect of international relations, safety can be treated as a certain value recognized by their participants.[6] Each entity perceives the state of safety differently because it is a subjective feeling of each of them. This means that in the same or similar circumstances, different entities will interpret the existing state or phenomenon differently. Pietraś notes that in international relations, the concept of safety is not only a need but a dynamic social process.[7] Safety can be divided according to various criteria. The most

1 Koziej S., *Bezpieczeństwo: istota, podstawowe kategorie i historyczna ewolucja*, Bezpieczeństwo narodowe, No. 2/2011, p. 18.
2 Czupryński A., *Bezpieczeństwo w ujęciu teoretycznym*, w: Czupryński A., Wiśniewski, Zboina (ed.), *Bezpieczeństwo – badania, teoria, praktyka*, Józefów 2015, p. 10.
3 Zdrodowski B., *Istota bezpieczeństwa państwa*, Annales Universitatis Paedagogicae Cracoviensis, Studia de Securitate 9(3) (2019), p. 50. See more: Evans G., Newnham J., The Penguin Dictionary of International Relations, London 1998, p. 39.
4 Grzywna Z., Limański A., Drabik I., *Zarządzanie bezpieczeństwem w portach lotniczych*, Zeszyty Naukowe Politeczhniki Śląskiej 2018, No. 118, p. 183.
5 Czupryński A., op .cit., p. 10.
6 Rosicki R., *O pojęciu i istocie bezpieczeństwa*, Przegląd Politologiczny, No. 3/2010, p. 28.
7 Pietraś M., *Bezpieczeństwo ekologiczne w Europie*, Lublin 1996, p. 20.

common is the division of safety according to the subject: international, regional, local, state, international organization, social group, etc. Zdrodowski states that in this approach, safety is always empowered, which means that it is attributed to a specific entity.[8] We can also point to the division of safety due to the subject of research: economic, military, ecological, social, aviation, etc.

Referring to the research issues in this monograph, the matter of aviation safety should be explained. It is a broad category with many doctrinal definitions arising from the extensive research spectrum of civil aviation. The state of aviation safety is influenced by many factors. In aviation, we can distinguish two terms: safety and security. In a narrow sense, "aviation safety" is understood as a set of legal regulations, actions, measures, and institutions aimed at ensuring that all entities to which it is addressed operate in accordance with the set standards. The term "aviation security" refers to a set of legal, organizational, operational, and technical rules related to the prevention of illegal acts against civil aviation safety and unlawful seizure of aircraft. The two terms are complementary, as ensuring an adequate level of aviation safety cannot take place without the adoption of appropriate measures and procedures to prevent acts of terrorism targeting the aviation sector. The European Parliament also points out that aviation and safety are inseparable, as air transport could not develop without strict rules guaranteeing a high level of safety.[9]

Based on the assumption that international safety has different dimensions, researchers point to the existence of many safety paradigms.[10] Therefore, safety paradigms – regional, subregional, and local – are part of the universal paradigm of international safety, considered in the context of both specific conditions and characteristics of the subject. The structure of the international environment and the processes taking place in it are decisive.[11] For the purposes of this study, attention will be focused on the aviation safety paradigm. It refers to the way of understanding issues related to safety in air transport. The aviation safety paradigm covers various issues related to air traffic safety, including the safety of air operations, air traffic management, and technical, navigational, and cyber operational issues. In order to ensure safety in air transport, a holistic approach is necessary, taking into account various aspects related to aviation safety, including technical, operational, and cyber aspects. An interesting reflection on the paradigm of aviation safety management is presented by Silva and Cardoso-Junior.[12] When considering

8 Zdrodowski B., op. cit., p.49.

9 European Parliament, https://www.europarl.europa.eu/factsheets/pl/sheet/134/bezpieczenstwo-lotnicze, accessed March 5, 2024.

10 Vide: Ziarko J., *Paradygmaty i orientacje badawcze w nauce o bezpieczeństwie*, Bezpieczeństwo. Teoria i praktyka, No. 1–2, 2008, pp. 9–21; Gryz J., *Współczesny paradygmat bezpieczeństwa międzynarodowego.* Rocznik Bezpieczeństwa Międzynarodowego, 2019, No. 1, pp. 11–27.

11 Gryz J., op. cit., pp. 11–27.

12 Silva M., Cardoso-Junior M., *Paradigm Shift in Safety Management in the Brazilian Army Aviation: Proposal and Validation of a Rag Questionnaire*, GEAR 2021, DOI: 10.13140/RG.2.2.36039.42405.

the aviation safety paradigm, it should be analyzed at the international level. One can distinguish a realistic, liberal, or constructivist approach here.

In a realistic approach, attention is focused on the interests of states and the rivalry between them. The basic assumption of this approach is the belief that states are the main subjects of international law, and relations between them are shaped based on their interests. This approach in aviation was particularly evident at a time when air transport was the domain of the state.[13] The point is that most air carriers and airports were state-owned at that time. This monopoly manifested itself in wide-ranging protectionist practices against its national carriers. States did not want to liberalize and take air transport out of their own regulatory and ownership control. Globalization processes and the general tendency to open international relations, to deepen international interdependencies, and the influence of other non-state participants in international relations caused a change in this approach. In the US, this process began to evolve in the late 1970s, and in Europe and other regions of the world from the end of the 1980s. The change in the perception of this sector by the state was also related to the change in geopolitics and the international system, which transformed from a bipolarization of forces at the turn of the 1980s and the 1990s to a multipolar system. The end of the Cold War and the East–West rivalry (the US-USSR) resulted in the "entry into the game" and greater importance of non-state participants, including international organizations. Therefore, the realistic paradigm of aviation safety no longer exists. Although states still retain their shares in the ownership capital of air carriers, in democratic countries these stakes rarely constitute a majority. In the twenty-first century, the strength of a state is not measured by a majority stake in a given carrier, the regulation of capacity, or the approval of airfares, but by the economic impact of air relations. The more open the aviation market, the greater the opportunities for the development of a carrier registered in a given country and identified with that country. The image of the state is perceived through the prism of the functioning and impact of the international air carrier registered in it, as well as the number of air passengers from other countries visited, or the ownership of airports of strategic passenger or cargo importance.

The liberal approach to aviation safety is characteristic of contemporary international relations. It emphasizes cooperation between states and international institutions (intergovernmental and non-governmental) and resolving conflicts through dialogue and exchange of experience or information. Global organizations such as ICAO and regional safety institutions cooperate at various levels and in various forms. The aim of such cooperation is to develop the best possible safety standards for all interested participants. This approach is dominated by common interests, not monopolization or hegemony in the area of aviation safety. There is a belief that the more countries cooperate and comply with international standards and recommendations, the greater the safety and the greater the economic and social benefits for the state. In air relations, there is no question of the hegemony

13 See more: Zając G., *Podstawy prawne i funkcjonowanie przewoźników lotniczych i lotnisk w Europie*, Wyd. Rambler, Warszawa 2016, p. 142.

of one carrier because, with the opening of competition and a free market, such practices are not realistic. Currently, air relations are liberalized in the vast majority of countries. The old restrictive bilateral agreements, which were characteristic of the bipolar system, are being modified and replaced by more liberal agreements that give greater freedom to provide services and to perform them by different entities, once the relevant safety requirements are met. The role of the state in the liberal paradigm is reduced to the function of supervising safety, and the regulatory function has been transferred to the international level. The state has transferred its regulation prerogatives to international organizations, which perform their role well by setting equal and non-discriminatory safety criteria for all.

In the constructivist approach, which is also characteristic of modern aviation safety, attention is focused on the role of international norms, values, and institutions in shaping international aviation relations and on their impact on political decision-making. Standards, both legally binding and in the form of soft law, are a key factor for aviation safety. In this approach, it is essential to assume that international institutions have a key role to play in creating norms and values. This is particularly important in civil aviation, where the adoption of uniform standards helps to build order, resolve conflicts, and develop better safety mechanisms. Thanks to mutual understanding and the dialogue that takes place between different cultures, an effective and comprehensive approach to aviation safety issues can be achieved. This can be seen in the example of air accident investigations, in which at least several countries and other entities are usually involved in order to determine the cause and prevent similar situations in the future. The overriding value is aviation safety, which is perceived similarly in different cultures. Therefore, there are similar regional institutional and regulatory mechanisms around the world, and in these regions, we can see almost identical aviation standards that build a community of entities focused on similar values.

It is worth noting that different paradigms of international safety often interpenetrate and complement each other. Therefore, a holistic and comprehensive approach to international safety issues is particularly important, as it allows us to analyze problems from different perspectives and to seek solutions that consider a variety of factors. The aviation safety paradigm can be used to create aviation policy and strategy. As a result, countries and international aviation organizations will be able to create better legal regulations, effectively address challenges and counter threats.

1.2 Legal definitions and understanding of aviation safety

As already mentioned, in aviation we distinguish aviation safety and security, which are two terms that refer to similar aspects, but at the same time differently understood legally and objectively.

The key concept from the point of view of the discussed research problem, i.e. safety, has been defined in many acts of international law, in multilateral and bilateral agreements. It is based on the provisions of the Convention on International Civil Aviation, signed in Chicago on December 7, 1944 (known as the Chicago Convention). Its main objective is to ensure the safety of international civil aviation. In light of the legal provisions of Article 3(d) of the Chicago Convention, it is only provided that the safety of navigation of civil aircraft will be considered when establishing regulations concerning state aircraft. Therefore, the obligation imposed on the state is to implement national legal regulations considering the safety of air transport, both civil and state. This laconic provision ceded the entire burden of introducing safety standards in air transport to individual countries. However, it is in vain to search for any definition of aviation safety in this document. Safety is determined by a number of rules and standards, the observance and implementation of which will determine safety. It is worth mentioning that it is difficult to define such a common term in an international agreement with a wide scope of subjects due to the diversity of countries that make up this global aviation system. Similarly, there is no definition of aviation safety or terrorism, as countries perceive the implementation of standards in these areas differently. Safety is conferred by enumerating specific actions and rules that will testify to its "existence". Nevertheless, in acts of lower legal rank or of regional importance, such definitions appear. First of all, we can point to legal regulations in the form of "annexes", which are adopted on the basis of Article 37 of the Chicago Convention. Furthermore, as defined in Annex 19 to the Chicago Convention (safety management), safety is a condition in which risks related directly or indirectly to aviation activities that occur during the operation of aircraft have been reduced to an acceptable level and are brought under control.[14] This document also contains many other safety-related definitions, such as:

1. safety information is safety data that is processed, organized, or analyzed in a given context to be useful for safety management purposes;
2. safety management system (SMS) is a systemic approach to safety management, that includes the organizational structure, responsibilities, policies, and procedures;
3. safety oversight refers to a function performed by a state to ensure compliance with national safety laws and regulations by individuals and aviation organizations;
4. safety performance should be defined as the level of safety achieved by a state or an aviation entity, defined by safety objectives and safety performance indicators (SPIs), i.e. parameters used to monitor and assess the level of safety;
5. safety risk is defined as the expected probability and severity of the consequences or effects of a hazard.

Other annexes also have definitions of safety that coincide, so it is not necessary to cite them here. It should be noted that some annexes deal with safety in a specific way. Safety as a process with changing conditions affects every aspect of civil aviation. Therefore, the research issues raised in this study, due to their

14 Annex 19 to the Chicago Convention (safety management).

broad issues, have been narrowed down to legal regulations and codification of issues or showing institutionalization and international influences. Annex 13 (the investigation of air accidents and incidents) concerns safety regulations related to the proper process of investigating these occurrences. In turn, Annex 1 (personnel licensing) refers to:

a) error, defined as the action or inaction of the flight crew leading to deviations from organizational or flight intentions or expectations;
b) error management, defined as the process of detecting and responding to errors by means of countermeasures that mitigate or eliminate the effects of errors and reduce the likelihood of errors or unwanted aircraft conditions;
c) a threat, defined as events or errors beyond the control of operational personnel, that increase the complexity of operations and that need to be managed to maintain a margin of safety.[15]

In civil aviation, due to its specific nature, in addition to the functioning of definitions and areas related to generally understood safety, we also distinguish the term aviation security. This is a category of international aviation law, which is not to be found in the provisions of the Chicago Convention. Only after 30 years, after numerous tragic events directly affecting civil aviation in the world, these issues were regulated by adopting Annex 17 to the Chicago Convention. Of course, a decade earlier, countries had taken international action to respond to the phenomenon of aviation terrorism. In 1963, the Convention on Offences and Certain Other Acts Committed on Board Aircraft, signed in Tokyo, was adopted. A few years later, in 1970, the Convention for the Suppression of Unlawful Seizure of Aircraft, signed in The Hague, was adopted, and in 1971, the Convention for the Suppression of Unlawful Acts Against the Safety of Civil Aviation, signed in Montreal, was adopted. All three conventions created the legal framework for aviation security, the so-called Tokyo-Hague-Montreal system (more on this later in the book). As defined in Annex 17 to the Chicago Convention, it is stated that this term refers to protection against acts of unlawful interference through a combination of means and human and material resources. The document goes on to state that the overriding duty of the state is to ensure the safety of passengers, crew, ground personnel, and the public in all matters related to protection against acts of unlawful interference in civil aviation.

Above all, legislation in the field of aviation security aims to prevent illegal acts against civil aviation and other illegal acts threatening safety or causing damage to aviation. In other words, these are legal regulations against aviation terrorism. It is a truism that terrorism and international civil aviation are closely linked. It is enough to note, for example, that after significant terrorist attacks for which aircraft is used, there is always an increase in legislative activities in the field of improving

15 Annex 1 to the Chicago Convention (aviation personnel licensing).

aviation security. In order to effectively counteract aviation terrorism, international legal regulations are adopted to protect civil aviation against such attacks.

So far, a number of international, regional, and national legal regulations have been adopted around the world regarding the protection of aviation against terrorist attacks. Effective control and operational instruments have been developed, which, although they do not guarantee complete protection, ensure that the terrorist threat is minimized. States are responsible for their implementation, but a great deal depends on the involvement of regional aviation safety institutions and entities from the aviation community, which should jointly make efforts to strengthen their capabilities regarding aviation safety and security.

1.3 Theoretical assumptions of aviation safety

Aviation safety is a comprehensive system of activities and procedures aimed at minimizing the risks associated with aircraft flights and ensuring the protection of passengers, crew, and people on the ground. The theory of aviation safety is based on many fields, including law, politics, technology, engineering, psychology, and management, as well as the analysis of data on aviation incidents and accidents.

Theory in research is a fundamental element of the scientific process.[16] When exploring aviation safety, the theory is a set of principles, rules, and recommendations that describe and explain phenomena relating to the functioning of civil aviation in the international context. Thanks to the theoretical approach, these phenomena and processes can be identified, and the outcome can be described, which corresponds to the level of safety, natural or social. This approach is essential in explaining and predicting phenomena and processes in scientific research.

Theory in civil aviation is built on the basis of observations, experiments, data analysis, and scientific conclusions. Due to the dynamic development of this field, the theory is also changing. It is empirical in nature, as it is based on the experience and observation of civil aviation. Events have repeatedly led to changes in legal regulations or have given rise to the establishment of regulations (codification) in a given area, as was the case after the events of September 11, 2001, when a number of provisions related to the protection of aviation against terrorist acts were established. In the study of civil aviation, employing a theoretical approach and understanding the conditions of a given phenomenon or process are crucial for safety and determining the right objectives of the strategy against the differentiation of threats.

The essence of scientific research in the field of civil aviation is to understand the complexity of the functioning of this discipline by learning theoretical aspects and translating them into practical application. Learning and explaining theories is a very important element of the scientific process.

Civil aviation, as noted earlier, is a multifaceted field of science. The explanation of phenomena, processes, interdependencies, and international influences

16 For more information, see Haig B., *Grounded Theory as Scientific Method*, Philosophy of Education 1995.

must be based on political aspects and legal regulations. Therefore, the normative aspects of aviation activity are the foundation for conducting scientific research and deepening analyses in various areas: economic (e.g. airport and air traffic management, navigation, and air traffic control systems), technical (e.g. aircraft design and production), safety (e.g. certification of aircraft and flight personnel, investigation of air accidents, protection against acts of unlawful interference, and other illegal acts), political science (e.g. determinants of shaping aviation policy, involvement of countries in international or regional activities) or environmental protection (e.g. aviation fuel taxation issues, the impact of air transport on climate change, noise issues around airports, ecological solutions). Civil aviation is a field of science that is constantly evolving and introducing new technologies to increase the safety, efficiency, and quality of services offered. With the development of technology, scientists in the field of civil aviation are also focusing on the reduction of greenhouse gas emissions and other aspects pertinent to the sustainable development of aviation.

The basic assumptions of aviation safety theory are:

a) preemptive safety;
b) just culture;
c) human factors.

1.3.1 Preemptive safety

The term "Preemptive Safety" means prevention against negative events in aviation, including incidents and accidents, through monitoring and data analysis and continuous improvement of the aviation safety system. Preventive safety in aviation is a proactive approach to avoiding accidents and incidents by identifying and mitigating potential safety risks before they become actual safety incidents. Preventive safety is a key component of an SMS, which represents a systematic approach to managing aviation safety hazards. This term includes the continuous monitoring and analysis of safety data to identify potential safety threats and the subsequent implementation of safety measures to prevent these threats from materializing in real safety events. This may include implementing new procedures and programs, cultivating training, improving equipment or infrastructure, or other measures that may reduce the likelihood of a safety incident occurring. Kopczewski *et al.* point out that the main task of preventive actions is to hinder or prevent the commission of criminal acts.[17]

The goal of preventive safety is to identify and manage safety risks before they lead to accidents or incidents, not just to respond to safety incidents when they occur. This helps to improve safety performance, reduce the occurrence of

17 Kopczewski M., Bednarczyk W., Niedźwiecki S., *Programy prewencyjne elementem bezpieczeństwa na szczeblu lokalnym*, in: Wilk-Woś Z. (ed.), *Bezpieczeństwo i zarządzanie kryzysowe. Bezpieczeństwo społeczności lokalnych*, Przedsiębiorczość i Zarządzanie 2017, Wyd. SAN, p. 56.

incidents, and foster the overall safety culture in the aviation industry. The most important element of safety is the prevention of undesirable situations and events through actions on many levels. These are primarily regulatory activities aimed at creating a coherent and harmonious system of functioning in a given area. The purpose of regulatory action is to comply with the contained regulations, recommendations, or guidelines in order to minimize the risk of error, misaction, or omission. In preventive safety, sanctions are not important as an instrument of influence on the entity for non-compliance with legal norms, but rather as a means to create a preventive legal, organizational, technical, or control mechanism to prevent negative consequences or events. A similar approach is implemented in other areas of society, as the role of the state and its institutions is to prevent undesirable or erroneous actions by entities and individuals that could cause greater harm.

Milligan, analyzing US aviation law, emphasizes that the use of preventive measures in the form of establishing federal aviation standards for aircraft manufacturers is necessary.[18] It should be noted that manufacturers usually do not know who will operate their machines after a single sale transaction has been made, as they can be used in different countries (via wet or dry lease) that have varying safety standards. In order to avoid unnecessary difficulties in aircraft certification procedures, manufacturers must "preemptively" adapt to different safety requirements in different countries before an aircraft is manufactured. Therefore, it is important at the construction and implementation stage to implement all legal and technical requirements so that the final product meets the provisions of minimum safety standards. However, this is a complicated task, as Milligan points out. According to him, the best solution is to harmonize regulations on a global scale, which would facilitate compliance with safety requirements in individual countries.[19] The unification of rules and requirements greatly facilitates the functioning of entities such as aircraft manufacturers, and producer responsibility is not hidden and is not delegated to other entities due to the lack of transparent legal criteria.

Another key element of preventive safety is the creation of training and information programs. They are aimed at improving the state of safety in civil aviation by raising awareness of the occurrence of various threats, risk areas, or challenges. Through the intensification and diversity of educational programs and information campaigns, measurable benefits are achieved by enhancing the quality of the holistic perception of safety. The essence of the importance of prevention programs is described by Kopczewski *et al.*[20]According to researchers, such programs can influence the formation of attitudes conducive to minimizing the effects of threats, provided they have clearly defined goals and strategies for achieving them.[21]

18 Milligan J., *Bet on the Field: Why Field Preemption Should Apply to the Federal Aviation Act*, Journal of Air Law and Commerce, Vol. 85 (3), 2020, p. 521.

19 *Ibidem*, p. 528.

20 Kopczewski *et al.*, op. cit., pp. 55–72.

21 *Ibidem*, p. 62.

Preventive safety is an important feature of aviation safety. It is a set of comprehensive activities of the state and international institutions along with appropriate measures and regulatory instruments affecting the reduction or prevention of threats in civil aviation. A holistic and harmonious approach and interdependencies in the application of these measures are crucial.

1.3.2 Just culture

Another important element of aviation safety theory is the "just culture" category. This term refers to an organizational culture that promotes fair treatment, where all employees are encouraged to participate in the aviation safety system by reporting incidents, errors, and irregularities without fear of reprisals. Just culture is a term used in aviation to describe a culture of responsibility for safety that encourages open and honest reporting of safety-related incidents and events without fear of retaliation or punishment. It is based on the principles of fairness, equality and learning from mistakes.

The term "culture of fair treatment" is regarded by scientists on the basis of theoretical considerations as part of the culture of safety. Although there is no single, universally accepted definition, various researchers highlight similar essential conditions. Jaworski and Raglewski emphasize that the term "culture of fair treatment" is of particular importance in the field of liability, including criminal law, in civil aviation.[22]

The basic international regulations governing just culture are Annex 13 (investigation of aviation accidents and incidents) and Annex 19 (safety management) to the Chicago Convention. The ICAO Safety Management Manual (Doc.9858) is also helpful. In line with the just culture philosophy adopted in the air accident investigation regulations, aviation organizations establish a safety incident and incident reporting system that is accessible and confidential to all employees. The system ensures that employees can report incidents and safety incidents without fear of disciplinary action or other forms of retaliation. Instead, the focus is on identifying the root cause of the incident and developing corrective actions to prevent similar incidents in the future. In Annex 19 to the Chicago Convention, states are required to establish a safety policy that reflects the state's commitment to a culture of safety. State activities should be aimed at fostering a positive safety culture, focusing on disseminating safety information, encouraging high standards, and raising safety awareness as part of training. A positive feature of the safety culture is that individuals are not only informed about threats and hazards, but also understand the essence of safety. The legal definition of a just culture can be found in European law. As defined in Regulation

22 Jaworski M., Raglewski J., *Polityka Just Culture w lotnictwie cywilnym z perspektywy podstaw odpowiedzialności karnej*, Kwartalnik Krajowej Szkoły Sądownictwa i Prokuratury, Zeszyt 4(24)/2016, Kraków 2016, p. 5.

No. 376/2014,[23] "just culture" means a policy in which operators or other people directly involved are not penalized for acts, omissions, or decisions taken by them that are commensurate with their experience and training. However, it does not tolerate gross negligence or intentional infringements and actions causing damage. In the US, there are also national regulations based on the principle of just culture. The Federal Aviation Administration (FAA) established a compliance program in 2015 that includes a just culture policy.[24] In other countries, equitable treatment procedures in line with international standards and recommendations should also be implemented at the national level.

The just culture concept recognizes that individuals are fallible and errors are an intrinsic part of human nature. James Reason shares this view. A culture of fair treatment, which is part of the broader term safety culture, is a situation in which, according to Reason, mistakes and dangerous actions will not be punished if the mistake was unintentional, while anyone who acts recklessly or takes deliberate and unreasonable risks will be subject to disciplinary action.[25] Similarly, Jaworski and Raglewski argue that trust must exist between the notifier and the entity responsible for collecting and evaluating information.[26]

Instead of blaming individuals for safety incidents, the focus shifts to identifying system issues that may have contributed to the incident and implementing corrective actions to improve safety. The concept of just culture is essential to promote a positive aviation safety culture. By encouraging employees to report incidents without fear of punishment, organizations can create an atmosphere of openness and transparency that supports the continuous improvement of safety performance. Moriarty believes that by establishing a culture of fair treatment, the overall safety culture is strengthened.[27] This approach applies not only within organizations but also at the state level.

1.3.3 Human factors

The third important element in the theoretical framework of aviation safety is human factors. The basic assumption in shaping a safe aviation environment is to

23 Regulation (EU) No 376/2014 of the European Parliament and of the Council of April 3, 2014, on the reporting, analysis and follow-up of occurrences in civil aviation, amending Regulation (EU) No 996/2010 of the European Parliament and of the Council and repealing Directive 2003/42/EC of the European Parliament and of the Council and Commission Regulations (EC) No 1321/2007 and (EC) No 1330/2007, OJ L 122, April 24, 2014.

24 The Compliance Program was modified in 2018 and in 2022. FAA's Compliance Program, July 7, 2022, https://www.faa.gov/about/initiatives/cp/compliance-program-and-airman-rights-brochure-e-mail-version, accessed February 16, 2024.

25 Reason J., *Human error*, op. cit., cited in https://www.airsafety.aero/safety-information-and-reporting/safety-management-systems/safety-culture, accessed February 27, 2024.

26 Jaworski M., Raglewski J., *Polityka…*, op. cit., p. 8.

27 Moriarty D., *Error management and standard operating procedures for organizations*, Practical Human Factors for Pilots, Academic Press 2015, pp. 119–132.

consider the human factor in the design of aviation systems and procedures and the training of personnel to minimize the impact of human error on aviation safety.

In scientific discourse, there are many definitions of human factors. Also on the legal ground, each state and international organization applies an interpretation based on different conditions. This is because it is a category that takes into account a wide range of impacts and includes numerous interdependencies. For instance, the US Federal Aviation Administration (FAA) defines human factors as a multidisciplinary approach to generating and compiling information about human capabilities and limitations and applying that information to equipment, systems, facilities, procedures, tasks, environments, training, personnel, and personnel management to ensure safe and effective human performance.[28]

Some of the most important human factors that affect flight safety are:

a) fatigue and overload of work – these factors can affect the ability to focus and make correct decisions, increasing the risk of mistakes and accidents, which is especially dangerous in aviation;[29]
b) situational awareness – the ability to understand and interpret the current situation, including the position of one's own aircraft and that of other machines in the airspace;[30]
c) communication – effective communication is crucial to maintain situational awareness and avoid misunderstandings that can lead to accidents; the exchange of constraints between system components is crucial for the safety of operations;[31]
d) teamwork and leadership – the ability to work effectively in a team and provide clear leadership is crucial for maintaining aviation safety;[32]
e) training and experience – relevant training and experience can help employees develop the skills and knowledge needed to perform their jobs safely and effectively.

Human factors are an integral part of aviation, and understanding them is crucial for creating effective safety strategies and minimizing the risk of accidents and incidents.

28 US Department of Transportation, Human Factors Policy, FAA Order 9550.8A. Human factors is a category included in the US federal regulations, Part 14 of the CFR.

29 You can find interesting scientific considerations of Stanley Mohler in: Mohler S., *Pilot fatigue manageable, but remains insidious threat*, Human Factors and Aviation Medicine, Vol. 45 (1), 1998, pp. 1–6.

30 Endsley Mica R., *Situation Awareness in Aviation Systems*, Handbook of Aviation Human Factors, 1999, pp. 257–276.

31 Harris D. and Stanton N. A, *Aviation as a system of systems: Preface to the special issue of human factors in aviation*, Ergonomics, Vol. 53 (2), 2010, DOI: 10.1080/00140130903521587.

32 For more information, see Muñoz-Marrón D., *Human Factors in Aviation: CRM (Crew Resource Management)*, Papeles del Psicólogo/Psychologist Papers, 2018, Vol. 39 (3), pp. 191–199.

1.4 Aviation safety theories

Aviation safety theory refers to a variety of principles, models, and frameworks employed to understand and improve safety in the aerospace industry. It also relies on the application of norms and standards in the aviation sector, such as international conventions, regulations governing flight safety, as well as certification and accreditation systems for aviation companies and personnel. Aviation safety is a multidisciplinary field that encompasses a wide range of factors, including human factors, technology, procedures, regulations, and organizational culture. Considering various safety determinants and factors, several detailed theories can be distinguished in aviation safety. These are:

a) system theory;
b) human factors theory;
c) safety culture theory;
d) risk management theory.

1.4.1 System theory

Aviation safety system theory refers to the general theory of systems in international relations. Various definitions of this phenomenon are provided by researchers, such as Kondrakiewicz.[33] According to Kukułka, a system is a set of elements between which there is a specific structure of couplings.[34] Similarly, Skyttner believes that system theory is characterized by interactions of independent elements.[35] Kulikowski defines a system as a set of elements or objects that are fused or linked together by specific relationships or dependencies.[36] In contrast, Balcerowicz states that the global system is a network of interconnected international participants, characterized by a high degree of complexity and hierarchical differentiation.[37] According to McKinney Jr., the theory of systems is presented as a complement to more traditional scientific approaches in aviation science.[38] He contrasts the assumptions of systems theory with traditional methods that rely on reductionism.

33 Kondrakiewicz D., *System międzynarodowy jako kategoria w nauce o stosunkach międzynarodowych*, Teka Politologii i Stosunków Międzynarodowych, Nr 11, 2016, s. 75–94. Kondrakiewicz recalls, that the creator of the general theory of systems was an outstanding representative of biological sciences Ludwig von Bertalanffy. See. Bertalanffy, L. von, *General Systems Theory: Foundation, Development, Applications*, New York 1968.

34 Kukułka J., *Problemy teorii stosunków międzynarodowych*, Warsaw 1978, p. 162.

35 Skyttner L., *General Systems Theory: Problems, Perspectives, Practice*, World Scientific Publishing 2005. See also: Burgess S., *A Systems Theory Approach for Studying Safety Management Systems for Operations of Small Helicopter Organizations*, Northcentral University ProQuest Dissertations Publishing, 2016, p. 5.

36 Kulikowski R., *Sterowanie w wielkich systemach*, Warszawa 1970, p. 9.

37 Balcerowicz B., *Pokój i "nie-pokój" na progu XXI wieku*, Warszawa 2002, s. 120.

38 McKinney, Earl H. Jr., *Systems Theory Implications for Human Factors in Aviation*, Proceedings of the Human Factors and Ergonomics Society Annual Meeting, Vol. 41 (1), 1997, pp. 85–89.

Therefore, a complementary method of study using groups or organizations as a unit of analysis is systems theory.[39] Particularly important considerations of the system theory of aviation safety are presented by Harris and Stanton. They believe that aviation is a system of systems.[40] They refer to Maier's theory of systems, in which he identified five features that a system must have:[41] operational independence of elements, managerial independence of elements, evolutionary development, emerging behavior, and geographical distribution of elements. In this context, Harris and Stanton highlight key features of the aviation safety system theory:[42]

a) clear operational independence (aircraft operations, air traffic management/control);
b) each element is independent in terms of management (provided by independent companies or service providers);
c) the various elements of this system are bound by a set of common operating principles and international rules governing their operation.

In the aviation system, there are many elements shaping and filling it. Each has its own operational distinctiveness. Suffice it to say that air carriers, airports, ground handling service providers, catering companies, cleaning companies, airport security, airport, air traffic control, airport fire brigades, and many other entities operate as separate, independent units, performing their tasks autonomously. Obviously, all these elements are interconnected within the legal and organizational framework, aiming to ensure the safety of air operations and foster cooperation for their uninterrupted and compliant operation, which must work together. Therefore, on the one hand, we have independence in carrying out our own tasks, but on the other hand, we have cooperation, the common denominator of which is safety and international legal regulations. The latter regulates how they operate and behave in certain circumstances in the system. All elements (entities) in aviation are developed in accordance with accepted standards (legal norms) to ensure the safety of all users.

Systems theory in civil aviation means interactions. These interactions involve a multitude of entities that, although separate, as shown above, share many common features and connections. Some scholars distinguish several interaction systems in aviation.[43] The main system is the global aviation system. It is noted that although carriers and their aircraft are separate entities, they all operate on the basis of one principle: safety, which is common to all. There is also an air traffic control system,

39 *Ibidem.*
40 Harris D., Stanton N. A., op. cit., pp. 145–148.
41 Maier, M. W., *Architecting principles for system of systems*, Systems Engineering, Vol. 1, 1998, pp. 267–284.
42 Harris D., Stanton N. A., op. cit., pp. 145–148.
43 Typical Systems in the Aviation Domain, https://ebrary.net/199963/engineering/typical_systems_aviation_domain, accessed February 25, 2024.

where the sole common denominator is safety. The purpose of air traffic control is to ensure that there are no collisions between individual aircraft. This system focuses on air traffic safety. The third system is the supply chain. This system begins with the initial phase of machine design, by providing appropriate components and technical subsystems, ensuring overall safety in the operation phase. Additionally, there is a socio-technical system that includes the aircraft environment as a place where the technical system interacts with the human factor (with cabin crew and flight crew responsible for onboard safety). In a broader sense, this system refers to the entire aircraft handling process related to ground handling. It is evident there are many layers of systems that are separate but independent and participate in the process of interaction. The most important thing is that safety depends on the consistency of these systems and complete interaction.[44]

The theory of system suggests that accidents and incidents in aviation are the results of complex interactions between different elements of an aviation system, including people, equipment, procedures, and organizational culture. According to this theory, safety can be improved by addressing the root causes of accidents and incidents, not just treating symptoms. Another element of the theory of the system is the system of technical service. Harris and Stanton present data from other researchers and the aircraft manufacturer Boeing which indicate that improper aircraft maintenance and technical errors are the cause of a large number of aviation accidents and incidents.[45] The authors indicate that the level of safety can be improved by enhancing maintenance performance through logging, categorizing, and monitoring errors.

1.4.2 Human factors theory

The basic scientific considerations in the context of aviation safety include the human factors theory, sometimes referred to as the theory of human mistakes. This theory focuses on the study of how people interact with machinery, equipment, and systems in aviation. It involves an understanding of human capabilities and limitations, as well as the cognitive and social factors that affect human performance.

The theory of human factors in aviation is a practical study of how human capabilities, limitations, and behaviors can affect aviation safety. The theory emphasizes the importance of designing aviation systems, equipment, and procedures, taking into account human capabilities and limitations, in order to reduce the risk of human mistakes. In aviation, human factors refer to the study of the interaction between humans and machines, equipment, and systems.

The human factor plays a key role in aviation safety, as human error is the leading cause of accidents and incidents in the industry. The theory of human factors recognizes that people are fallible and can make mistakes, especially in

44 *Ibidem*.
45 Harris D., Stanton N. A., op. cit., pp. 145–148.

cases of high-stress or demanding situations.[46] It has been suggested that many aviation accidents and incidents are the result of human error, which can be caused by various factors including fatigue, stress, communication failures, and inadequate training or experience. One of the key concepts in this theory is that mistakes are a normal part of human behavior and should be expected, rather than immediately seeking to punish the guilty. This way does not lead to solving the problem, but it is the easiest shortcut. This theory is based on the assumption that people are fallible and can make errors even if they strive to avoid them. Instead of blaming individuals for errors, the focus should be on identifying and eliminating the underlying causes, such as inadequate training or improper design of equipment or procedures.

Theoretical considerations of human factors help in better understanding and prevention of the causes of errors. Human factors theory aims to explain the causes, conditions, and circumstances of a specific event, behavior, error, or mistake. By understanding the human factor in aviation, it is possible to design better equipment and systems, develop more effective training programs, and create a safer working environment for pilots, crew members, and ground personnel. A thorough, comprehensive, multifaceted analysis of human factors, along with a set of various connections and interactions, can provide a holistic picture of the phenomenon under consideration.

From a scientific perspective, researchers try to explain the impact of human factors on aviation safety by considering psychological conditions, including cognitive, behavioral, physical, and social aspects. Moriarty notes that there are many organizational factors that can lead to dangerous activities.[47] He emphasizes that it was once believed that every error was attributable to humans because the system was inherently good and functioned correctly. According to Moriarty, this is a misconception that is no longer acceptable, because systems are not foolproof, and people strive to make the entity function properly, without disruption.[48] Therefore, a multifaceted approach to addressing errors and deficiencies in the functioning of the entity is necessary.

There are various models used in the study and explanation of human factors theory to understand the causes of errors and develop strategies for reducing them. One of them is Reason's Model, which suggests two approaches to the problem of human error: the individual approach and the systems approach. The former focuses on the traditional understanding that every mistake results from inappropriate or dangerous human action, thereby blaming the individual. On the other hand, the systemic approach focuses on the conditions in which individuals work, i.e. external factors and environment. These are often hidden mistakes that reveal themselves in the least expected situation. They can be latent for many years

46 For more on theoretical and practical considerations of human factors and human error, see *Human Factors Training Manual*, Doc 9683iAN/950, ICAO 1998.

47 For more on error management, see Moriarty D., op. cit., pp. 119–132.

48 *Ibidem*.

and only erupt when they react with active failures or triggers. The system model is also known as the Swiss cheese model. According to this theory, each system has multiple protective layers (e.g. technical solutions, people, procedures), whose role is to guard against threats. These layers resemble Swiss cheese, which has many holes. These holes do not necessarily cause bad results. However, if these holes overlap, then one can notice the "leakage" of the system; these holes can contribute to a potential accident.[49] Therefore, understanding both of these theories leads to proactive risk management.

Another model is the Human Factors Analysis and Classification System (HFACS), which was developed by Shappel and Wiegmann.[50] This model is used to analyze accidents and incidents in aviation and to identify the human factors that contributed to them. HFACS categorizes human factors into four levels:

a) unsafe acts;
b) preconditions for unsafe acts;
c) organizational influence;
d) unsafe supervision.

Dangerous activities fall into two categories: errors and violations. Errors can be attributed to skill-based issues (such as executing procedures in the wrong sequence), decision-making errors (in aviation, not all situations have proper procedures and sometimes one must choose from several options – some choices may be good, while others are not), and perceptual biases (where one's perception of the world differs from reality; for example, due to visual illusions or spatial disorientation). Violations, on the other hand, primarily concern breaches of rules and procedures. They can result from routine violations (habitually disregarding rules) or exceptional violations (isolated cases of deliberate non-compliance with regulations).[51]

Prerequisites influencing dangerous actions or behaviors include: adverse mental states, adverse physical conditions, and mental/physical limitations.[52]

Organizational impact comprises three factors: resource management (human, financial, technical, operational), the work atmosphere (work climate, relationships between employees, forms of interpersonal communication), and the operational process (system of maintaining supervision and balance between employees and management, incentive system, work schedule).[53]

49 Reason J., *Human error: models and management*, BMJ 3/18/2000; Vol. 320 (7237), pp. 768–770. DOI: 10.1136/bmj.320.7237.768.
50 Shappel S., Wiegamnn D., *The Human Factors Analysis and Classification System–HFACS*, Washington 2000.
51 *Ibidem.*
52 *Ibidem.*
53 *Ibidem.*

Unsafe surveillance in aviation concerns the following four elements: inadequate supervision, inadequately planned operations, failure to rectify/remedy the problem, and regulatory breaches by regulators.[54]

By understanding the causes of human error in aviation and developing strategies to reduce it, aviation organizations can improve safety and minimize the risk of accidents and incidents. Such strategies may include enhancing training and experience requirements, designing equipment and procedures to be more user-friendly, and promoting a safety culture that prioritizes communication, teamwork, and continuous improvement.

The theory of human factors in aviation has led to the development of many tools and techniques to improve aviation safety, including crew resource management (CRM), threat and error management (TEM), and fatigue risk management systems (FRMS). By incorporating human factors principles into flight design, training, and operations, organizations can improve safety performance, reduce the risk of accidents and incidents, and increase the overall efficiency and effectiveness of aeronautical systems. Theoretical scientific analyses of human factors have been reflected in international, regional, and national regulations. They have become the basis for the development of an aviation safety management system at various horizontal levels. They are the foundation for considering the causes analyzing events in aviation and drawing conclusions for the future.

1.4.3 Safety culture theory

Safety culture theory emphasizes the importance of organizational culture in promoting safety. This suggests that safety is not only the responsibility of individual employees, but also falls under the values, attitudes, and behavior of the organization as a whole. A positive safety culture can lead to improved safety performance, while a negative safety culture can increase the risk of accidents and incidents. In civil aviation, safety culture is unique and crucial.

There is no universally accepted single definition of this term. The literature indicates that the term "safety culture" was first used in connection with the Chernobyl nuclear reactor disaster in 1986.[55] Eeckelaert *et al.* point out that the report from the investigation by the International Nuclear Safety Advisory Group (INSAG) of the International Atomic Energy Agency (IAEA) indicated identified a "poor safety culture" as one of the factors that contributed to the largest and most tragic nuclear power plant accident in history. In many subsequent cases, cultural aspects were similarly highlighted as causal factors. Studies of other serious, tragic

54 *Ibidem.*

55 The Chernobyl disaster of April 26, 1986, is widely described in the literature. The most valuable works include: Sekuła P., CZARN*OBYL. Społeczno-gospodarcze, polityczne i kulturowe konsekwencje katastrofy jądrowej dla Ukrainy*, Kraków 2014; Yablokov A. V., Nesterenko V. B., Nesterenko A. V., *Chernobyl: consequences of the catastrophe for people and the environment*, Annals of the New York Academy of Sciences, Vol. 1181 (1), 2009; *Chernobyl: Looking back to go forward*, IAEA, Vienna 2008.

accidents in the following years also identified cultural aspects as contributing factors. Since then, the concept of safety culture has been increasingly used in safety research, particularly in air transport.[56]

There are many scientific interpretations of safety culture. Reason, a prominent British psychologist, argues that safety culture refers to "what people at all levels of an organization do and say when their commitment to safety is not tested".[57] Reason lists five elements that constitute a safety culture: informed culture, reporting culture, learning culture, just culture, and flexible culture.[58] Uttal, on the other hand, defines safety culture as a set of values and beliefs that interact with an organization's structures and control systems to produce behavioral norms.[59] According to Turner, there are four dimensions to a "good" safety culture:[60]

a) establishing specific actions and reactions of the entity to a given phenomenon;
b) ensuring full involvement in the response of all people, including management;
c) providing feedback from incidents to relevant stakeholders;
d) establishing flexible and comprehensive legal rules, policies, and procedures for resolving safety issues.

The ICAO Safety Management Manual (Doc.9858) indicates how the issue of safety culture is understood. The interdependencies and interactions between the culture of safety and the cultural diversity of people shall be emphasized. Each nation has a different culture, so people of different nationalities, ethnicities, races, or religions, in other words, from different cultures, can work in a given organization. Therefore, interactions between people and communication are crucial.[61]

A safety culture requires constant monitoring. Each entity should develop and implement its own system for monitoring compliance with the principles of safety culture by personnel. Various tools, such as data analysis or questionnaires, are designed to improve the functioning of the organization, contribute to a better understanding of safety regulations, understand threats, and be able to identify them.[62]

It is worth paying attention to one more aspect when analyzing the scientific determinants of safety culture. It is often pointed out that "goal zero" is essential

56 Eeckelaert L., Starren A., Scheppingen A. van, Fox D., and Brück C., *Occupational safety and health culture assessment – a review of main approaches and selected tools. Working environment information working paper*, European Agency for Safety and Health at Work, 2011, p. 12.
57 For more information: Reason J., *Human error*, Cambridge University Press 1990.
58 *Ibidem*, see also: https://www.airsafety.aero/safety-information-and-reporting/safety-management-systems/safety-culture, accessed February 27, 2024.
59 Vide: Uttal, B. *The corporate culture vultures*, Fortune Magazine, 17 October 1983, Reason James, *Achieving a safe culture: theory and practice*, Work and Stress 1998, Vol. 12 (3), pp. 293–306.
60 Turner Barry A., *The sociology of safety*, in: Blockley D. I. (ed.), Engineering Safety, London 1992, pp. 186–204. Cited by: Marsden E., *Safety culture. A contentious and confused notion*, https://risk-engineering.org/concept/safety-culture#ref-Turner1992, accessed February 18, 2024.
61 Safety Management Manual, ICAO, Doc.9858, point 3.2.
62 Eeckelaert, *et al.*, op. cit., p. 5.

in aviation safety. This applies to frequent situations where states and international organizations establish policies aimed at reducing the number of fatal accidents to zero, reducing the carbon dioxide emissions from aircraft into the atmosphere to zero, or eliminating victims, accidents, incidents, and any negative phenomena affecting aviation safety. To achieve these objectives, regulations are introduced that align with this policy. Reason offered interesting considerations on this subject when he discussed the paradox of goal zero.[63] Many entities strive to achieve this goal by setting a decreasing target every year until the number "zero" is reached. According to Reason, this is a dangerous approach, as it focuses solely on winning the fight for goal zero. Unquestioning belief in the possibility of achieving absolute safety (zero accidents or goal zero) can lead to defeat in this war. The participants of this struggle are under constant external and internal pressure, and the anticipation of defeat can only accelerate it. That is why the culture of safety is crucial because the concerns of the individual subject are transferred to everyone and together we can deal with achieving the goal.

Civil aviation safety culture theory refers to the shared values, attitudes, beliefs, and behaviors within an organization that influence safety-related decisions and actions. A strong safety culture is essential to ensure safety in civil aviation, as it helps to promote a proactive approach to safety and encourages employees to take responsibility for safety. In order to foster a positive safety culture in civil aviation, entities (including state authorities) must prioritize safety and create a safety culture that emphasizes communication, cooperation, and continuous improvement. This can be achieved through various methods, including the involvement of people (management and employees), effective communication, systematic and periodic training conducted by qualified specialists, or continuous improvement.

1.4.4 Risk management theory

Risk management theory involves the identification, assessment, and management of risk in aviation. It involves the development of strategies to reduce or eliminate risks and the monitoring of the effectiveness of these strategies. This theory refers to the process of identifying, assessing, and managing risks to reduce the likelihood or severity of accidents and incidents. In aviation, risk can result from a variety of factors, including technical faults, environmental conditions, and human error.

The safety policy contains objectives, strategies, principles, procedures, legal provisions, and rules of conduct to ensure order or desired order of a given system or entity. Since safety is a dynamic category, it varies according to internal and external conditions, as well as political, economic, social, and other factors. The risk of threats should always be considered when creating such a policy. Accurate identification of risk of threats facilitates the implementation of appropriate measures with the right choice of tools to solve an existing crisis. The literature

63 Reason J., Safety *paradoxes and safety culture*, Injury Control & Safety Promotion, Vol. 7 (1), 2000, pp. 3–14.

offers many definitions of risk and its many divisions.[64] Based on scientific research, the risk is analyzed differently in various fields, including economics, law, and others. Risks in the field of legal science can be perceived as an action inconsistent with the applicable legal regulations. Risk in safety studies is a factor or phenomenon affecting the safety of a given entity or system, and causing threats in its regular (peaceful) functioning.

Risk exists in every area of social life, so the role of the state, as well as other international organizations, as entities responsible for regulating the area of civil aviation and shaping aviation safety policy, is one of risk management. In particular, this responsibility lies with the state as the principal subject of international law. According to Eeckelaert *et al.*, the more complex the organization, the greater the potential risk.[65] Thus, the authors draw attention to the fact that the larger the entity, the greater the risk or the greater the number of them. In aviation particularly, there are many risk factors and threats that need to be properly identified, estimated, assessed, and controlled. Muller and Drax contend that in civil aviation risk exists at two different levels, namely the strategic level (encompassing entity policy, expectations, preferences, alliances, reputation, reporting) and the process level (including regulatory, operational, and financial aspects).[66]

Annex 19 to the Chicago Convention (safety management) indicates that the obligation of the state in the field of aviation safety oversight is to establish a national civil aviation safety program, one of the four elements of which is risk management. The risk management process is an inseparable element of any safety system in the contemporary world. Ciekanowski and Wyrębek believe that a model risk management system includes establishing a risk management policy (with clearly defined objectives and tasks as part of an overall strategy), fostering a "common understanding" (ensuring proper and effective communication between participants in each system or entity), and defining the appropriate organizational structure (clarifying the role and tasks of system participants).[67] The risk management process typically involves several key stages, including:

a) risk identification (includes identification of potential hazards that may lead to accidents or incidents; this can be achieved through various methods, including safety audits, incident reporting, and hazard analysis);

64 Vide: Gędek S., *Definiowanie ryzyka*, Prace Naukowe Uniwersytetu Ekonomicznego we Wrocławiu/ Research Papers of Wrocław University of Economics, Nr 513, 2018, s. 119–130; Bashev. H., *Upravlenie na agrarniya risk.* Ikonomicheska misal. Issue 2, Bulgarian Academy of Science. Sofia 2013; Hu Buwei, Shen Siqi, *An Overall Analysis of Risk and Risk Mane*, BCP Business & Management, Vol. 38, 2023.

65 Eeckelaert *et al.*, op.c it., p. 28.

66 Muller R., Wittmer A., Drax C., *Aviation Risk and Safety Management. Methods and Applications in Aviation Organizations*, Springer 2014, p. 24.

67 Ciekanowski Z., Wyrębek H., *Zarządzanie ryzykiem*, in: De Securitate, Nr 2(2), 2016, s. 18–19.

b) risk assessment (involves an assessment of the likelihood and severity of the identified risk based on factors such as frequency, consequences, and available safeguards);
c) risk mitigation (entails developing strategies to mitigate or eliminate identified risks; this may include improving equipment or procedures, implementing new training or education programs, or changing organizational policy or culture);
d) risk monitoring (refers to ongoing observation of risk and its effectiveness in mitigating or eliminating through regular safety audits, incident reporting, and data analysis);
e) continuous improvement (involves continuous efforts to improve the risk management process and the use of new information or the application of best practices).

An interesting theoretical consideration of risk management is presented by Muller and Drax, according to which, strategic risk management can be described as the process of identifying, assessing, and managing risk anywhere in the strategy, in order to protect and create value for stakeholders.[68] According to the researchers, it is necessary to take a strategic view of risk to understand how external and internal events or scenarios will affect the organization in pursuit of its strategic goals.[69]

One of the key concepts in risk management theory is the idea of risk acceptance, which involves making decisions about the level of risk that is acceptable in a given situation. This may include balancing factors such as safety, operational efficiency, and economic considerations. The ICAO Safety Management Handbook presents a classification of civil aviation safety risk probabilities comprising five categories: frequent, sporadic, far, improbable, and extremely unlikely. Once the assessment of the likelihood of the risk occurring has been completed, its severity should be determined, which can be defined as the extent of the damage that can be expected as a consequence of the identified hazard. There are five categories indicating the level of risk severity: catastrophic, dangerous, serious, minor, and irrelevant.[70] All entities should develop a safety risk matrix combining risk probability results and risk severity.

In aviation, risk management is a key element in ensuring safety and minimizing the risk of accidents and incidents. By identifying and eliminating potential risks and hazards, aviation organizations can improve safety and prevent accidents before they occur.

Adequate risk management is essential for the safe and smooth operation of civil aviation. This is significantly influenced by the legislation of the countries or organizations to which these countries belong. Global organizations such as ICAO, or regional ones like the EU or EUROCONTROL, create a legal system for risk management - not to hinder the activities of entities but to take care of their

68 Muller R., Wittmer A., Drax C., op. cit., p. 22.
69 *Ibidem*.
70 Safety Management Manual, ICAO, Doc.9858, op. cit., point 2.5.

safety and eliminate dangerous situations, behaviors, machines, and systems from the market. Risk is inherent in the nature of aviation. The risks are not diminishing, and the fact that air travel is the safest means of transport is due to the international and regional rules that have been adopted and their effective enforcement. In some regions, the risk of threats is greater, influenced by many factors, such as the legal culture of some countries (lack of a proper safety oversight system), insufficient involvement of some entities, cultural conditions (safety culture), and many others.

In Europe, there is a high awareness and commitment of entities in shaping a safe space for the functioning of civil aviation. An effective control mechanism is established and appropriate risk management procedures are implemented in accordance with international standards and recommendations. One of the elements of this mechanism is a system of control of carriers from third countries that wish to operate in Europe.[71] This is vital because, in terms of implemented legislation, the whole safety system functions very well. However, it cannot be said that this is sufficient. Threats cannot always be predicted (technical problems, human error, or the issue of terrorist attacks).

Risk management in this matter refers to the skillful recognition of external and internal threats as well as their prevention in the future. It can be said that this is a formal approach to dealing with danger. Carriers have systems in aircraft to prevent unauthorized intrusion into the cockpit, and appropriate emergency notification mechanisms have been installed in aircraft. On the other hand, until recently, little attention has been paid to the issues of threats coming from within, i.e. terrorist attacks that can be carried out by pilots themselves. For example, the case of March 24, 2015, when pilot Andreas Lubitz of the German carrier *Germanwings* belonging to the *Lufthansa Group* carried out a terrorist attack by crashing a plane in the Alps. The plane was flying from Barcelona in Spain to Dusseldorf in Germany. All of the people onboard died: 148 passengers, including children returning from a school exchange, and six crew members.[72] The pilot committed this terrorist act

71 Establishment of the so-called "blacklist of air carriers". It is a European list of those carriers that do not meet, according to the European approach, the minimum safety requirements and are prohibited from operating to any EU member state, or to Iceland, Liechtenstein, Norway, and Switzerland. The list was first developed in 2005. It is updated periodically, including the removal of a given carrier from the list or the additionof a new one. Legal basis: Regulation (EC) No. 2111/2005 of the European Parliament and of the Council of December 14, 2005 on the establishment of a community list of air carriers subject to an operating ban within the community and informing air transport passengers of the identity of the operating air carrier and repealing Article 9 of Directive 2004/36/EC, OJ EC, L 344 of December 27, 2005, in connection with: Commission Delegated Regulation (EU) 2023/660 of December 2, 2022, laying down detailed rules on the list of air carriers subject to an operating ban or operating restrictions in the Union referred to in Chapter II of Regulation (EC) No 2111/2005 of the European Parliament and of the Council, OJ EU, L 83, March 22, 2023.

72 Campbell S., *Germanwings A320 crash: Rescuers continue search amid reports plane's black box is damaged,* March 25, 2015, Express (http://www.express.co.uk/news/world/566001/Plane-crash-horror-two-babies-among-150-dead-in-Germanwings-Alps-crash?_ga=1.63829675.581465833.1438252774), accessed: May 11, 2015.

when the co-pilot exited the cockpit and then locked the door, preventing him from re-entering. While much has been said about the mental disorder of this attacker, he should be treated as a terrorist rather than as merely a sick man. A sick person certainly deserves sympathy, but a terrorist acts knowingly with the intention of destroying or killing people. There have been no European or even international regulations on this issue so far. Following this event, legislative work began on the implementation of relevant provisions to eliminate such a risk. This example clearly demonstrates that the entire safety management system of carriers was imperfect, ranging from training, and periodic specialist examinations, to the system of internal control of flight personnel and technical solutions. Consequently, greater emphasis has been placed on risk management issues. Under international rules, states are required to establish a national civil aviation safety program, of which risk management is an essential component. Additionally, it is the state's responsibility to enforce and supervise the effective compliance of all relevant aviation entities operating within it with safety management programs. Entities are required to develop a process for hazard identification, and for assessing and controlling safety risks in the context of individual hazards.[73]

Nowadays, the high risk associated with terrorist attacks requires maintaining proper supervision by state authorities in the field of aviation security to counter illegal acts targeting flight safety. Therefore, there is an obligation to implement and maintain national aviation security programs in accordance with the international regulations set out in Annex 17 to the Chicago Convention (aviation security). Risks also arise in the area of air traffic management. Risk factors include, for example, the problem of "congestion" in the sky and at the airport, delays in flight operations, meteorological factors, and inadequate aviation infrastructure to the intensity of air traffic. In this context, it is important to continuously improve the air traffic management system, ensuring it is adapted to the risks associated with the growing demand for air services.

A proper understanding of risk management theory allows for the adequate development of safety strategies and the selection of effective measures and instruments to limit the occurrence of a threat. Risk management is a dynamic and interdependent process. All factors that could potentially affect the risk must be addressed and taken into account.

1.5 International nature of air relations and aviation law

The issues discussed in this study concern the normativity and institutionalization of aviation safety as part of international aviation relations and international aviation law. Civil aviation is an area in which the interdependencies of its constituent entities are noticeable, manifested on different scales of symmetry and asymmetry. Kukułka notes that the regulation, coordination, and balancing

73 Annex 19 to the Chicago Convention (safety management), point 2, Appendix 2, and point 3.3 of Chapter 3.

of the interdependence of international entities are dealt with by an increasingly dense network of institutional frameworks worldwide[74] covering the diversity of legal, organizational, technical, and operational issues. Civil aviation is an interdisciplinary field of science dealing with the study and development of the interdependence of entities and processes occurring within it. It covers legal, political, economic, and technical aspects. First of all, research focuses on the legal regulation of civil aviation and the unification of regulations, which contributes to greater integration and development of interdependence among entities and has an important stabilization and safety function. Air relations take the form of bilateral and multilateral relations between states and international organizations of an intergovernmental nature. Non-state forms, such as professional NGOs, whose aim is to pursue the goal of specific interest groups or common objectives, also play a very important role in international aviation relations. In contemporary international relations, their role is increasing, which is related to the dynamic processes of globalization, regionalization, and international influences. Rysińska's reflections on the international activity of non-state participants are particularly noteworthy.[75] Each type of international relation operates on a legal basis that underpins future cooperation and interdependence of the entities concerned. Antonowicz points out that international law is a system of legal norms regulating relations between its subjects, which are primarily states, but also, to a certain extent, other entities recognized by states.[76] These are, of course, mainly international organizations whose members are states.[77]

International aviation law serves as the legal foundation for the functioning of global aviation relations. It comprises a set of legal regulations, standards of conduct, and methods of action adopted by states and international organizations in the field of aviation. Essentially, it forms the framework for regulating aviation relations and must be considered in international terms due to its inherently global nature. Aviation law is an integral part of both domestic and international legal systems. It is a young and dynamically developing discipline of scientific research. Aviation law is a field of study covering many elements falling within the scope of individual parts of both international and domestic law.[78] It is characterized by internationalization because it is part of the legal systems of states (also referred to as multi-state law).[79]Therefore, creating exclusively national standards of aviation

74 Kukułka J., *Teoria stosunków...*, op. cit., Warsaw 2000, p. 239.

75 Rysińska I., *Uczestnicy stosunków międzynarodowych, ich interesy i oddziaływania*, in: Haliżak E., Kuźniar R. (eds), *Stosunki międzynarodowe: geneza, struktura, dynamika*, Warsaw 2000, pp. 86–106.

76 Antonowicz L., *Podręcznik prawa międzynarodowego*, Warsaw 1998, p. 20.

77 Antonowicz points out that the issue of subjects of international law, other than the state, is complicated. However, entities with international legal capacity and the capacity to act in international law also include the Holy See, the constituent parts of complex states, insurgent communities, and dependent territories. According to the author, the criterion of subjectivity is the ability to enter into treaties. See more: Antonowicz L., op. cit., pp. 21–23.

78 Żylicz M., *Prawo lotnicze międzynarodowe, europejskie i krajowe*, Warszawa 2002, p. 21.

79 See more: Antonowicz L., op. cit., p. 20.

law would be illogical and would hinder the processes of internationalization and coexistence of nations in the modern world. Moreover, it also covers other aspects of law, including elements of constitutional, administrative, civil, and criminal law.

1.6 The process of codification and hierarchization of international aviation law

Since its inception, global aviation relations have been governed by international standards. According to Antonowicz, the codification of international law involves states concluding international agreements that systematically arrange rules regulating the conduct of its subjects.[80] The first attempts to codify aviation law on an international scale took place before World War I. In 1910, attempts were made at the Paris Conference to work out a document, but due to criticism from some countries, this initiative was postponed. It was not until after World War I, in 1919, that the first convention regulating air navigation was adopted.[81]

It is worth pointing out here that the sources of international law are international customs and agreements. It should be noted that from the beginning of the codification of aviation law, states did not rely on custom because, as such, it did not exist. Very quickly, when matters not regulated by written law emerged, efforts were made to codify them. Therefore, almost from the moment the first aircraft appeared in the first decade of the twentieth century, work began on the process of codification of this area. The use of international custom is not common in civil aviation. Żylicz, like other researchers, argues that the responsibility of states and the recognition of their jurisdiction are sometimes identified as customary law. However, according to Żylicz, these are not aviation law issues but rather a derivative or manifestation of sovereignty related to the nationality of aircraft.[82] Nowadays, even this principle is no longer applied because aircraft are recognized as the subject of affiliation of a specific carrier, and the issue of registration is key issue in aviation law. The principle that an aircraft or carrier is the property of the state and is a specially protected national asset is archaic. Such terms can still be found in a political context but not in legal ones. In the era of open and equal competition, economic freedom, liberalization of air transport, and equal rules for all entrepreneurs, such an approach is not justified. The 1919 Paris Convention was based on the principle derived from the law of the sea concerning the freedom of airspace, analogous to the freedom of the seas. This principle, however, was confined to the state's jurisdiction over its airspace within its administrative boundaries, which was promptly codified. In international aviation law, the principle of state sovereignty in the airspace above its territory is already established. The process initiated in 1919 by the Paris Convention concerning the regulation of the basic issues of the activities of

80 *Ibidem*, p. 33.

81 Convention Relating to the Regulation of Aerial Navigation, signed October 13, 1919, in Paris (Paris Convention), in: *The American Journal of International Law*, Vol. 17 (4), Supplement: Official Documents (October 1923).

82 Żylicz M., op. cit., p. 46.

the previously mentioned entities and the function of the state as a regulator and guardian of air transport safety was developed in the following years based on subsequent conventions that addressed other issues.

Żylicz indicates that the structure of aviation law is very complex because it is shaped on many levels, has different sources of origin, and its acts have different subjective, objective, and territorial scopes of application.[83] Aviation law is characterized by hierarchy. The most important standards are multilateral international agreements, followed by regional international agreements, bilateral international agreements, and national regulations. This hierarchy is presented in Figure 1.1. Hierarchy is important for international aviation relations, as it helps to determine which pieces of legislation are more important and which should take precedence in the event of a conflict between them. At the top of the hierarchy of international aviation law is the 1944 Chicago Convention, which is the cornerstone of aviation law at the international level. Other acts include international agreements concluded at the regional level (e.g. European Union law, African Civil Aviation Commission law). These agreements can be classified as either primary or secondary law. Depending on the legal structure of the regional system, they may be legally binding or non-binding. Acts with legally binding force will be applied in states, either directly or transposed into domestic legislation. There are also bilateral international agreements, which are concluded based on multilateral regulations. Finally, states retain the prerogative to create their own legislation, albeit limited in the scope of tasks delegated to regional or global organizations, which are negotiated and ratified by states. International agreements generally hold a higher status than national laws and regulations that are incompatible with them. In the event of

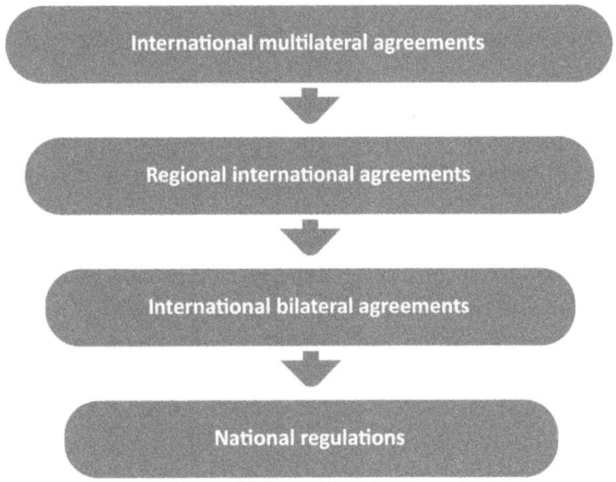

Figure 1.1 Hierarchical structure of aviation law.

83 *Ibidem*, s. 33.

a conflict between an international agreement and national law, according to the principle *pacta sunt servanda*, states must comply with their obligations under the international agreement. Antonowicz emphasizes the primary role of international agreements as a source of international law, as they represent a direct expression of the will of states to establish mutual rights and obligations.[84]

It is worth emphasizing that the hierarchy of international law is not unambiguous and it is not always clear which legal act takes precedence in the event of a conflict. In such cases, it is necessary to carefully analyze each case and pay attention to the specific circumstances that contributed to the conflict. However, the codification of international aviation law and its hierarchy have a direct impact on enhancing safety in civil aviation. The International Civil Aviation Organization (ICAO) has an important regulatory function. The law established by this institution is respected in all member states. Uniform norms and standards developed by the ICAO in the form of hard law (legally binding provisions) and soft law (recommendations) affect the safety and practice of countries that adapt national law to international regulations.

1.7 Legitimacy and importance of harmonizing aviation law

Harmonization of aviation safety rules is a process of cooperation between various international and regional organizations and agencies, such as the global intergovernmental organization ICAO, the International Air Transport Association (IATA), and the European Union Aviation Safety Agency (EASA), in order to establish uniform aviation safety standards worldwide. The main axis towards the harmonization of regulations is based on international standards derived from Chicago Convention and regulations, laws, and procedures issued on its basis. This constitutes a comprehensive system of hard and soft law created by the institutional mechanism of ICAO.

The aim of harmonization is to ensure a uniform level of safety for all flights, regardless of the place of take-off and landing. The unification of aviation safety rules covers the following areas:

1. technical: standards for aircraft construction and equipment;
2. operational: standards for operational procedures and practices, such as air traffic management and on-board safety management;
3. personnel: standards for the qualification and training of personnel, including pilots and cabin crew;
4. environmental: environmental standards such as those governing noise and exhaust emissions.

Harmonization of aviation safety rules is necessary to ensure the safety of all entities of the international law, first and foremost states, but also other users and

84 Antonowicz L., op. cit., pp. 28–29.

entities, including passengers and crew, air carriers, airports, air navigation services, and other services (including air traffic control, meteorology, information, airspace management). It should also ensure flight continuity and the efficiency of international flights. This is an ongoing process as safety standards and requirements are constantly evolving and improving to adapt to the changing environment and emerging threats.

Milligan also points out that among the various sectors regulated by the government, there is the greatest need for a uniform system of laws and regulations in civil aviation. According to Milligan, the aviation industry is an integral part of interstate commerce and it would be contrary to its essence if it were not subject to a uniform set of laws and regulations.[85] Not all countries have a uniform system of aviation law. This applies particularly to federal states, where federal and state laws coexist. Milligan notes that there is still no single system of air law in the US; each state has different safety standards governed by its own tort laws. According to Milligan, the US aerospace industry requires uniform rules and regulations, which would simplify litigation for negligence and product liability claims.[86] It's important to note that while each state in the US may have different laws regarding torts, the Federal Aviation Administration (FAA) plays a central role in regulating aviation safety across the entire country.

1.8 Summary

In general, aviation safety theories provide a framework for understanding and improving the performance of air transport by comprehensively considering the interdependencies between the various factors that contribute to hazards or cause dangerous situations or incidents. By putting these theories into practice, both states and aviation organizations can develop more effective safety strategies, foster a positive safety culture, and minimize the risk of accidents and incidents.

The aim presented at the beginning of the chapter was to show the theoretical aspects of aviation safety. This goal was subordinated to the explanation of aviation safety theory and international and aviation safety paradigms. The essence of the considerations in this chapter also encompassed the issues of codification of international aviation law and the international nature of air relations. These considerations will contribute to clarifying the complexity of normative and institutional issues in civil aviation.

Structure and hierarchy also play an important role in the codification of aviation law. The most important are the international regulations that create the legal frameworks for aviation safety in each country. These standards are primarily defined by the ICAO and its associated institutional structure. An important role

85 Milligan J., op. cit., p. 521.
86 *Ibidem*, p. 534.

in the process of codification and harmonization of aviation law is also played by regional institutions, as well as industry organizations operating in the field of aviation (aviation safety). They serve as an integrating factor for the environment and inspire the codification of specific areas where legal gaps exist or regulations need updating or modification.

2 The global institutional and legal system for aviation safety

In modern international aviation law, many areas have been harmonized in the field of aviation safety. The process of institutionalizing aviation safety is also developed, which ensures continuous monitoring of compliance with international regulations by states and entities providing air services and is also responsible for modifying existing international legal rules, and adapting them to the current challenges and threats facing civil aviation in the world.

The purpose of the present chapter is to analyze the global institutional and legal system of aviation safety. Consideration will be given to existing international agreements that regulate civil aviation safety, as well as the nature and legal conditions of international institutions responsible for performing primarily regulatory and control functions concerning aviation safety issues. In particular, consideration will be given within the ICAO system to coordinate and regulate civil aviation activities worldwide. The characteristics and legal aspects of the activities of ICAO, which develops standards and guidelines for flight safety and supervises their implementation by the member states, will also be discussed. The multilateral system, which includes various legal subsystems on aviation safety issues, will also be discussed, as well as a system of bilateral agreements that are essential for the performance of safe air operations between stakeholders. All these institutions and agreements are aimed at ensuring aviation safety worldwide and preventing aviation incidents and accidents.

The global aviation safety system is an integrated and comprehensive system of activities. It consists of such elements as: international organizations (both intergovernmental – of the utmost importance, because they have a regulatory and control function for all entities operating in the field of aviation – and non-governmental, which contribute to the improvement of the global safety system); safety standards and procedures developed mainly by ICAO; and supervision and control, which are the main prerogatives of states, or rather, of bodies responsible for the control and supervision of aviation safety. The analysis in this chapter has been carried out on the basis of current international legal regulations and reflects the current practice of states and organizations in the application of safety regulations.

DOI: 10.4324/9781003557876-3

2.1 Codification of aviation safety in the multilateral regime

Legislation and the regulatory framework in the field of civil aviation are necessary for the establishment and effective implementation of aviation safety norms and standards on every continent. The basic regulation for aviation law is the Chicago Convention and its annexes. International aviation law also includes other instruments, such as conventions and protocols, in specific areas, including aviation safety and security, regulation and liberalization of the aviation market, passenger and third-party liability, etc. At the national level, countries must adopt legislation that complies with international and regional law regulations.

It is of utmost importance that states also adopt in their internal legislation appropriate provisions that clarify general international standards or recommendations resulting from relevant recommendations of international bodies. National procedures and enforcement mechanisms must include instructions, rules, guidelines, requirements, and policies adopted by these institutions. The main purpose of issuing various non-legally binding acts by international bodies is to standardize certain areas of action and to harmonize legislation. Aviation is international in nature, and the rules in individual countries must not differ significantly from one country to another, as this could lead to difficulties in the functioning of air transport. Thus, harmonization of aviation regulations is essential and is linked to ensuring a higher level of safety. That is why an aviation policy is important, as it sets the direction for legislative action and regulatory framework in the areas of civil aviation.

The term "regulation" refers to an official rule issued by an authority. The use of this term is not limited to the narrow meaning of the creation of legally binding acts. The term "regulations" refers to a wide range of various instruments such as: legal regulations, instructions, guidelines, requirements, principles, standards, declarations, recommendations, policies, and sets of these instruments adopted by state authorities and/or national and international institutions for the purpose of specific behavior or action of the entities to which they are addressed. All these instruments have their own meaning and consequences, legal and/or political. Regulations are created so that the institutions responsible for the area concerned can implement them. The aim is to harmonize legislation and take an integrated approach in a given area. The legislative nature of the adopted regulations is based on their practical application in the future and broad, subjective recognition. Air safety regulations are introduced to ensure the safety of people (flight personnel, crews, passengers, third parties), places (airports, buildings, and aviation installations), and things (luggage, equipment used at airports, aircraft).

Civil aviation regulations are standards or norms that regulate a phenomenon (e.g. terrorist threat), product (e.g. aircraft), process (e.g. impact on climate change), or scheme (e.g. compensation scheme for lost and/or damaged air baggage). Standards are used to homogenize and systematize practices and procedures, which can improve quality, safety, and efficiency. Regulations can be developed by governments, and international and regional aviation organizations, both intergovernmental and non-governmental. They are often used as criteria for the certification of products and services in aviation (e.g. aviation personnel licensing, aircraft certification, air operator certification). The standards serve as a benchmark of quality and help to ensure uniform and consistent requirements at the national and international levels.

Aviation safety codification in a multilateral regime refers to a set of international aviation safety standards and rules established by various international organizations and agreements. These standards and rules aim to ensure a uniform and consistent framework for civil aviation safety and security worldwide.

One of the basic objectives of international civil aviation is to ensure the highest possible safety standards. Zając claims that safety is one of the major challenges of contemporary aviation and should be considered in the context of ground handling, passenger service and check-in, aircraft takeoff and landing, air navigation, technical, and operational safety of aircraft, among others.[1] International legal regulations in this area do not have a long history, because the establishment of the regulatory framework in aviation began at the beginning of the twentieth century, with the emergence and development of aviation. Creating regulations governing the overall functioning of civil aviation strengthens safety in legal, organizational, and operational aspects. We can point to several levels of safety regulation in this matter.

First of all, due to the number of parties, we can point to the multilateral level (where law is created on the basis of adopted international agreements – conventions and treaties, which are signed either as part of an intergovernmental organization or by countries associated in an international conference devoted to a specific topic) and the bilateral level (law concluded by two subjects of international law,[2] i.e., states, or international organizations of an intergovernmental nature).

Secondly, due to the regulatory entity (a regulator), one can distinguish between the institutional level (law-making by intergovernmental international organizations and specialized agencies) and the national level (regulations created by the state as public law).

Thirdly, due to the scope of impact, one can point to global regulations (affecting all entities around the world, without geographical restrictions), regional regulations (laws limited to a continent or a part of it, or to a geographical area), local regulations (laws created by several neighboring entities with a smaller scope than of a region), and national regulations.

Fourthly, due to the addressee, the law is either general-abstract (norms are addressed to multiple entities, with no specific addressee, and refer to the repetitive behavior of these entities) or concrete-individual (the addressee is specified by name, or the norms relate to a specific circumstance or situation).

1 Zając G., *Contemporary political, legal and economic aspects of aviation safety*, International Journal of Social Science and Economic Research, Vol. 5, No. 9, September 2020, p. 2418.

2 Perkowski M., *Podmiotowość prawa międzynarodowego współczesnego uniwersalizmu w złożonym modelu klasyfikacyjnym*, Białystok 2008, p. 342.

Multilateral regulations on the international safety of civil aviation have the widest impact. Establishing an adequate level of safety requires the implementation of global legal instruments that constitute the "backbone" of safe flight operations. Within the framework of the international legal regime, we can point to the leading role played by the ICAO. Its main aim is to promote aviation safety and support the development of civil aviation worldwide by setting aviation safety standards and rules in various areas. ICAO member states are required to incorporate these standards and principles into their national aviation safety systems. Another important document codifying aviation safety in a multilateral regime is the Chicago Convention, which was signed in 1944 and is the legal basis for ICAO's activities. This Convention defines the basic principles and obligations of states in the field of aviation safety. In addition, there are other international agreements and conventions regulating other aspects of civil aviation. They form the legal system in each area.

The multilateral system is based primarily on the regulations resulting from the Convention on International Civil Aviation, signed in Chicago on December 7, 1944, (commonly called the Chicago Convention). On the basis of its provisions, the ICAO became the regulator of the global aviation system. This organization shall adopt, in accordance with Article 37 of the Convention, international standards and rules of conduct in the form of annexes to the Convention. This is a very important legal instrument that regulates individual areas of international civil aviation, with a view to ensuring and maintaining a high level of aviation safety as a priority. ICAO also adopts soft law, i.e. recommendations and a number of acts which, while constituting international standards, are not legally binding, but are of great importance. An effective aviation safety legal system must be based on four pillars:[3]

a) state policy and safety goals;
b) safety risk management;
c) ensuring safety;
d) promoting safety.

The multilateral system of international civil aviation safety is based on a several systems that define performance standards in specific areas:

a) The Chicago system – a system that forms the backbone of international civil aviation safety and establishes a comprehensive regulatory framework for global air transport;

3 Based on Chapter 3 'State responsibility for security management' of Annex 19 to the Chicago Convention.

b) The Tokyo-Hague-Montreal-Beijing system – a system for safeguarding aviation against acts of unlawful interference and preventing acts against the safety of international civil aviation;[4]
c) The Warsaw-Montreal system – a system defining the conditions for the safe air carriage of passengers and baggage, including the liability of the air carrier for damage caused in connection with such carriage;[5]
d) compensation scheme – a system concerning compensation for damage caused by aircraft and for damage inflicted on third parties in connection with broadly understood terrorist acts.[6]

2.1.1 The Chicago system

The Chicago system is the most important, fundamental aviation safety system in the world, which regulates the basic issues of performing safe flight operations and the obligations of countries responsible for the implementation of tasks related to safety supervision. The system comprises the Chicago Convention and 19 annexes, which are created by the ICAO Council. The Chicago Convention is the basic document governing international aviation law, although it is not the first in the world to regulate international civil aviation. It should be recalled that as early as in 1910, attempts were made to enact a multilateral international agreement that would regulate the basis for the functioning of air relations. Thanks to the efforts of France and Great Britain, which were aware of the dangers posed by the lack of regulation of air transport, a diplomatic conference was convened in Paris in 1910. Its main purpose was to legally regulate the movement in airspace, which was an innovative approach due to the lack of existing regulations in this area. The result was a draft convention consisting of 55 articles and three annexes. Despite the submission of the applicable project during the conference, it could not be passed, so it did not become law. The failure was politically related to the fact that states would have to apply the principle of equal treatment to all aircraft, regardless of

4 This system is based on: the Convention on Offences and Certain Other Acts Committed on Board Aircraft, signed in Tokyo on September 14, 1963 (Tokyo Convention); the Convention for the Suppression of Unlawful Seizure of Aircraft, signed in The Hague on December 16, 1970 (Hague Convention); the Convention for the Suppression of Unlawful Acts Against Civil Aviation Safety, signed in Montreal on September 23, 1971 (Montreal Convention); the Protocol for the Suppression of Unlawful Acts of Violence at Airports Serving International Civil Aviation, signed in Montreal on December 24, 1988; and the Convention for the Suppression of Unlawful Acts in Relation to International Civil Aviation, signed in Beijing on 10 September 2010 (Beijing Convention), which replaced and extends the Montreal Convention and the Montreal Protocol.

5 This system consists of two conventions: the Convention for the Unification of Certain Rules for International Carriage by Air, signed in Warsaw on 12 October 1929, and the Convention for the Unification of Certain Rules for International Carriage by Air, signed in Montreal on 28 May 1999.

6 This system includes: the Convention on Compensation for Damage to Third Parties Resulting from Acts of Unlawful Interference Involving Aircraft, signed in Montreal on May 2, 2009. In addition, it incorporates the compensation provisions for the carriage of passengers, goods and baggage as set out in the Warsaw Convention of 1929 and the Montreal Convention of 1999.

nationality.[7] However, the conference did not end in a complete fiasco, as the result was the formulation of two concepts that were later adopted in multilateral and bilateral agreements:[8]

a) the national status of airspace, which implies the need to develop international regulations on flights between the parties concerned;
b) the nationality of aircraft, which meant that each aircraft had to have only one nationality, i.e., be registered in one country.

It was only after World War I that attempts were made to create an international aviation law. In 1919, the world's first multilateral civil aviation agreement was adopted. It was the convention organizing air navigation, signed on October 13, 1919, in Paris (called the Paris Convention).[9] The multilateral agreement was intended to regulate the issues of movement in the airspace of the state and customs exemptions. On the other hand, more detailed solutions concerning the frequency of operations, the designation of routes and carriers to operate them, the procedure for approving air fares, among others, were to be included in bilateral agreements between states. Such a model of air relations existed throughout the whole interwar period.[10] In addition to addressing the fundamental issues of air operations at the multilateral international level, a mechanism for the legal governance of air relations between the countries concerned through bilateral agreements was also established. This is how the bilateral system was born, which became the basis for air connections between countries for many years. The period of World War II remodeled the existing international relations at that time. At the end of hostilities, in 1944, efforts were made by states to permanently restore peace between nations by establishing a solid legal framework for new international organizations in various areas of life of nations and states, including finance, safety, and civil aviation. It is precisely in the scope of the latter that it was decided to create a new system that would be more durable and regulate in more detail the area of aviation law on an international scale. Thus, a conference was convened in Chicago in November and December 1944, which resulted in the adoption of a new Convention on International Civil Aviation.[11] The Convention has become the legal basis for a new air order, or a new system, which has developed over the years within the newly established ICAO. This system, called the Chicago system, primarily regulated all aspects of aviation law, and above all prioritized

7 Sand P., de Sousa Freitas J., Pratt G.N., *An historical Survey on international Air Law before the Second World War*, McGill Law Journal, Vol. 7 (1) 1960–61, p. 30.

8 Zając G., *Podstawy prawne*..., op. cit., pp. 45–46.

9 Convention Relating to the Regulation of Aerial Navigation, signed in Paris, on October 13, 1919, The American Journal of International Law, Vol. 17, No. 4, Supplement: Official Documents (October 1923), pp. 195–212.

10 Zając G., *Podstawy prawne*..., op. cit., p. 46.

11 Kraśnicka I., *Air navigation standards in the activities of the International Civil Aviation Organization (ICAO)*, Wyd. CH Beck 2019, p. 19.

safety, thereby conditioning the development of the entire sector. The Chicago system is very important for aviation safety and the facilitation of international air transport, as it provides uniform standards and rules that are applied worldwide. It also led to the development of a system for concluding bilateral air services agreements between the two countries (e.g. agreement between the Government of the United Kingdom of Great Britain and Northern Ireland and the Government of the Republic of Singapore concerning air services, signed in London, November 21, 2007), which is why it is often referred to as the Chicago-bilateral system. More on the system of bilateral agreements will be discussed later in this study.

2.1.1.1 The Chicago Convention and its provisions

The Chicago Convention is an international agreement that sets out the rules governing air traffic and the safe operation of civil aviation worldwide. It was signed in Chicago in 1944 and is one of the most important legal acts regulating aviation. The goals of the Chicago Convention are:

a) ensuring safety in air traffic: the Convention obliges states to ensure flight safety by establishing common safety standards and procedures;
b) promoting international cooperation: the Convention stipulates the need for cooperation between countries in the field of aviation to permit efficient and safe air traffic;
c) development of civil aviation: the Convention obliges states to develop and improve civil aviation throughout the world,
d) regulation of certain aspects of aviation activities: the Convention regulates air traffic control, airport management, the carriage of goods and passengers, and the responsibility for damage arising from aviation activities;
e) facilitatingcasual commercial exchanges and air services: the Convention obliges nations to allow casual commercial exchanges and air services between countries in order to contribute to economic development.

The Chicago Convention is the basic regulatory act for the safety of air operations with the widest range of subjects. Initially signed by 52 countries,[12] it is currently legally binding for 193 countries.[13] This convention is considered one of the most important documents regulating civil aviation at the international level. Flight safety standards defined within its framework are valid worldwide. It is worth pointing out important safety provisions.

Article 3(d) of the Convention requires states to implement in their internal legislation the measures necessary to ensure the safe exploitation of aircraft.

12 Kraśnicka I., *66 Years of the Chicago Convention on international civil aviation – new trends in the international law of the air*, Analele Universităţii "Constantin Brâncuşi" din Târgu Jiu, Seria Ştiinţe Juridice, Nr. 1/2010, p. 196.
13 ICAO members include 192 countries and the Cook Islands, a dependent territory of New Zealand.

National rules should be compatible and complementary to international rules. In accordance with Article 3bis, all states shall refrain from using weapons against civilian ships in flight so as not to endanger the lives of passengers and crew.[14] Each state shall have the right to require an aircraft to land at a designated location if there are reasonable grounds for fear that it is being used for purposes inconsistent with the Convention. The Convention prohibits the use of air transport for purposes incompatible with the Convention, i.e. aviation must be subject to safe rules, and any action in breach of the safety standards is unacceptable.[15] With regard to the safety of all users and third parties, states have the right to impose restrictions on the performance of air operations in certain zones within their territory.[16] States shall have the prerogative, based on the principle of sovereignty and jurisdiction over airspace, to establish such prohibited zones permanently or temporarily.[17] The conditions that may necessitate the establishment of such zones are related to public safety (e.g. threats arising from the existence of an epidemic, natural disasters, chemical threats, or biological threats, as well as the occurrence or threat of a terrorist attack), and military issues (e.g. the existence of an armed conflict in all or part of the territory of the state, a state of war, martial law, or other armed activities carried out in part or in whole territory).

The provisions of the Convention also provide for state authorities to inspect aircraft in order to maintain the safety of air navigation.[18] Inspections are an extremely important legal instrument for ensuring the aviation safety and are carried out by qualified inspectors and technical specialists. Security inspections are conducted at various stages, including before each flight (a pre-flight check),

14 Article 3a was adopted by the ICAO Assembly on May 10, 1984. In accordance with Article 94(a), this amendment entered into force on October 1, 1998.

15 Article 4 of the Chicago Convention.

16 Article 9 of the Chicago Convention.

17 In terms of establishment of restricted zones, each state has exclusive competence to make such decisions. There are no international regulations requiring states to operate in these zones. International aviation law merely designates such zones, leaving the decision whether to conduct air operations at the discretion of each country. States may, in their domestic legislation, permit operations in restricted areas only under strictly defined conditions. For example, in the US, the existing Code of Federal Regulations (CFR) precisely indicates the procedures for obtaining permission to perform an air operation in a special air zone, i.e. a restricted zone (legal basis: Chapter 14 CFR Section 93.339 C). Furthermore, under the provisions of P56 of Chapter 14 CFR, there are restricted areas covering the White House, the National Mall, and the Vice President's residence in Washington, D.C., as outlined in P-56A regulations, and the area surrounding the Navy Observatory in Washington, D.C., as specified by P-56B regulations. The only aircraft that can operate in these no-go zones under special authorization are those used by the US Secret Service, the President's Office, or other government agencies performing special missions. In another country, Poland, it is possible to perform air operations in restricted zones, but only in exceptional situations, based on a special authorization issued by the national air traffic management authority (legal basis: Guidelines No. 4 of the President of the Civil Aviation Office of July 21, 2005, on flights in restricted zones) According to the regulations, there are 13 special restricted zones in Poland. The situation is similar in the US. In the UKregulations also address restricted zones, specifically in section 239 of The Air Navigation Order 2016, No 765, issued under the Civil Aviation Act 1982 (Civil Aviation Act 1982).

18 Article 16 of the Chicago Convention.

and after a certain number of flight hours or according to a schedule determined by regulations and standards. Aircraft safety inspections are strictly regulated and monitored by aviation authorities. Aircraft inspections are carried out under regulations established by national regulatory authorities such as the Federal Aviation Administration (FAA) in the US[19] or by regional intergovernmental organizations dealing with aviation safety regulations, such as the European Union Aviation Safety Agency (EASA) in Europe.[20] In spite of these regulations, many countries have their own normative rules for the inspection and maintenance of aircraft that are in line with the international standards set by ICAO.

All states parties to the Convention are obliged to adopt rules of conduct in areas to be determined by the ICAO Council, in accordance with Article 54, paragraph 1, of the Convention. The provisions of the Convention impose on states the obligation to comply with international regulations, subject to Article 38 of the Convention. On its basis, if a state is unable to fully implement international rules and bring them into line with its internal legislation, it is obliged to notify the ICAO Council. In that case, the Council shall notify the other member states of the differences between the adopted rules and the actual practice and law in question in that state. Another obligation of the state in the field of flight safety is the requirement to meet certain safety standards before issuing an airport operating permit or issuing certificates of airworthiness to aircraft and air carriers.[21] In addition, the Convention requires states to ensure that appropriate personnel are trained and that appropriate procedures and technical equipment are in place to minimize the risk of air accidents.[22] In the event of a breach of safety standards, ICAO has the power to apply sanctions, such as banning international flights or imposing financial penalties.[23] Article 64 also provides ICAO with an instrument for concluding safety agreements with any international organization. Furthermore, ICAO, together with regional aviation safety providers, shall sign appropriate agreements to cooperate in order to increase safety awareness and develop better and more effective safety standards.

19 As regards the US, the aircraft inspection and maintenance regulations are outlined in Title 14 CFR, Chapter 1, Section C, Part 43, which governs the inspection, repair, and maintenance obligations of aircraft operators, owners, and mechanics. In addition, the provisions of Title 14 CFR Chapter 1, Section F, Part 91 govern the requirements for pre-flight checks before each flight and for periodic inspections as well as inspections related to an aircraft's service.

20 In the case of the EU, the rules for the inspection and maintenance of aircraft are laid down in Part M of Commission Regulation (EU) No 1321/2014 of 26 November 2014 on the continuing airworthiness of aircraft and aeronautical products, parts, and appliances, and on the approval of organizations and personnel involved in these tasks (OJ EU, *L* 362, 17.12.2014), which sets out the requirements for maintaining aircraft airworthiness, as well as in Part 145 of the above-mentioned regulation, which governs organizations responsible for keeping aircraft airworthy. Under these provisions, entities must carry out regular technical inspections, and reviews related to the duration of the aircraft as well as pre-flight checks before each flight.

21 Article 33 of the Chicago Convention.

22 Article 32 of the Chicago Convention.

23 Article 54 (k) of the Chicago Convention.

Along with the Chicago Convention, two other agreements establishingthe so-called air freedoms were adopted. These were the International Air Services Transit Agreement and the International Air Transport Treaty. The former regulated the provisions on technical freedoms,[24] while the latter, in addition to reiterating technical freedoms also included three commercial freedoms.[25]

In international aviation law, the Chicago Convention and the annexes adopted pursuant thereto constitute the regulatory framework for aviation safety. While the convention was agreed upon 52 countries, it laid a foundation for a new institutional system based on the ICAO. Of course, the multilateral system in civil aviation is not based solely on the regulations of this institution. For aviation safety, it is crucial to consider both the legal solutions that existed before ICAO began its operations and those that were developed in later years to address gaps not covered by the Chicago Convention, reflecting the evolving and dynamic nature of international civil aviation. Each of these multilateral systems is designed to ensure the safety of this sensitive and vulnerable sector, incorporating diverse elements from a variety of backgrounds.

The annexes to the Chicago Convention have a unique legal status as they are binding on ICAO member states and are treated as integral parts of the convention itself. This legal nature aligns with the principles established in the Vienna Convention on the Law of Treaties (1969). The Vienna Convention provides a framework for interpreting and applying treaties, including international agreements like the Chicago Convention and its annexes. According to Article 2(1)(a) of the Vienna Convention, a "treaty" is an international agreement concluded between states in written form and governed by international law. The Chicago Convention qualifies as a treaty under this definition. Article 2(1)(b) further states that if a treaty includes annexes that form an integral part of the main text, they are considered inseparable from the treaty. Therefore, the annexes to the Chicago Convention are seen as part of the Convention itself, and any modifications or amendments to these annexes are treated as modifications to the treaty. This means that member states are obligated to incorporate and adhere to the standards, recommendations, and procedures contained in these annexes into their national regulations. They are legally binding and must be implemented by each contracting state as part of their national law or aviation regulations. Article 27 of the Vienna Convention

24 In civil aviation there are nine so-called air freedoms. They are peculiar privileges that allow an aircraft from one country to use the airspace of another. The International Air Services Transit Agreement introduces into aviation law two technical freedoms: the first freedom – the right to fly over the territory of another country without landing; the second freedom – the right to land in the territory of another country in order to refuel or carry out necessary repairs.

25 The International Air Transport Agreement introduces three new commercial freedoms (although it lists five in total, including technical freedoms): the third freedom – the right to embark and disembark passengers or to load and unload goods on the territory of another country; the fourth freedom – the right to carry passengers or goods between two points in the territory of another state, without having to pass through the carrier's home country; the fifth freedom – the right to carry passengers or goods between two points in the carrier's country, through the territory of another country.

emphasizes that a party to a treaty cannot invoke its internal law as an excuse for failure to perform a treaty. This principle applies to the annexes of the Chicago Convention, which member states are required to incorporate into their national aviation laws to comply with international obligations. Article 19 of the Vienna Convention allows for reservations to be made when signing, ratifying, or acceding to a treaty, but this does not apply to annexes unless explicitly permitted by the treaty. Since the Chicago Convention and its annexes do not allow reservations, member states are bound to implement all provisions and standards contained therein. Article 30 of the Vienna Convention addresses the relationship between treaties and their annexes, particularly in the event of a dispute. If a dispute arises regarding the interpretation or application of an annex, it should be resolved in accordance with the procedures established under the treaty. The ICAO Council plays a key role in interpreting the annexes and resolving disputes related to their implementation.

In conclusion, the Vienna Convention provides a legal framework that underscores the binding nature of the annexes to the Chicago Convention, ensuring that member states are obligated to comply with their provisions and that amendments are made following a specific and agreed-upon procedure.

2.1.1.2 Legal aspects and competences of ICAO in the codification of aviation safety

It is worth outlining the institutional principles underlying the functioning and codification of the global aviation safety system based on the ICAO. Its legal basis lies in the Chicago Convention of December 7, 1944. ICAO began operations as the Provisional International Civil Aviation Organization (PICAO) until the Convention entered into force on April 7, 1947.[26] Its main aims are set out in Article 44 of the Convention, of which those relating to safety are:

a) ensuring the safe and proper development of international civil aviation worldwide (Article 44.a);
b) promoting the safe construction and operation of aircraft (Article 44.b);
c) ensuring safe and regular air transport for all people (Article 44.d);
d) increasing the safety of international flight (Article 44.h).

In carrying out its tasks, ICAO has several key functions. The most important of these is the regulatory function. ICAO develops international aviation safety standards,

26 The provisions of the Convention include legal regulations concerning the provisional application of this Convention and the temporary ICAO (PICAO). PICAO operated from December 7, 1944, to April 7, 1947, i.e. until the Convention entered into force. In accordance with Article 91(b) of the Convention, it came into effect on the thirtieth day of the date of obtaining 26 ratifications and depositing the last instrument with the depositary, which was the US. The last state that was required for the entry into force of the Convention was Spain, which deposited its instrument of ratification on March 5, 1947.

such as annexes to the Chicago Convention. Under its auspices, international agreements are drawn up on various aspects of aviation safety and security around the world. Another is the coordination function. ICAO helps member states to comply with aviation safety standards by training staff, providing information, and supporting infrastructure development. ICAO also has a promotional function. It provides a platform for member states to exchange information and experience on aviation safety, leading to improved aviation practices and procedures. Finally, ICAO performs a control function. The organization monitors the activities of states in the field of compliance with safety standards and regulations. In addition, it prepares cyclical reports on civil aviation safety and issues recommendations and guidelines for improving safety at the national or regional level as part of the institutional structures of safety supervision.

The ICAO structure is extensive and consists of main and subsidiary bodies (advisory, technical). The Chicago Convention lists the following bodies;

a) Assembly (Articles 43, 48–50, 54, 61–66, 73, 75, 88, 93–94);
b) Council (Articles 38, 43, 48–56, 58–61, 65, 69–71, 73–74, 77–78, 84–88, 90);
c) Secretary General (Articles 48, 54, 58–60);
d) Air Navigation Commission (Articles 51, 54–57);
e) Air Transport Committee (Articles 51, 54).

The General Assembly is a plenary body of ICAO attended by delegates from all member states. The General Assembly meets in ordinary session every three years.[27] Extraordinary sessions may be convened at the request of the Council or at the request of at least one fifth of all member states (Article 48(a)).[28] During voting, each country has one vote, which is a manifestation of the principle of equality of states.[29] As a rule, resolutions of the Assembly are adopted by a majority of votes of the states present and voting at the session. This body deals with a number of matters, including, in accordance with Article 49 of the Chicago Convention, among others:

a) the election of the board chairman;
b) the selection of representative nations in the Council;

27 Between 1947 and 2023, 33 ordinary (regular) sessions were held. The first ordinary session was held in Montreal from May 6 to 27, 1947, and the last of this period (41. Session) from September 27 to October 7, 2022. The first ten sessions, up to 1956, were held annually in accordance with the original regulations. The 11th session was held in 1958, and since the 12th session in 1959, each subsequent session has been held every three years.

28 In the years 1947–2023, nine extraordinary sessions were held. Extraordinary sessions were held in 1961, 1970, 1971, 1973 (twice), 1984, 1990, 1993, and 2003.

29 The principle of sovereign equality of states is laid down in Article 2(1) of the Charter of the United Nations. The opposite of this is the principle of weighted voting, or the principle of veto (a system that privileges certain states, e.g. those in the UN Security Council).

c) the consideration of the Council's reports and decisions by the Council, the adoption of strategies, and an action plan of the organization;
d) the enactment of annual budgets and making decisions on financial matters, including the examination of expenses;
e) the adoption of resolutions for concluding agreements with other international organizations acting for the benefit of aviation safety.

The Council is the executive body of the ICAO, which consists of 36 members elected for a three-year term by the General Assembly. The Council elects from among its members a chairman, and one or more vice-chairmen. However, if a state representative is elected as chairman, the chairman does not have the right to vote.[30] The seat vacated is therefore filled by a representative of another state. The President of the Council serves a rather ceremonial function. His duties include merely convening meetings of the Council, the Air Transport Committee, and the Air Navigation Commission, as well as representing the Council externally, and carrying out tasks assigned by the Council.[31] The composition of the Council must reflect the nations' affiliation to one of three groups:[32]

1) a group of the most important countries in air transport;
2) a group of countries that contribute most to the provision of facilities for international civil air navigation;
3) a group of countries representing the main geographical regions of the world.

The Council deals with the day-to-day management of ICAO, develops standards and recommendations, oversees the budget of the organization, and makes decisions on matters related to civil aviation. The Council's most important competences, as defined in Article 54 of the Chicago Convention are, for example:

a) submission of the annual report to the Assembly;
b) handling the recommendations and resolutions of the Assembly;
c) designation of the Air Transport Committee, the Air Navigation Commission, and the Secretary-General;
d) management of the finances of the organization;
e) notification of all parties of any violation of the Convention and of any failure to comply with recommendations or rulings of the Council;

30 Article 51 of the Chicago Convention.
31 *Ibidem.*
32 For the 2022–2025 Council term, the following states were elected: Group 1: Australia, Brazil, France, Germany, Italy, Japan, PRC, the UK, and the US; Group 2: Argentina, Austria, Egypt, Iceland, India, Mexico, Nigeria, Saudi Arabia, Singapore, South Africa, and Venezuela; Group 3: Bolivia, Chile, Equatorial Guinea, Ethiopia, Ghana, Jamaica, Malaysia, Mauritania, Qatar, Republic of Korea, Romania, El Salvador, United Arab Emirates, and Zimbabwe.

f) adoption in accordance with the provisions of Chapter VI of the Chicago Convention, international standards and recommended practices (annexes), as well as amendments thereto, based on a two-thirds majority of states present and voting.

The Secretary-General is the chief official of the organization. He heads the Secretariat, which is based in Montreal. With the assistance of the administrative apparatus (the Secretariat), the Secretary is responsible for the day-to-day work of the organization and implements the decisions taken by the Council and the General Assembly. The Secretariat consists of five departments, such as the Air Navigation Bureau, the Air Transport Bureau, the Technical Cooperation Bureau, the Legal Affairs and External Relations Bureau, and the Bureau of Administration and Services. The staff of the Secretariat and the Secretary are independent of the performance in their duties and cannot receive instructions from any state. With this in mind, they enjoy privileges and immunities for international officials in accordance with international regulations in this regard. Augustyniak notes that the privileges and immunities of international officials, unlike diplomatic ones, are functional in nature, granted only to protect these persons in relation to the performance of their official duties.[33] In addition, Augustyniak emphasizes that there are no uniform legal regulations in the world regarding the status of all international officials, however, states customarily or on the basis of international courtesy grant appropriate privileges and immunities to officials of international organizations operating on their territory.[34]

The Secretary-General is also responsible for supervising the work of the seven ICAO regional offices. In order to better carry out its activities and respond to national needs, seven regional offices have been established to maintain closer contacts with the countries of the region and to cooperate with local and regional safety oversight organizations and other intergovernmental or non-governmental organizations active in the field of civil aviation. ICAO has the following regional offices:

1. North America and Caribbean Office (NACC) – headquarters Mexico City (Mexico);
2. South America Office (SAM) – headquarters: Lima (Peru);
3. Europe and North Atlantic Office (EUR/NAT) – headquarters: Paris (France);
4. West and Central Africa Office (WACAF) – headquarters: Dakar (Senegal);
5. Eastern and Southern Africa Office (ESAF) – headquarters: Nairobi (Kenya);
6. Middle East Office (MID) – headquarters: Cairo (Egypt);
7. Asia-Pacific Office (APAC) – headquarters: Bangkok (Thailand).

33 For more information, Augustyniak Ł., *Immunity from jurisdiction of international organizations and the immunity of their officers*, Ruch prawniczy, ekonomiczne i socjologiczny, Tom LXIX - zeszyt 3 – 2007, p. 49.

34 *Ibidem*, p. 50.

The Chicago Convention also mentions two other bodies, albeit of an advisory and technical nature. These are the Air Navigation Commission (ANC) and the Air Transport Committee. The former consists of 21 persons nominated by the member states and appointed by the Council.[35] These persons should have appropriate qualifications and experience in civil aviation (Article 56 of the Chicago Convention). The Commission meets in three sessions per year, each lasting about nine weeks. The main tasks of the ANC are to draft annexes to the Chicago Convention and amendments thereto, and to issue opinions on the maintenance and improvement of aviation safety and the efficiency of air navigation. However, the Air Transport Committee is not the main organ of the organization, it is one of the advisory and technical bodies, whose members are also elected by the Council. While the ANC performs key tasks related to the development and amendment of annexes as an important legal instrument for aviation safety regulation, the Air Transport Committee mainly deals with economic matters and aviation facilitation.

In addition, ICAO has a number of committees, subcommittees and working groups that deal with specific issues related to civil aviation, such as flight safety standards and procedures, greenhouse gas emissions, flight crew training, passenger safety, etc. These subsidiary bodies are responsible for developing standards and recommendations in their respective fields and submitting them to the Council for approval.

Kilar points to three areas that ICAO deals with: legal, technical, and economic issues.[36] Its regulatory activity involves establishing legally binding rules, such as standards in the form of annexes, and multilateral and bilateral agreements (concluded between ICAO and a state, or between ICAO and another organization), or issuing recommendations (for example, manuals on specific aviation issues or recommendations contained in annexes) addressed to member states, and, through them, *de facto* to all entities operating in the aviation sector (airports, air carriers, services, intergovernmental and non-governmental aviation organizations). Activity in the area of technical issues involves developing uniform technical standards in the field of construction, use and maintenance of aircraft, as well as for the technical aspects of the design and operation of airports, and establishing appropriate technical parameters for aviation equipment and installations necessary to maintain safety in air traffic. The economic activity of ICAO includes the development of rules regulating the functioning of entities in civil aviation, including air traffic management, air traffic control, competition rules, and rules of conduct for business by carriers, airports, or other entities. In addition, it addresses

35 The composition of the Air Navigation Commission has been expanded three times by the ICAO Assembly. Initially, it had 12 representatives. As a result of the change in 1971, the composition was expanded to 15 people, then in 1989 to 19 people, and finally in 2016 the composition was increased to 21 people. See: https://applications.icao.int/postalhistory/the_air_navigation_commission.htm, accessed 20.02.2024.

36 Kilar I., *Geneza funkcjonowanie Organizacji Międzynarodowego Lotnictwa Cywilnego*, op. cit., p. 32., cited in Zajas S., *Organizacja Międzynarodowego Lotnictwa Cywilnego i jej wpływ na funkcjonowanie i rozwój lotnictwa*, Zeszyty Naukowe AON No. 4(101) 2015, p. 51.

customs and tax issues related to international civil aviation. Zajas argues that, so far, there is no uniform and universal codification of economic issues within ICAO, because many countries still maintain a restrictive aviation policy that limits other entities' access to a country's airspace, including not opening up to free competition.[37] However, ICAO issues many regulations relating to economic matters that do not raise general concerns, and in this respect it promotes and encourages states and regional aviation organizations to adopt uniform standards in economic matters in the interests of transparency, competition, and development of the sector. ICAO also promotes the conclusion of "open market" agreements that liberalize the aviation market, contributing to the development of air connections and the aviation-related sector or the local economy.

This division seems to be limited to these most important areas of ICAO's activity, but the specific conditions and its functions in the modern world should be considered. It should also be appropriate to include the area of administrative issues or matters related to environmental protection. In the administrative sphere, ICAO coordinates and develops cooperation amongvarious aviation organizations in the world, serves as a platform for the exchange of experience, provides technical and expert support, organizes international conferences, and provides a forum for discussion devoted to various aspects of civil aviation. It should also be added that, in carrying out its administrative activities, ICAO manages various programs and initiatives related to aviation safety, environmental protection, air traffic management, and other key areas.

ICAO increases its focus on environmental issues by regulating factors such as excessive noise and carbon dioxide emissions from aircraft. It undertakes numerous activities to promote the sustainable development of civil aviation and minimize the environmental impact of its operations. To this end, it develops standards and recommendations for environmental protection in aviation, such as standards for emissions, noise, and fuel consumption. It also supports efforts to improve fuel efficiency and reduce greenhouse gas emissions from aircraft by promoting greener technologies. ICAO monitors and assesses the environmental impact of aviation activities in order to identify areas for further action and adapt its standards to new requirements. All activities in the area of environmental protection aim to minimize the negative impact of civil aviation on the environment, improve air quality, and reduce greenhouse gas emissions, thereby enhancing the sustainable development of the aviation sector.

To sum up, ICAO's activities focus on such areas as legal issues, economic issues, technical issues, administrative issues, and environmental issues. The unifying principle behind all these areas is the safety of civil aviation. ICAO subordinates all its activities to this guiding idea, which is enshrined not only in the Chicago Convention but also in the provisions of its annexes and in other normative acts. It would be trivial to state that if the level of safety decreases, air transport will lose its significance and development. No one would pursue such a thesis, as it is not in

37 Zajas S., *Organizacja…*, op. cit., pp. 51–52.

the interest of any state, international institution, or other users. The development of civil aviation, which is facilitated by ICAO, is intended to respond and adapt to the changing conditions of the global environment, including meeting demands resulting from processes such as globalization and digitization. Civil aviation is inherently international, and in recent years the issues of digitization in the aspect of Information Communication Technologies (ICT) security as well as the technical safety of machinery and communications have acquired new significance. All legal acts adopted, as well as cooperation with states and international organizations, aim not only at monitor compliance with concluded legal agreements, and to establish or modify legal provisions in specific areas, but also to develop good practices in the field of safety management and promote greater engagement by states in maintaining air transport safety.

All these activities contribute to maintaining aviation safety worldwide and make ICAO an indispensable organization in the aviation industry. The developed uniform standards and norms contribute to a high level of safety globally. Thanks to the harmonization of the codification of aviation standards in all countries around the world (except Liechtenstein and the Vatican, which are not ICAO members) the same rules serve as the basis for the functioning of civil aviation.

It is also worth noting ICAO's promotional and educational activities in the field of aviation safety. It publishes annual reports on the state of safety and the challenges facing international civil aviation. These reports are prepared in connection with the Global Aviation Safety Plan (GASP). Aviation safety reports (ASR) contain information about air accidents, incidents, and dangerous occurrences related to flights, including analysis of their causes and recommendations for improving safety in the future. They also address safety in air traffic management systems and the operational safety of civil aviation. ICAO also publishes reports on the Universal Safety Oversight Audit Program (USOAP), which are the results of audits conducted by ICAO in the member states assessing the quality of national oversight of civil aviation safety and compliance with international standards. Overall, both the ASR and USOAP report serve as essential tools in the process of improving civil aviation safety by identifying critical areas for enhancement and providing actionable recommendations to help prevent future accidents and incidents.

2.1.1.3 Aviation safety regulations in the annexes to the Chicago Convention

From the perspective of the book's subject matter, the regulations created in the form of annexes to the Chicago Convention are of particular interest. Annexes are a form of legal acts that contain international standards and rules of conduct in the area defined thematically in such a document. It is worth pointing out the legal conditions for adopting annexes. At the outset, it is necessary to define the essence of annexes. An annex contains standards and recommended practices. Standards are provisions whose has been deemed necessary for ensuring the safety and proper functioning of international air navigation. They can regulate areas such as physical characteristics, configuration, materials, operation, personnel, or procedures. On the other hand, prescribed methods of action are provisions that have been deemed desirable in the interests of ensuring safety, regularity, and the proper functioning of international civil aviation. They pertain to areas similar to those covered by the norms.

The legal nature of the annexes is laid down in the Chicago Convention, which clearly states in Article 54 that international standards and recommended practices are to be adopted by the ICAO Council in the form of annexes to the Convention, in particular with regard to civil aviation safety. The annex therefore has the force of international law and is an act binding on the states parties to the Convention upon its entry into force. The annexes shall be adopted by the Council in the form of a decision in accordance with the procedure referred to in Article 90 by a two-thirds majority of the members of the Council. They are then presented to the member states. States have the right to raise objections within 60 days of receipt of the document. Subject to Article 38, if a provision cannot be introduced into national legislation by a state, it must report this fact to the ICAO Council. The annex shall enter into force three months after it has been submitted to the member states or after a period scheduled by the Council. The Council shall inform each country of any amendment to the annex. The standards set out in the annex shall become binding on the ICAO states.

The legal status of the annexes is not entirely clear. It should be noted that the annexes are legal acts adopted in accordance with the procedure set forth in the Chicago Convention. They contain standards which the member states are obliged to apply. This is in line with the definition of standards that are necessary for the safe functioning of civil aviation. However, if a state has objections to certain provisions in an annex, it shall notify ICAO in accordance with the established procedures. Therefore, unless a state raises objections, the annex is fully implemented. It should be stressed, however, that an annex itself also contains recommendations which are not legally binding and serve merely as guidance for the state to follow, albeit without a legal obligation. This does not change the fact that the standards contained in the annex are legally binding and carry the most important regulatory force.

So far, 19 annexes to the Chicago Convention have been adopted, which are presented in Table 2.1.

At the multilateral level within ICAO, aviation safety standards are mainly contained in Annexes 1, 2, 6, 8, 9, 12, 13, 14, 17, 18, and 19. Although *de facto* each annex contains provisions defining the safe functioning of transport in a given area, several of the previously mentioned annexes deserve special attention.

Annex 1 to the Chicago Convention contains provisions regarding the licensing of aviation personnel, including pilots of various types of aircraft, aircraft navigators, flight engineers, air traffic controllers, and technical personnel. The requirements for licencing aviation personnel have been developed to ensure that individuals with appropriate qualifications and experience are responsible for safe flight operations. The licensing requirements encompass both theoretical and practical training and assessments and they require applicants for a license to demonstrate specific skills and experience. Licensing is also dependent on the candidate's

Table 2.1 List of annexes to the Chicago Convention and the date of their adoption

Number	*Title*	*First release date*
Annex No. 1	Personnel Licensing	1948
Annex No. 2	Rules of the Air	1948
Annex No. 3	Meteorological Service for International Air Navigation	1948
Annex No. 4	Aeronautical Charts	1948
Annex No. 5	Units of Measurement to be Used in Air and Ground Operations	1948
Annex No. 6	Operation of Aircraft	(1948)[a]
Part 1	International Commercial Air Transport – Aeroplanes	1948 (1969)[a]
Part 2	International General Aviation – Aeroplanes	1948 (1965)[a]
Part 3	International operations – Helicopters	1986
Annex No. 7	Aircraft Nationality and Registration Marks	1949
Annex No. 8	Airworthiness of Aircraft	1949
Annex No. 9	Facilitation	1949
Annex No. 10	Aeronautical Telecommunications	(1949)[b]
Volume 1	Radio Navigation Aids	1949 (1965)[b]
Volume 2	Communication Procedures including those with PANS status	1949 (1965)[b]
Volume 3	Communication Systems	1949 (1965)[b]
Volume 4	Surveillance and Collision Avoidance Systems	1949 (1965)[b]
Volume 5	Aeronautical Radio Frequency Spectrum Utilization	1949 (1965)[b]
Annex No. 11	Air Traffic Services	1950
Annex No. 12	Search and Rescue	1950
Annex No. 13	Aircraft Accident and Incident Investigation	1951
Annex No. 14	Aerodromes	
Volume 1	Aerodrome Design and Operations	1951
Volume 2	Heliports	1990
Annex No. 15	Aeronautical Information Services	1953
Annex No. 16	Environmental Protection	
Volume 1	Aircraft Noise	1971
Volume 2	Aircraft Engine Emissions	1981
Volume 3	Aeroplanc CO_2 Emissions	2017
Volume 4	Carbon Offsetting and Reduction Scheme for International Aviation (CORSIA)	2018
Annex No. 17	Aviation Security: Safeguarding International Civil Aviation Against Acts of Unlawful Interference	1975
Annex No. 18	Safe Transport of Dangerous Goods by Air	1984
Annex No. 19	Safety Management	2013

[a]Annex No. 6 was issued in 1948 as a single volume. In 1965, further amendments were introduced, from which, four years later, Volume 2 was separated. In 1969, the entire document was divided into two volumes. Although Volume 2was created in 1969, its provisions had already been included in 1965 and it is therefore considered that this is the date of creation of this annex.

[b]Annex No. 10 was issued in 1949 as a single volume. As a result of numerous amendments, in 1995 it was divided into five volumes.

age and other factors, such as health. In the context of the medical regulations set out in Chapter 6 of Annex 1 to the Convention, essential health specifications are specified that enable a person to properly and correctly perform the duties associated with a given position. Moreover, the conditions that would prevent the acquisition of a license which may pose a threat to flight safety, have also been described. Therefore, holding a license indicates the holder's awareness of safety regulations and ensures they have acquired the thorough knowledge necessary to safely perform tasks in air transport. Flight crew licensing requirements are constantly updated to reflect the latest technologies, procedures and safety standards. Certification of aviation personnel is important not only for flight safety, but also for ensuring consistency in standards and procedures across the aviation sector.

Annex 2, "Rules of the Air" sets out air traffic regulations that are intended to ensure safety in air traffic. These regulations define the rules for performing aerial maneuvers and using airspace, as well as the requirements for crews and on-board equipment. The guidelinesfor the safe operation of Visual Flight Rules (VFR) flights (in accordance with the regulations for visual flights) and Instrument Flight Rules (IFR) flights (operating by instrument indications) are specifiedbased on weather conditions. This issue is extremely important for the safety of air operations, as it standardizes the conditions under which specific flights may be performed. These regulations constitute an important procedural and technical indication for all air operators, ensuring uniform requirements for VFR and IFR flights, such as rules for maneuvering and use of airspace, navigational procedures, minimum required weather conditions, as well as the principles governing flights over controlled and non-controlled areas. The rules for conducting night flights (including requirements for lighting and on-board equipment) and for flights using drones have also been harmonized. It is precisely with regard to the latter that the legislation clearly stipulates that operations of remotely piloted aircraft shall be carried out in such a way as to minimize, as far as possible, risks and threats to persons, property, and other aircraft in accordance with the provisions laid down in that annex. In general, the provisions of that annex establish guidelines for the use of different categories of airspace, such as controlled or uncontrolled airspace. Thanks to this document, air traffic around the world is safer and more effectively regulated.

Annex 6 to the Chicago Convention "Operation of Aircraft" consists of three parts: the first part concerns the performance of aircraft operations in regular and commercial air transport, the second part regulates operations in general aviation, and the third part coversoperations performed by helicopters. Each carrier must operate aircraft that are safe, i.e. meet certain basic safety standards. To this end, Annex 6 enacts provisions for the design, production, operation, and maintenance of aircraft, as well as for the training of aviation personnel and flight safety management. It contains standards relating to:

a) aircraft design and production, including technical and structural safety requirements;
b) operating regulations, including aircraft maintenance and repair requirements;

c) flight crew training, including requirements for staff qualifications,experience and periodic training;
d) flight safety management, including requirements for risk analysis and assessment, safety procedures, and incident reporting.

The introduction of international regulations and recommendations referred to in Annex 6 is aimed at ensuring the highest level of flight safety worldwide by developing uniform standards and rules for aircraft operation and for the training and qualifications of aviation personnel. This allows each ICAO member state to apply the same standards and principles, thereby making international flights safer.

Annex 8, "Airworthiness of Aircraft", sets out standards and recommendations for the airworthiness of aircraft. In accordance with Annex 8, each aircraft must obtain appropriate certificate(s) of airworthiness before commencing service, confirming that the aircraft meets the specified technical and safety requirements. Each state must incorporate into its national legislation provisions concerning the supervision of air carriers, including compliance with appropriate safety standards when obtaining an airworthiness certificate. The law of each state must comply with international regulations, or establish standards that are generally recognized as sufficient to conducting international operations. The EU prohibits flights within its territory from aircraft whose safety level does not comply with EU standards, including international standards defined by ICAO, by placing such carriers or aircraft on a special "black list".[38] These carriers are either completely banned from operating within the EU or certain aircraft are removed from service in the EU. This is an effective legal mechanism that ensures carriers operating in the EU adhere to stringent safety standards, thereby protecting the safety of states and citizens.

Returning to the safety regulations, Annex 8 to the Chicago Convention establishes standards related to aircraft design and construction, including requirements for materials, installations, systems, and equipment, as well as for aircraft production and quality control, certification procedures, and technical inspections. The regulations also set out requirements for the maintenance and repair of aircraft, including maintenance, repair, and replacement of aircraft components. Overall, these regulations aimto develop uniform safety standards for the design, production, quality control, testing, certification, and maintenance of aircraft.

The purpose of Annex 9 "Facilitation" is to ensure the safe implementation of efficient administrative and control procedures for the crossing of borders by persons, the clearance of goods, and the inspection of aircraft. The aim of these international regulations is to guarantee an optimal level of safety while simultaneously facilitating border-crossing procedures at airports. It is in the interest of every party that the

38 The black list of air carriers in the EU is a safety instrument established by Regulation (EC) 2111/2005 of the European Parliament and of the Council of December 14, 2005, on the establishment of a Community list of air carriers subject to an operating ban within the Community and on informing air transport passengers of the identity of the operating air carrier, and repealing Article 9 of Directive 2004/36/EC, OJ EC, *L* 344, 27.12.2005.

rules in this area do not cause disruption to air traffic, that they are harmonized, and that they minimize administrative and control inconveniences. According to Annex 9, the member states of the Chicago Convention are obliged to ensure the highest level of facilitation for the movement of passengers, baggage, goods, and aircraft across their borders. The annex contains standards for the facilitation of entry and exit procedures for passengers, baggage, and goods, as well as for documentation and border control procedures. The adopted rules facilitate the implementation of procedures ensuring safety during the movement of persons, goods, and aircraft, while under no circumstances do they reduce the level of safety. To this end, states should apply procedures that facilitate the exchange of information and shorten the processing time.

The introduction of the regulations in Annex 9 is intended to ensure the application of uniform standards and procedures for the movement of people, goods, and aircraft across national borders, thereby facilitating trade and tourism, while ensuring safety and protection of public health. The provisions of Annex 9 are designed to help countries worldwide develop and harmonize civil aviation standards. Previously, differing procedures in each statecaused difficulties for aircraft manufacturers or air carriers operating these machines when navigating various administrative procedures related to certification or aircraft inspection. Therefore, ICAO has decided to develop standards and recommendations aimed at facilitating safe operations for all interested parties.

Annex 12 "Search and Rescue" is important for air navigation safety, as it outlines standards related to search and rescue in aviation. It describes the standards and procedures to be followed during the four phases of air search and rescue, i.e. the phase of uncertainty, the alert phase, the danger phase, and the threat phase. Member states are obliged to establish appropriate search and rescue services. In the normative aspect, states must implement the necessary legal regulations in this area, designate the public administration authority responsible for air search and rescue, and establish appropriate communication system to coordinate the actions of various services. The creation of this system is crucial for aviation safety, as it enables rapid response in the event of aviation accidents or other emergency situations.

The provisions of Annex 12 set out the procedures for coordinating search and rescue operations during different phases of threat within a single state or in cases where search and rescue actions must be undertaken across the territory of at least two states. Moreover, member states should ensure that their aviation search and rescue systems are equipped with adequate equipment and personnel to effectively carry out rescue operations in the event of air accidents. These systems should also be optimized for rapid response in order to provide assistance to those affected as quickly as possible.

One of the legal requirements set out in these provisions is the establishment of appropriate training standards for personnel involved in air search and rescue. Such personnel shall be required to have appropriate qualifications and experience and be trained in air search and rescue techniques. In order to increase the safety of persons for whom rescue operations are required, the signaling system has been normalized and standardized, both for communication with vehicles and ground units as well as for "ground-to-air" and "air-to-ground" visual communication. It should also be added that all states are obliged to provide information on their air search and rescue systems to ICAO. This information shall then be made available to other member states in order to improve cooperation and coordination in the event of air accidents or other emergencies. Thus, the provisions of Annex 12 on air search and rescue are intended to ensure that appropriate legislation exists in each country to ensure rapid and effective assistance in the event of air accidents or other emergency situations, thereby minimizing the effects of such events on passengers, crew, and ground personnel.

Annex 13 entitled "Aircraft Accident and Incident Investigation", specifies standards and procedures for the investigation of air accidents and incidents.[39] It contains definitions of an accident and an incident, which are of great importance for the legal consequences of such events. The purpose of the investigation conducted in accordance with the annex's standards is solely to prevent similar situations in the future, and not to determine or assign blame for an accident or incident. According to its regulations, ICAO member states are required to establish a system for the investigation of air accidents and incidents and to set up the appropriate national investigative bodies. States should also ensure the independence of these investigative bodies and provide them with adequate human, financial, and technical resources.

Annex 13 also specifies standards for the collection, analysis, and reporting of data related to air accidents and incidents. The legal framework regulates the process of investigating aviation accidents and incidents. In accordance with these provisions, the investigation shall include the participation of representatives of the states involved in the case, e.g. the state of occurrence – where the accident occurred (as the state responsible for conducting an investigation, or the state entrusted with the investigation), the state of manufacture of the aircraft, the state of design of the aircraft, the state of aircraft operator, the state of registration of the aircraft, or any state expressing interest in relation to fatalities. The regulations also address formal issues, such as final conclusions, which are prepared in the form of a final report. According to the regulations, the final report should contain four elements: a factual information of the event, an analysis of the event, final conclusions and preventive recommendations. The standards set forth in Annex 13 are intended to ensure that investigation is carried out accurately and efficiently and that the collected data is used to improve flight safety. Annex 13 also outlines the principles regarding the exchange of information between member states in the field of air accident and incident investigation, with the aim to enhance flight safety at the international level. It can therefore be concluded that the purpose of Annex 13 is to provide consistent standards and procedures for the investigation of air accidents and incidents, thereby improving flight safety worldwide.

39 See more: Zając G., *Rules and procedures of accident investigation in civil aviation*, Science & Military, Vol. 10, No. 2, 2015, s. 36–45.

The provisions of Annex 14, titled "Aerodromes", aim to ensure that aerodromes meet appropriate safety standards so that carriers operate safely and are securely located within aerodrome areas. The aim is also to guarantee the safe operation of all services at the airport, including ground handling services. The regulations cover standards and requirements for the construction, operation, and maintenance of airports and their equipment, including navigation and safety systems. These requirements address various aspects, such as minimum runway length, necessary airport equipment (including lighting, marking, and signaling systems), as well as minimum standards for ground handling, among others. States must ensure that airports comply with all the norms and standards set out in these regulations to be permitted to handle international traffic. Moreover, the legislation requires states to set up a control system to ensure the effective implementation of the requirements in Annex 14. Each member state is required to carry out regular inspections and checks in this regard. It is therefore recommended that states set upspecial safety oversight bodies and adopt appropriate legal regulations, to effectively perform the safety oversight function at airports.

Accordingly, the provisions of Annex 14 require states to carry out a certification procedure for aerodromes intended for international civil aviation. Each stateis obliged to apply the relevant criteria specified in Annex 14 and in the Aerodrome Certification Manual (Doc 9774) to certify its aerodromes. In addition, the standards in Annex 14 define a signaling and marking system as an important element of aviation safety at airports. This system is regulated by Annex 14 to ensure that all airport users (pilots, passengers, airport staff, and any other individualsauthorized to be in certain areas of the airport) can move safely around the airport. The provisions on airport signaling system include lighting systems designed to provide information to pilots about the position and direction of movement at the aerodrome, as well as warning of dangers and other situations. The signaling requirements include, among other things, minimum standardsfor light intensity, color, and signaling duration. In turn, the airport marking system includes signs, lines, symbols, and other markings designed to convey information to pilots and other airport users, such as ground staff, passengers, and aircraft crew. The marking system must be suitably positioned and maintained to ensure adequate visibility and legibility under various weather and lighting conditions. All airports must comply with the marking and signaling standards and requirements set out in Annex 14 to ensure the safe movement of aircraft at the airport. Member states are obliged to carry out regular inspections and controls to ensure that these standards are being observed by the authorities managing the airports.

Important provisions on aviation safety and security are contained in Annex 17, "Aviation Security: Safeguarding International Civil Aviation Against Acts of Unlawful Interference". It contains provisions regarding the protection of aviation against illegal breaches of flight safety. This annex sets forth the standards, requirements and procedures that states and aviation operators must comply with in order to ensure aviation safety. Under Annex 17, member states are obliged to develop and implement aviation security plans aimed at preventing acts of illegal breaches of civil aviation safety. These plans must take into account the threats arising from terrorist activities, theft, sabotage, and other forms of flight safety breaches. Each airport serving international civil aviation must develop, implement, and update a written aerodrome security program in accordance with the requirements of the national aviation security program, pursuant to Chapter 3, point 3.2 of Annex 17. The legislation also lays down requirements for the training of aviation and ground staff in security matters and for cooperation between the different agencies and bodies responsible for ensuring aviation security. Annex 17 is an important tool for ensuring aviation safety, and in light of the dynamics of international relations and emerging new threats, including hybrid ones, it is frequently updated to take account of new dangers and challenges. Member states are obliged to comply with the requirements and standards set out in that annex and to regularly assess and improve their aviation security plans to ensure safety and protection against threats.

Annex 18 "Safe Transport of Dangerous Goods by Air" sets out standards and procedures for the air transport of dangerous goods. These norms are supplemented and detailed by the Technical Instructions for the Safe Transport of Dangerous Goods by Air issued by ICAO.[40] The purpose of the provisions in Annex 18 is to ensure the safety of air transport and the protection of human and animal health, as well as the environment by setting standards and requirements for the transport of dangerous goods by air. The general rule is a prohibition on the carriage of hazardous materials by air, with the exception of those materials strictly defined in the technical instructions issued pursuant to Annex 18 of the Chicago Convention. In accordance with the international regulations set out in Annex 18, the transport of these specific materials by air must be carried out under specific and strict standards and requirements for classification, packaging, labelling, documentation, handling, transport, and procedures in the event of a breakdown or other unfortunate event. Hazardous materials are classified based on their chemical and physical properties into specific hazard groups, which allows for the determination of the appropriate requirements and procedures for their transport. Before shipment by air, it is necessary to obtain the appropriate certificates and permits, as well as ensure that individuals involved in transport are properly trained and certified. The provisions of Annex 18 in Chapter 7 also address the shipper's responsibility and the requirement to possessthe appropriate transport documents for dangerous goods. The provisions constitute uniform and consistent international norms and standards that contribute to enhanced safety in the transport of goods considered dangerous or likely to pose a potential risk to persons or the environment.

Finally, Annex 19 "Safety Management" concerns aviation safety management. It defines the requirements for safety management system (SMS) in aviation organizations and civil aviation authorities. SMS aims to ensure flight safety by identifying, assessing, and controlling risks in aviation. As part of SMS, aviation organizations must conduct risk analysis, determine appropriate preventive measures, monitor and report incidents, and conduct regular safety audits.

40 ICAO Doc.9284.

Annex 19 also establishes the requirements for the training of personnel in safety management. According to the regulations set out therein, aviation organizations must regularly assess the effectiveness of their safety management system. The purpose of the provisions of Annex 19 is to provide safety management standards and requirements that help prevent incidents and accidents. Thus, the safety management system can be an effective tool in ensuring aviation safety and minimizing risks associated with aviation.

Furthermore, the Annex contains regulations concerning the obligation of the state to develop and maintain the National Civil Aviation Safety Program, which will include the following elements: state policy and objectives in the field of aviation safety, risk management, ensuring safety, and promoting safety. Under the provisions of Annex 19, states are required to introduce effective aviation legislation into their national legal frameworks for the oversight and management of civil aviation safety and to establish an enforcement mechanism through designated national authorities.

2.1.2 The Tokyo-Hague-Montreal-Beijing system

The Tokyo-Hague-Montreal-Beijing system concerns the protection of aviation against acts of unlawful interference and the prevents acts aimed at the safety of international civil aviation. This multilateral system is based on four key conventions along with a protocol:

a) The Convention on Offences and Certain Other Acts Committed on Board Aircraft, signed in Tokyo on September 14, 1963 (Tokyo Convention);
b) The Convention for the Suppression of Unlawful Seizure of Aircraft, signed in The Hague on December 16, 1970 (Hague Convention);
c) The Convention for the Suppression of Unlawful Acts Against the Safety of Civil Aviation, signed in Montreal on September 23, 1971 (Montreal Convention);
d) The Protocol for the Suppression of Unlawful Acts of Violence at Airports serving International Civil Aviation, signed in Montreal on December 24, 1988;
e) The Convention on the Suppression of Unlawful Acts Relating to International Civil Aviation, signed in Beijing on September 10, 2010 (Beijing Convention).

The multilateral system of aviation security was adopted as a response to the large number of acts of aviation terrorism occurring in various places around the world.[41] This phenomenon intensified during the 1950s, 1960s, and 1970s. States

41 There is no single definition of terrorism, nor of aviation terrorism, in international law. The Montreal Convention and its supplementary Montreal Protocol, and the new Beijing Convention, indicate acts subject to criminal sanctions and which are, in fact, acts of aviation terrorism. However, this list is only an enumeration of specific acts that qualify as aviation terrorism, and does not provide a comprehensive definition of this phenomenon.

agreed to take immediate action to radically reduce this phenomenon. The best platform for developing international regulations was ICAO. Therefore, in 1963, the Tokyo Convention was signed. Nevertheless, states delayed its ratification until 1969, after it had been ratified by 12 states (a requirement set out in Article 21 of the Convention),[42] by which time the number of terrorist attacks involving the hijacking of aircraft or their use as bombs had increased.

The Tokyo Convention primarily defines the rules of conduct for state authorities in the event of an illicit act committed by any person on board an aircraft. This provision leaves considerable discretion in interpreting the actions of the perpetrator. A significant shortcoming of the Convention is the absence of the obligation to punish criminals; instead, according to its provisions, the commander of the aircraft is given the option to hand the perpetrator over to justice. In addition, the Convention provides for the prosecution of acts that are considered crimes under the domestic criminal law of the state concerned. The Tokyo Convention covers the narrowest scope of regulation. It confines itself to determining which acts fall under its application and does not provide a definition of crime. Under the provisions of Article 1(1), it applies to "offences under the criminal law of each signatory State" and to acts "which, whether or not they are offences, may or do jeopardize the safety of an aircraft or of persons or property therein, or which jeopardizegood order and discipline on board". In such cases, the aircraft commander or crew members and, in special cases, even passengers, may take all necessary measures, including coercive ones, against a person who commits or attempts to commit an act endangering the safety of the aircraft, persons, or property on board. Another option available to the commander is to remove the offender from the aircraft or, if the act constitutes a serious offence under the criminal law of the state of registry of the aircraft, to surrender the offender to the competent authorities of any state party after landing in that state's territory.

In view of the numerous threats and acts of aviation terrorism in the 1960s, a decision was made to adopt broader legal regulations to combat the unlawful seizure of aircraft. In 1970, the Hague Convention was signed. It entered into force in 1971 after ratification by ten states, in accordance with Article 13(3).[43] The Convention sets out the definition of "crime". According to Article 1,

> any person who, on board an aircraft in flight, unlawfully, by force or threat thereof, or by any other form of intimidation, seizes, or exercises control of, that aircraft, or attempts to perform any such act, or is an accomplice

42 As of January 31, 2025, 187 states (including two dependent territories: the Cook Islands and Niue) had ratified the Tokyo Convention. The Vatican is a signatory to the convention, but has not yet ratified it. https://www.icao.int/secretariat/legal/List%20of%20Parties/Tokyo_EN.pdf, accessed 20.02.2025.

43 As of January 31, 2025, 185 states (including two dependent territories: the Cook Islands and Niue) have ratified the Hague Convention. Burundi is a signatory to the convention but has not yet ratified it. https://www.icao.int/secretariat/legal/List%20of%20Parties/Hague_EN.pdf, accessed 20.02.2025.

of a person who performs or attempts to perform any such act commits an offence.

It should be noted that, for the first time in international aviation regulations, even theattempt to commit such an offence was classified as a crime. In addition, any person assisting the perpetrator is also considered as an accomplice and will be held accountable to the same extent and under the same criteria as the main offender. The Hague Convention regulates offences in international civil aviation. As a multilateral international agreement, it applies only if the place of take-off or final landing of the aircraft, on board which an offence, as defined by the Convention was committed, is situated outside the territory of the state of registry of that aircraft. This applies to both international flights (i.e. those under the so-called fifth, sixth, or seventh freedoms of the air) and domestic flights (the so-called eighth freedom, i.e. cabotage). Such treaty language appears justified, because if an act occurs on board an aircraft, operating solely domestic flights within the territory of the state of registration of that aircraft, then the domestic law of that state applies. The only exception to this rule is if the perpetrator or alleged offender is located in the territory of a state other than the state of registry of that aircraft. Regardless of the location of the perpetrator or alleged perpetrator of the offence, states signatories to the Hague Convention are obliged to detain such a person. Action should be taken immediately to clarify all the circumstances and establish the facts. If the offender turns out to be a citizen of a country other than the one in which they were detained, extradition must be carried out. According to the provisions of the Convention, this may occur if an extradition agreement exists between the two states. However, if the state refuses to extradite the offender, who is a citizen of another state, it is obliged to immediately initiate criminal proceedings against that person under its own internal regulations. Similarly, Feller submits that, although the Convention does not impose an extradition obligation on any state, it is obliged to prosecute such a person in accordance with national law.[44]

The Tokyo and Hague Conventions differ from each other substantively in at least two essential elements. While the former enigmatically refers to the situation of unlawful seizure of an aircraft, the latter defines an offense in *expressis verbis,* including an attempt to commit it.

The Hague Convention is an important milestone in the codification of international aviation law concerning the protection of aviation against acts of terrorism. States are obliged to prosecute offences related to the unlawful seizure of civil aircraft.

In 2010, ICAO member states decided to modify the existing legal regulations in the 1970 Hague Convention as 40 years had passed since its adoption and the conditions of aviation safety had changed. New security threats have emerged, including cyber threats related to the development of the Internet and modern

44 Feller S. Z., *Comment on "Criminal Jurisdiction Over Aircraft Hijacking"*, Israel Law Review, Vol. 7, 2015, p. 210.

information technologies. States decided to supplement the provisions of the Hague Convention with new forms of aircraft hijacking, including those carried out using modern technological means. As a result of the conference held in Beijing from August 30 to September 20, 2010, a Supplementary Protocol to the Convention for the Suppression of Unlawful Seizure of Aircraft was adopted on the last day of the meeting. According to Article 23 of the Beijing Protocol, entry into force will take place after 22 ratifications have been obtained. The Protocol entered into force on July 1, 2018, following ratification by Turkey.[45]

The Protocol explicitly provides for criminal liability for the perpetrators of a crime, as well as for those who knowingly assist the offender in evading prosecution or punishment. According to the provisions, any person threatening to commit a crime can be held criminally responsible if the circumstances indicate that the threat is credible.[46] Moreover, a legal person may also be held criminally liable, provided that such a possibility is stipulated by national law.[47] The bases of jurisdiction of the state have been extended to cover situations in which the crime is committed by one of its citizens and when the victim is also its citizen.[48] The grounds for extradition have been clarified. The protocol includes a clause stating that a contracting party may not refuse to extradite a criminal solely on the grounds that the offence is of a political nature.[49] The Beijing Protocol is the result of efforts by the international community to modernize the legal framework for the protection of aviation. The new regulations adopted are intended to strengthen the ability of states to prevent crimes against civil aviation safety. As a modern instrument of international aviation law, the Beijing Protocol also represents a response to the Global Counter-Terrorism Strategy of September 8, 2006, which aims to improve and modernize existing international aviation safety regulations.

Alongside the regulation of issues related to the hijacking of aircraft (the Hague Convention), work was underway on a convention to regulate the issue of combating unlawful acts directed against the safety of civil aviation. In 1971, the Montreal Convention in this regard was signed.[50] The acts defined as offences have been exhaustively enumerated (Article 1 of the Montreal Convention). These are:

a) an act of violence against a person on board an aircraft in flight;
b) the destruction or damage of an aircraft, rendering it incapable of flight;
c) the placement on board an aircraft of devices or substances that could destroy it or endanger flight safety;

45 As of January 31, 2025, 46 states have ratified the international agreement.
46 Article 2 of the Beijing Protocol amending Article 1 of the Hague Convention.
47 Article 4 of the Beijing Protocol adding Article 2 bis to the Hague Convention.
48 Article 7 of the Beijing Protocol amending Article 4 of the Hague Convention.
49 Article 12 of the Beijing Protocol adding Article 8 bis to the Hague Convention.
50 The Convention entered into force in 1973, in accordance with Article 15(3) thereof, i.e. after ten ratifications. As of January 31, 2025, 188 states are signatories to the Convention (including two dependent territories: the Cook Islands and Niue). https://www.icao.int/secretariat/legal/List%20of%20Parties/Mtl71_EN.pdf, accessed 20.02.2025.

d) the destruction, damage, or disruption of the operation of aviation navigational devices;
e) the spread of misinformation that could affect flight safety.

According to the provisions of the Convention, a person commits a crime, if they carry out even one act that endangers the safety of the aircraft. In addition, the Montreal Protocol of 1988[51] adds to the category of offences two acts committed at the airport:

a) an act of violence committed intentionally against a person at an airport causing or likely to cause serious injury or death;
b) the destruction or serious damage of an airport installation or an aircraft located therein, or the disruption of airport operations causing a security risk at that airport.

The Montreal Convention and the Montreal Protocol introduce a category of acts classified as a criminal offence, on the condition that the act is committed unlawfully and intentionally. Jurisdictional competences and extradition matters under the Montreal Convention are identical to those in the Hague Convention.

Overall, aviation security under the multilateral Tokyo-Hague-Montreal-Beijing system is a comprehensive approach to ensuring safety at airports and in the air, based on international cooperation and rigorous control and security procedures. International aviation security regulations are not merely contained in the previously mentioned conventions or protocols. The global legal system of civil aviation security is also reflected in Annex 17 of the Chicago Convention (Aviation Security). The ICAO has adopted a number of procedures and standards to counteract and prevent threats to aviation safety as outlined in the other annexes. In addition, aviation security is reinforced by the regulations of Annex 18 to the Chicago Convention (Safe Transport of Dangerous Goods by Air) and the provisions of the Civil Aviation Security Manual (ICAO Document 8973) containing detailed procedures and guidelines on aviation security aspects along with a list of items prohibited for carriage on board an aircraft. The provisions of ICAO Document 8973 are restricted for the public, but any entity involved in aviation security has access to these regulations.

The discussed legal regulations aim to support states in protecting aviation against illegal acts targeting the safety of civil aviation. In addition, ICAO also supports states in implementing their own national civil aviation security programs as required by the provisions of Annex 17 to the Chicago Convention. International

51 The Montreal Protocol entered into force in 1989, in accordance with Article 6 thereof, i.e. after ten ratifications. As of January 31, 2025, 176 states are signatories to the Convention (including two dependent territories: the Cook Islands and Niue). https://www.icao.int/secretariat/legal/List%20of%20Parties/Mtl71_EN.pdf, accessed 20.02.2025.

regulations on protection against aviation terrorism are very important because these threats pose a real challenge to aviation safety.

2.1.3 Warsaw-Montreal system

The Warsaw-Montreal system defines the conditions for the safe carriage of passengers and baggage by air, including the liability of the air carrier for damage incurred in connection with such carriage. It is formally comprised of two conventions:

1. the Convention for the Unification of Certain Rules relating to International Carriage by Air, signed in Warsaw on October 12, 1929;
2. the Convention for the Unification of Certain Rules for International Carriage by Air, signed in Montreal on May 28, 1999.

This multilateral system is de facto based on a single Montreal Convention. It should be noted that the Warsaw Convention is of a purely formal nature (since it has not been repealed) and in current practice the Montreal Convention applies.[52]

Air safety is one of key aspects of the Montreal Convention, as it pertains to the safe international transport of passengers, baggage, and cargo. This Convention establishes that air carriers are obliged to ensure the broadly understood safety of passengers and their baggage. The air carrier is also liable for damage resulting from air accidents or other incidents, including losses associated with delays or loss of baggage. The Montreal Convention requires member states to establish and maintain high standards of air safety for the international carriage of passengers, baggage, and goods and to adhere to the standards set by the ICAO. International requirements have been established regarding the types and content of travel documents for passengers, baggage receipts, and air waybills for the carriage of goods, with the aim of harmonizing procedures and standards on a global scale and thereby improving aviation safety. The Convention also regulates the conditions and principles of the financial liability of air carriers for the carriage of passengers, baggage, and goods, including the obligation to compensate in the event of death, bodily injury, or health disorder of a passenger, as well as for damage, destruction, loss, or delay of baggage or goods. Furthermore, the Convention also lays down the maximum amounts of compensation that an air carrier must pay in the event of such incidents.[53]

52 The Montreal Convention entered into force on November 4, 2003. As of January 2025, 141 parties have ratified, including 140 states and the EU. https://www.icao.int/secretariat/legal/List%20of%20Parties/Mtl99_EN.pdf, accessed 20.02.2025.

53 Article 21 of the Montreal Convention limits the carrier's compensation to a passenger up to 100,000 SDR (Special Drawing Rights – SDR). Article 22, on the other hand, deals with the carrier's liability for destruction, loss, damage or delay of baggage up to 1,000 SDR in case of goods, the carrier's liability is limited to 17 SDR per kilogram.

In summary, the Montreal Convention establishes air safety standards for the international carriage of passengers, baggage, and cargo. It also defines the rules of legal liability for carriers regarding damage caused to passengers, baggage, and goods in connection with the performance of international air transport services. The Convention also introduces mechanisms for air carriers to compensate passengers as well as their baggage and goods in the event of damage during carriage.

2.1.4 Compensation system

The multilateral compensation system is a set of tools and measures set out in several international agreements concerning the normalization of the compensation system for damages caused to persons, baggage, and goods in international civil aviation. There are four conventions that regulate these issues:

a) The Convention on Damage caused by Foreign Aircraft to Third Parties on the Surface, signed in Rome, Italy, on October 7, 1952 (Rome convention of 1952);
b) The Convention on Compensation for Damage to Third Parties resulting from Acts of Unlawful Interference Involving Aircraft, signed in Montreal on May 2, 2009 (for the purposes of this book, this is referred to as the 2009 Montreal convention);
c) The Convention on Compensation for Damage caused by Aircraft to Third Parties, signed in Montreal on May 2, 2009 (for the purposes of this book, this is referred to as the 2009 Montreal convention bis);
d) The Convention for the Unification of Certain Rules for International Carriage by Air, signed in Montreal on May 28, 1999.

This legal system, although partially in force, has its origins in 1933. For the first time, compensation issues were regulated in the Convention for the Unification of Certain Rules Relating to Damage Caused by Aircraft to Third Parties on the Surface, signed in Rome on May 29, 1933. Its purpose was to establish uniform rules on the liability of persons operating aircraft for any damage caused by civil aircraft air to third parties or their property on the surface of the earth. The provisions of that Convention also imposed an obligation on the aircraft operator to maintain insurance to cover compensation for damages incurred under the Convention. Despite the fact that only five states ratified it, the Convention did not enter into force.

After World War II, it was decided to revive the idea of this convention and in 1952 another convention concerning damage caused to third parties on the surface of the earth by a foreign aircraft[54] was adopted, along with the Protocol amending the provisions of that Convention, signed in Montreal on September

54 Convention on damage caused by foreign aircraft to third parties on the surface, signed in Rome (Italy) on October 7, 1952, entered into force on February 4, 1958. As of January 31, 2025, there

23, 1978. Therefore, in the current state of international law, this convention is binding on the signatory states. Haanappel points out that in states where the 1952 Rome Convention does not apply, national law is applied either under tort or under liability arising from specific legal provisions.[55] The Convention regulates the following aspects:[56]

a) responsibility of the operator of the aircraft;
b) damages caused by an aircraft registered in a state different from the state where damage occurred;
c) the amount of compensation;
d) the requirement to have insurance as a guarantee for covering liability for damages.

The supplementary protocol adopted in 1978 introduced new compensation limits and modified insurance regulations.

Nevertheless, it was decided to modify the existing provisions of the 1952 Rome Convention and during the conference on aviation law in Beijing in 2009, two new conventions were adopted to adjust them to the current international legal conditions. The two Montreal Conventions of 2009 are not yet in force, according to their ratification status in the beginning of 2025. However, it is worth outlining their legal scope and essence.

The Convention on Compensation for Damage to Third Parties Resulting from Acts of Unlawful Interference Involving Aircraft is an international document that was adopted in Montreal in 2009 under the auspices of ICAO. It contains two legal conditions for its entry into force. The first is the requirement for the number of ratifications – according to Article 40(1) of the Convention, it will enter into force 180 days after ratifications have been submitted by 35 states. The second condition is that air traffic at all airports in these states must be no less than 750 million in the year preceding the deposit of the instrument of ratification.[57]

The purpose of that convention is to unify the rules on the liability of states for damage caused to third parties as a result of unlawful interference by aircraft. It applies to damage caused by third parties that occurs within the territory of a state party to the Convention and was caused by an act of unlawful interference by aircraft during an international flight.[58] Thus, the provisions of the Convention pertain to events related to international flights, but states may submit an additional

are 51 signatory states., https://treaties.un.org/Pages/showDetails.aspx?objid=08000002801406bd&clang=_en, accessed: 20.02.2025.

55 Haanappel P. P. C., *The Law and Policy of Air Space and Outer Space: A Comparative Approach*, Wolters Kluwer, 2003, p. 86.

56 Zylicz M., *Prawo lotnicze międzynarodowe, europejskie i krajowe*, Warszawa 2002, p. 95.

57 As of January 2024, nine states have deposited their instruments of ratification with the depositary of the Convention. https://www.icao.int/secretariat/legal/list%20of%20parties/2009_uicc_en.pdf, accessed 20.02.2024.

58 Article 2(1) of the 2009 Montreal Convention.

declaration that domestic flights will also be liable for compensation. If damage related to an aircraft occurs on the high seas or within an exclusive economic zone, then according to the regulations, it is deemed to have occurred in the territory of the state in which the aircraft is registered. Conversely, if the state of registration of an aircraft differs from the principal place of business of the operator of that aircraft, then the law of the state in which the principal operator is located applies.[59] The provisions also specify that damage to an oil platform or other installation permanently fixed to the ground located in the exclusive economic zone or on the continental shelf is regarded as damage caused in the territory of the state to which that platform or installation belongs, in accordance with the international law of the sea.[60]

The Convention regulates the liability of an aircraft operator for the payment of compensation for damages caused directly by its aircraft while in flight.[61] Personal injuries (resulting from death, bodily injury, and health disorder solely related to mental illness as a result of bodily injury), material damages and environmental damage are subject to compensation.[62] Precise limits of the operator's liability have been established, ranging from 750,000 SDRs for damage caused by aircraft with a maximum takeoff mass of 500 kg or less, up to 700 million SDRs for aircraft with a maximum takeoff mass exceeding 500,000 kg.[63] The Convention also imposes an obligation on states to enforce the requirement that the aircraft operator maintain insurance to cover any potential damage.

Moreover, in order to provide compensation to victims, an institutional mechanism was established in the form of the International Civil Aviation Compensation Fund. The fund is a separate institution with a defined organizational structure and set of prerogatives. Its headquarters is located in the same place as the ICAO (Montreal). It possesses international legal personality and the capacity to engage in legal transactions. The structure of the fund shall consist of the Conference of the Parties as its plenary body, a permanent Secretariat, and a Director of the fund who manages its day-to-day operations.[64] The provisions of the Convention also regulate the collection of contributions, including their amount, the basis for their determination, and the obligation of states to collect these contributions from operators and transfer them to the fund. States are further required to provide information on the number of passengers and cargo in international transport, general aviation data, and information identifying operators

59 Article 2(3)(a) of the 2009 Montreal Convention.

60 United Nations Convention on the Law of the Sea, signed in Montego Bay (Jamaica) on December 10, 1982

61 In accordance with Article 1(c) of the 2009 Montreal Convention, an aircraft is deemed to be in flight from the moment all its exterior doors are closed upon boarding or loading, until any of those doors are opened for disembarkation or unloading.

62 Article 3 of the 2009 Montreal Convention.

63 Article 4 of the 2009 Montreal Convention.

64 Articles 8–11 of the 2009 Montreal Convention.

regarding the implementation of the Convention's provisions.[65] The fund is an organization to achieve the objectives of the 2009 Montreal Convention. The scope of activities of this fund covers all matters concerning the compensation system. The provisions also define the right of recourse both for the operator against any person (in particular those who committed, organized or financed the act of unlawful interference) and for the International Civil Aviation Compensation Fund, which is entitled to recourse against both the persons involved and the aircraft operator.[66] Finally, the Convention limits the period of the right to compensation to two years from the date of the event causing the damage.[67]

The second Convention on Compensation for Damages caused by Aircraft to Third Parties (2009 Montreal Convention bis), covers a similar scope of regulation as the 1952 Rome Convention. It defines the liability of the aircraft operator and states in the same way as the 2009 Montreal Convention.

Żylicz points out that the low number of ratifications by states of conventions concerning the international legal system with regard to damage on the surface of the earth results from the traditional subjection of these issues to territorial law (*lex loci delicti commissi*).[68] It is believed that this issue is not significant enough to necessitate the development of international standards common to all states, unlike other areas of civil aviation. The issue of liability for damages and the system of compensation has been a constant topic in legal and political discourse since the interwar period in the twentieth century. The 1952 Rome Convention, which remains in force, and the 2009 Montreal Conventions are important legal tools to ensure compensation for victims caused by acts involving aircraft. Once the 2009 Montreal Conventions come into force, they will take precedence over the 1952 Rome Convention or the 1978 Montreal Protocol in cases of conflict.

The 1999 Montreal Convention has already been discussed in the context of the international carriage of passengers, baggage, and goods. It is a binding international agreement with a broad scope in terms of both subjects and geographical coverage. The Warsaw Convention of 1929, whose provisions for the compensation system were amended by the Montreal Convention, and which take precedence in application, of the provisions of those two conventions cannot be irreconciled, will be deliberately omitted here. For formal reasons, the Warsaw Convention still functions because it has not yet been repealed, and it essentially regulates the same subject matter as the later Montreal Convention.

It is the Montreal Convention that contains important provisions on the compensation system. A legal mechanism has been established that holds the carrier's liability for damages caused to persons, baggage, and cargo. In accordance with Article 21 and in conjunction with Article 17(1) of the Montreal Convention, an air carrier is liable for damages caused to a passenger in the event of his death,

65 Article 16 of the 2009 Montreal Convention.
66 Articles 24–27 of the 2009 Montreal Convention.
67 Article 36 of the 2009 Montreal Convention.
68 Zylicz M., op. cit., p. 94.

bodily injury or health deterioration provided that the incident occurred on board the aircraft or during the embarkation or disembarkation process. In such a situation, the carrier is obliged to pay compensation up to 100,000 SDRs per passenger. However, there are two circumstances excluding the carrier's liability for damages if the amount of damage exceeds 100,000 SDR. One is when an event did not result from the carrier's negligence, improper action, or omission. The second is when an event was caused by the negligence, improper action, or omission of third parties over which the carrier had no control. If the carrier wishes to rely on either of these exemptions excluding its liability, it must prove them.

The issue of compensation for delays in the carriage of passengers has also been regulated. The Convention also stipulates that the carrier's liability is up to 4,150 SDRs per passenger unless the carrier proves that it took all possible measures to avoid the delay or that taking the appropriate measures was impossible in the particular situation. This international mechanism for delay compensation applies in all states parties to the Convention, i.e. in 138 States and in the EU. This provides passengers with the assurance that they will receive compensation for losses incurred due to delays. This instrument is universally applicable, so any citizen of a state party to the Montreal Convention may invoke it, regardless of whether their country's legislation specifically regulates these matters. It is worth noting that within the EU, a much broader and more comprehensive system of protection of passenger rights has been established in connection with delays, denied boarding, and cancellation of flights than that provided in international regulations.[69]

What is more, in accordance with Article 22(2) of the Montreal Convention, the carrier is liable for compensation for the loss, damage, or delay of baggage up to 1,000 SDR per passenger. However, if the passenger has submitted a special declaration regarding the value of the baggage, the carrier shall be liable only up to the amount of this declared amount.

The Montreal Convention also regulates the carrier's liability for goods. In the event of the destruction, loss, damage, or delay of the goods, the carrier must pay compensation up to 17 SDR per kilogram of goods, unless the consignor has submitted a special declaration regarding the total value of the goods. In that case, the carrier shall be liable only up to the amount specified in that declaration.

In any case, to receive compensation, the passenger (or, in the event of passenger's death, the family or a legally authorized person) or the consignor must prove that the damage was caused by the air carrier. The passenger or consignor must also file a claim with the air carrier immediately, upon discovering the damage or discrepancy, but no later than 7 days from the date of receipt of the baggage and 14

69 The European provisions are based on Regulation (EC) No 261/2004 of the European Parliament and of the Council of February 11, 2004, establishing common rules on compensation and assistance to passengers in the event of denied boarding and of cancellation or long delay of flights, and repealing Regulation (EEC) No 295/91. L 46, 17.02.2004.

days in the case of receipt of cargo. If a delay has occurred, it must be reported no later than 21 days after the delay.[70]

The compensation system characterized in the abovementioned international agreements guarantees the safety of air carriage services for all parties. It protects the interests of passengers, cargo consignors, as well as third parties who have suffered damages related to the aviation activities of the carrier or airport. It also safeguards the interests of the carriers themselves, who are liable only up to the limits set by international regulations. The development of modern technologies in air transport, including unmanned aerial vehicles, makes it necessary to regulate all potential threats that they may pose. States are obliged to monitor compliance with these provisions by air carriers andother aviation entities in relation to any damage they cause. Moreover, each state has effective legal mechanisms to hold those responsible for the damage caused. The multilateral compensation system constitutes an important component of the safety and security of international air transport.

2.2 Legal scope and significance of the Global Aviation Safety Plan (GASP)

The main aviation safety instruments on a global scale are the Global Aviation Safety Plan (GASP) and the Global Air Navigation Plan (GANP). Both serve as essential frameworks for harmonizing the international civil aviation system and ensuring its safety and efficiency. They guide the actions of states and regional aviation organizations should focus, and they undoubtedly form the foundation for new legal regulations in the field of aviation safety.

During the 41st ordinary session of the ICAO General Assembly, the GASP and the GANP for the period 2023–2025, with objectives extending to 2030, were adopted.[71]

The GASP is a plan developed by the ICAO to ensure aviation safety worldwide. The GASP defines the priorities and actions that should be undertaken by governments and aviation organizations to improve flight safety. The plan takes into account the latest threats and challenges to flight safety, such as climate change, cyber-attacks, and growing air traffic, and sets out ways to minimize these risks. The GASP's goal is to ensure that aviation remains one of the safest and most efficient modes of transport in the world.

The GASP was adopted in 1997 by ICAO. It is a document of strategic importance concerning aviation safety policy. It serves as a vital component in the development of aviation law for member states and regional organizations. In addition to specifying the strategic objectives of air navigation safety and priorities for these entities, it establishes a legal framework for the implementation of national and regional standards improving aviation safety.

70 Article 31 of the Montreal Convention.

71 Resolution A41-6.

Under the GASP, states are required to implement national aviation safety plans, while regional safety oversight organizations develop regional plans.

The GASP is a document adopted at each ordinary session of the ICAO Assembly, which then formally approves it. The GASP is prepared by the ICAO Air Navigation Commission and subsequently distributed to all member states and aviation (non-governmental) organizations for consultation. Upon completion of these consultations, the Commission submits to the ICAO Council its conclusions and a proposal for modifications of the GASP based on the feedback received. After reviewing the proposed amendments, the Council approves the draft GASP and submits it for final approval by the General Assembly at its next ordinary session. The GASP is adopted every three years and it must reflect the challenges faced by international civil aviation and the needs of both member states and regional aviation safety organizations.

The GASP version adopted in 2022 contains the strategic goal to be achieved by 2030, namely zero accidents in commercial civil aviation. This is an ambitious target, but as statistics from the second decade of the 21st century show, the number of accidents and fatalities has significantly decreased. In order to achieve this goal, and based on an analysis of the causes of fatal accidents, five global high-risk categories have been identified that must be mitigated:[72]

a) controlled flight onto terrain (CFIT);
b) loss of control in flight (LOC-I);
c) mid-air collision (MAC);
d) runway excustion (RE);
e) runway incursion (RI).

The strategic vision combined with the identification of risk areas, should be accompanied by the specification of tools and means to achieve the intended goals. There are six areas identified in the Global Aviation Safety Plan:

Goal 1: continuously mitigate operational safety risks;
Goal 2: strengthen safety oversight capabilities in all states;
Goal 3: effectively implement national safety programs;
Goal 4: strengthen regional cooperation in the area of safety;
Goal 5: expand industry programs and initiatives and promote exchange of safety information;
Goal 6: improve the infrastructure needed to support safe air operations;

The implementation of these objectives is supported by specific tasks.

Goal 1 can be achieved through the effective implementation of measures aimed at reducing or eliminating the causes of fatal accidents, which have been identified in the five global high-risk categories mentioned above. The goal for 2030 is to

72 Global high-risk categories are identified in the GASP and in the 2022 ICAO Annual Safety Report.

reduce the number of fatal accidents to zero. It is a goal that is easily measurable as it is based on statistics regarding the number of accidents, incidents and serious incidents.

Goal 2 focuses on increasing the efficiency of implementating the critical safety surveillance system components. These critical elements encompass the entire spectrum of the activities required to build this system,, covering legal, organizational, and technical issues. Eight such critical elements can be distinguished:

1. basic aviation legislation,
2. specific operational rules,
3. the state system and its functions,
4. qualified technical personnel,
5. technical procedures and expert support,
6. the process of certification, licensing, and state approval,
7. monitoring procedures, and
8. the resolution of safety-related issues.

The effectiveness of the implementation of these critical elements is expressed as a percentage. It is evaluated by regional safety oversight authorities and on a global level, they are assessed by ICAO as part of the Universal Safety Oversight Audit Programme (USOAP).[73]

Goal 3 is aimed at states to effectively implement their national safety programs. This concerns the legal aspect of operation, which involves adopting appropriate legal regulations based on international norms and guidelines, as well as the creation of an organizational structure of the safety management system. In order to achieve this goal, it was expected that stateswould develop national safety programs that reflect current and future challenges and threats to their civil aviation. In each state, there are specific safety conditions related to geographical, geopolitical, cultural, or social factors.

Objective 4 refers to regional integration as a crucial factor in shaping safety. Regional safety oversight organizations should cooperate with other institutions and organizations, both intergovernmental and non-governmental, to develop a program tailored to the needs and circumstances of the region and to meet the demands of the relevant stakeholders. The key to adopting appropriate legal solutions is cooperation and mutual interaction. ICAO Regional Offices, which play a significant regulatory function, can serve as integration platform for entities operating within a given region or even beyond it. Goal 4 also requires states to provide regional aviation safety groups (RASGs) with information on operational safety risks by 2025.

Goal 5 imposes on regions and states to collaborate with the business and institutional environment in the creation of new initiatives or the development of aviation safety plans. It is considered that non-governmental (industry)

73 USOAP was established in 1999 in response to the low safety standards in global civil aviation.

organizations by conducting internal safety audits, make a positive contribution to enhancing operational safety. By sharing these findings with states and institutions such as the RASG, a better strategy, policy, standards, and quality of service can be developed. ICAO stresses the importance of organizations and initiatives,[74] including:

a) the Airport Excellence (APEX) safety program developed by Airports Council International (ACI);
b) the standard of excellence for safety management systems developed jointly developed by CANSO and EUROCONTROL;
c) the Operational Safety Audit (IOSA) of the International Air Transport Association (IATA);
d) the IATA Safety Audit for Ground Operations (ISAGO);
e) the International Standard for Business Aircraft Operations (IS-BAO) developed by the International Business Aviation Council (IBAC).

Goal 6 refers to the need to provide adequate infrastructure that supports safe operations. States must ensure that airport infrastructure open to international civil aviation is continuously improved to meet the highest ICAO standards. The infrastructure must be maintained in accordance with the technical parameters set out in ICAO regulations to ensure the safety of airport operations. With an increase in air traffic, the existing infrastructure must be adapted and expanded to meet current and future needs.

States are obliged to implement a national civil aviation safety program in their internal legislation, in accordance with the provisions of Annex 19 to the Chicago Convention (Safety Management) as well as based on the recommendations set forth in the GASP. Both documents, Annex 19 and GASP, are complementary and regulate the establishment of an efficient safety management and oversight system within the state.

It can be concluded that the adopted international legal regulations adequately constitute and secure proper safety procedures. However, problems may arise from the improper implementation of international standards into domestic legislation, or the ineffective enforcement of sanctions for non-compliance with these norms and procedures. Much depends on the willingness of states to address these issues. Since the rules are uniform for all, and some states exhibit low accident or incident rates while others have rates several times higher, the problem does not lie with the absence or inadequacy of international rules, but rather with the failure to create an effective and consistent legal mechanism in those states where the level of aviation safety remains unsatisfactory. That is why, the guidelines and principles outlined in international legal and political documents are crucial, as, with the support of regional safety organizations, industry associations or other entities, they can materialize into an effective legal system for safety management.

74 Global Aviation Safety Plan 2023–2025, Doc 10004, ICAO 2022, paragraph 4.2.

The essence of the GASP is to ensure the highest level of safety in air transport, which can be done by reducing the number of air accidents and minimizing the risk to passengers, crew, and people on the ground. It is also important to achieve sustainable growth in the aviation sector. In this context, the GASP aims to increase the efficiency and safety of the aviation system, while minimizing its impact on natural environment. It should be noted that the provisions of international aviation law take into account the approach of sustainable development of civil aviation through the adoption of a new Part 3 of Annex 16 to the Chicago Convention which addresses the reduction of greenhouse gas emissions (the CORSIA system). Moreover, the GASP seeks to increase the effectiveness of aviation safety management at both the global and national levels by strengthening incident reporting systems, monitoring preventive actions, and sharing safety information. Strengthening the aviation safety capabilities of states is necessary in this case, and GASP guidelines and procedures are intended to improve these capabilities through personnel training, technical support, and coordinated actions between states. Reflecting current civilizational and technological progress, the GASP, also supports innovative solutions in civil aviation safety, such as new technologies and operational procedures. All actions taken on the basis of and in accordance with GASP serve to ensure the highest level of aviation safety.

The GASP sets out political objectives, objectives, challenges, threats, and proposals for legislative and operational changes to strengthen aviation safety in states. It is also intended to support regional safety organizations in developing the highest possible standards and framework to ensure the safety of air operations. The adoption of such a document by ICAO serves as a legal and political guideline for states and institutions to minimize threats and address any irregularities and legal gaps in the international civil aviation safety system. The targets set out in the 2022 GASP include various instruments to achieve the intended results by 2030. The GASP provides the framework for cooperation among states and other entities involved in civil aviation regarding risk management and responses to aviation threats and crises, including the aviation crisis triggeredby the coronavirus pandemic between 2020 and 2022.

GASP is an international strategy for which the Global Aviation Safety Roadmap (GASR) has been established.[75] Its primary aim is to support states and regional organizations in developing their respective national and regional safety programs. It contains concrete initiatives that can be applied. The document is divided into two parts: an organizational part and an operational part. The first includes states, regional organizations, and industry entities. The second part outlines the main global high-risk categories. In each part, the following actions are listed in each section:

75 Global Aviation Safety Roadmap, 2023–2025, ICAO Doc.10161. For the first time, the Global Aviation Safety Roadmap was developed as a separate document in 2022. Until then, it functioned as part of GASP.

a) the types of initiatives that should be undertaken to improve safety;
b) identification of actions to be carried out in an appropriate order;
c) the legal basis – international rules to be used in formulating specific actions.

The GASR is a long-term and holistic strategy developed by ICAO to improve aviation safety worldwide. The use of the Global Roadmap by the entities to which it is addressed will improve coordination between them, thus reducing inconsistencies or duplication of efforts in the development of national and regional aviation safety plans. The GASR is an instrument to encourage different forms of entities to continuously improve their performance in aviation safety.

To sum up, the GASP together with the GASR are not only political targets and strategies, but also a scheme for taking new actions in the area of legislation and modification of existing legal solutions. The GASP is adopted to reduce negative incidents in civil aviation and address real and potential threats, including the reduction of accidents and incidents by promoting a proactive approach to safety, involving various entities in dialogue, and fostering cooperation to raise safety awareness, as well as by implementing new technologies facilitating and improving safety procedures.

More and more states are involved in implementing safety oversight provisions into national legislation and enforcing compliance with accepted international safety standards. Achieving this goal requires not only legal solutions, as international regulations exist, but also the adaptation of national aviation legislation to those standards, as well as greater involvement by regional aviation organizations in supporting states and entities in developing good practices, or promoting unified standards to improve quality and safety in civil aviation.

2.3 Legal nature and importance of Regional Aviation Safety Groups

Regional Aviation Safety Groups (RASGs) worldwide play a key role in an integrated approach to safety. The RASG institutions were established by the ICAO Council in 2010. Their main task is to develop a harmonized strategy and implement a work program that supports regional performance frameworks in safety management. RASG is the key player in the entire safety management value chain.[76]

The initiative to establish such regional groups dates back to the creation of the Global Aviation Safety Plan (GASP) in 1997. In 2005, ICAO initiated a process of amendment to this plan in order to adapt it to current legal conditions and challenges facing civil aviation safety. One of the legal and institutional elements of the proposed changes was the establishment of regional groups that would initiate and promote progress in operational safety, as referred to in the Global Aviation Safety Roadmap (GASR).

RASGs are groups comprised of representatives from governments, aviation operators, industry organizations, and the ICAO that operate at the regional level to

76 Mechanism for Monitoring Implementation of Safety Systems & Initiatives, AFCAC 2019, p. 12.

improve flight safety. The goal of RASG is to foster collaboration between governments and the aviation industry to address safety issues, exchange information and good practices, and support the implementation of global aviation safety standards. RASG works on rchallenges and threats specific to their region, providing support and advice on flight safety to member states. Cooperation within the RASG helps to ensure that flight safety is maintained at high and uniform level throughout the region.

Nowadays, in every region of the world, there are institutions supporting national authorities in strengthening safety at the regional level. Such groups consist not only of state representatives but also of representatives from non-governmental organizations, scientific institutions, and companies operating in aviation. Their aim is to address challenges related to flight safety and promote good practices. Some examples of RASGs are:

a) EASA – a European organization established in 2002 which serves as both an RASG and Regional Safety Oversight Organisation (RSOO); its role is the most comprehensive in regulatory, institutional, and functional aspects among all similar organizations;
b) RASG-PA – a Pan-American organization created in 2008;
c) RASG-AFI – an African organization established in 2010;
d) RASG-APAC – an organization for the Asia-Pacific region established in 2010;
e) RASG-MID – an organization of the Middle East region established in 2011.

The RASGs serve as a forum for discussing regional aviation safety problems and developing initiatives in this area. Each group covers a different geographical region. The aim of these groups is to enhance aviation safety worldwide by fostering cooperation between stakeholders in aviation safety at the regional level.

The essence and scope of the activities of individual oversight groups are discussed in more detail in Chapter 3.

2.4 Aviation safety oversight provisions

The legal basis for establishing safety oversight and its institutionalization in the form of regional and national bodies are found in the Chicago Convention. It should be noted that, according to Article 1 of the Chicago Convention, each state has complete and exclusive jurisdiction over the airspace above its territory. The exercise of this duty requires control in that area within the context of international civil aviation. This condition is confirmed by further provisions of the Convention. Accordingto Article 12, each state must take appropriate measures to ensure that every aircraft, regardless of its nationality (i.e. state of registration), conducts a safe flight within the state's jurisdiction. This obligation also extends to ensuring that the aircraft's crew complies with all the rules and regulations of the state in which it is operating. The provision of Article 12 contains an important stipulation that the regulations adopted by the state in this matter should, as far as possible, conform to the provisions of international aviation law, based on the Chicago Convention and other legal regulations issued thereunder. The provision should be read in conjunction with Article 37 of the Chicago Convention, which imposes on states the obligation to cooperate in the creation of uniform rules, legal regulations, procedures, and rules of conduct.

This process of standardizing international aviation law is intended not only to facilitate the functioning of air transport worldwide but also to make it safer for all users. Since the entry into force of the Chicago Convention, as well as subsequent regulations, states and other entities have incorporated international standards into their domestic legislation. However, these standards have continued to differ and have not achieved the expected level of legal harmonization.

The performance of safety oversight functions is a means of achieving a safe global air transport system. This is the fundamental responsibility of the state for the legal and organizational shape of civil aviation. Although there is a noticeable downward trend in the number of air accidents, the figures remain too high depending on the regions of the world. It should be remembered that air traffic will continue to grow, despite the temporary difficulties experienced during 2020–2022 due to the COVID-19 pandemic and the numerous bans and restrictions on air travel imposed by most states in the world.

The volatility and dynamics of international civil aviation necessitate the constant adaptation of current regulations to address emerging challenges in the industry. The legal framework must also follow this dynamic and respond to the development of air transport, the deepening of interdependencies, the process of institutionalization of civil aviation, and threats stemming from civilizational progress (e.g. cyberterrorism). Therefore, despite previous efforts to implement safety procedures and regulations in domestic legislation, discrepancies in the measures and instruments applied by individual states persist. Consideringthe varying levels of sophistication in the implementation of legislation, ICAO identified a statistical correlation between states' safety oversight capabilities and accident rates. Audits on the implementation of safety oversight procedures revealed that the main reason states do not develop effective safety oversight capabilities is the lack of adequate resources, particularly in terms of qualified staff and experts with in-depth technical knowledge. The ICAO concluded that the only effective way to overcome these shortcomings is to set up regional or subregional safety oversight systems based on common objectives, strategies, and action plans.[77]

In the 1990s, within ICAO discussions took place on the creation of a legal framework to encourage states to harmonize their safety oversight system and establish an effective enforcement mechanism for the implemented regulations. In 1992, the ICAO Assembly raised the issue that safety oversight is one of

77 Safety Oversight Manual, Part B. Establishment and Management of a Regional Safety Oversight Organization, ICAO 2011, Doc.9734, s. VI.

the fundamental principles set out in the Chicago Convention.[78] The resolution recognized that, until then, states had struggled to implement this principle for financial or technical limitations. This problem affected not only to the least developed states, but also many highly developed ones. As a result of discussions held in ICAO's technical groups, the Universal Safety Oversight Audit Program (USOAP) was adopted in 1998.[79] The decision was taken by the ICAO Assembly in resolution A32-11. The entry into force of these regulations was scheduled for January 1, 1999.

It is worth considering what a Universal Safety Oversight Program is, what its goals and essence are. The USOAP is an initiative developed by the ICAO to help ensure that member states have effective safety oversight systems in place. The USOAP consists of two components: the Safety Oversight Audit and the Continuous Monitoring Approach. The Safety Oversight Audit is a comprehensive on-site examination of a member state's civil aviation system, including its aviation legislation, organizational structure, personnel licensing, aircraft airworthiness, aircraft operations, and air navigation services. The audit is conducted by ICAO auditors who assess the member state's compliance with international standards and recommended practices for civil aviation safety. The Continuous Monitoring Approach is a process that involves ongoing evaluation of a member state's safety oversight system between audits. This is done through the collection and analysis of safety-related data and information, such as accident and incident reports, safety surveys, and other relevant data. The USOAP helps to identify areas where safety oversight systems need improvement and provides guidance and support to member states to help them meet international safety standards.

It should be emphasized that the safety oversight regulations issued by the ICAO, in the form of manuals,[80] contain legal provisions, a set of rights and obligations for the state and guidelines establishing the framework for the state's safety oversight system in the field of civil aviation:

1. Universal Safety Oversight Audit Program - Continuous Monitoring Manual, ICAO 1998, Doc 9735;[81]
2. Safety Oversight Manual, Part A: Establishment and Management of a State's Safety Oversight System, ICAO 2000, Doc.9734;[82]

78 Resolution A29-13 adopted at the 29th Ordinary Session of the ICAO Assembly, September 22 to October 8, 1992.

79 Resolution A32-11 adopted at the 32nd Ordinary Session of the ICAO Assembly, September 22 to October 2, 1998.

80 The ICAO manuals serve as a reference for states to harmonize their regulations and practices regarding civil aviation, with the aim of promoting the safe, efficient, and orderly development of international civil aviation.

81 Three updated editions have been released so far: the second in 2006 and the third in 2011.

82 The second updated edition of these rules was published in 2006.

3. Safety Oversight Manual, Part B. Establishment and Management of a Regional Safety Oversight System, ICAO 2000, Doc.9734.[83]

The USOAP Manual was first issued in 1998 (modified twice: in 2006 and 2011). This document provides guidelines for flight safety audits. Its goal is to standardize and improve the processes of conducting safety audits in international civil aviation. This document contains the following information:

1. an introduction to the safety audit program and its objectives;
2. the safety audit process and evaluation criteria;
3. requirements for safety audits for states and aviation organizations;
4. the audit preparation process, including planning and conducting audits;
5. methods of evaluation and reporting of audit results;
6. recommendations for improving flight safety based on audit results;
7. the process of continuity and enhancement of the safety audit program.

The document is important for states and aviation organizations because it provides them with guidelines for carrying out flight safety audits, as well as enables them to adapt their regulations and practices to meet ICAO safety standards. In accordance with provision 2.4 of Doc.9735, eight areas subject to audit have been identified:[84]

1. primary legislation on civil aviation;
2. structure and organization of civil aviation;
3. licensing and training of personnel;
4. flight operations;
5. aircraft airworthiness;
6. investigation of aviation accidents and incidents;
7. air navigation services;
8. airports and ground facilities.

According to provision 2.7 of Doc.9735, the following principles have been defined when conducting a safety oversight audit: ethics (professionalism in the audit process, confidentiality, and trust), justice (obligation to report honestly and fairly), diligence (care in handling obtained information and ensuring that those conducting the audits possess the necessary competence), and independence (the ability to provide an objective assessment and impartial conclusions based on collected material).[85] An important provision from the perspective of institutionalization and codification on a broad subject level appears in provision 4.5 of Doc.9735. It defines the role and responsibilities of regional safety oversight bodies. It is noted that ICAO has a strong interest in establishing such institutions that would perform

83 The second updated edition of these rules was published in 2011.
84 USOAP Manual, ICAO 2011, Ed.3, Doc 9735, paragraph 2.4.
85 *Ibidem*, clause.2.7.

safety oversight tasks on behalf of individual states. Such regional institutions should primarily focus on:

a) the unification of rules and regulations;
b) the formulation and implementation of detailed procedures;
c) training qualified and experienced inspectors to carry out safety inspections on behalf of member states.[86]

The Safety Oversight Manual, Part A, Doc.9734 was created to establish guidelines and procedures for the effective implementation of a safety program. It is addressed to ICAO member states, but it also applies to every entity in the aviation industry, as the state has an instrument to carry out appropriate audits of such entities. The Chicago Convention and its 19 annexes define various obligations for states, since international law is applied directly to them, but also indirectly to air operators. The state, and more specifically its aviation authorities or other authorized state institutions responsible for specific tasks, must monitor the compliance with safety standards by individual entities in the aviation industry. Therefore, the provisions set forth in the Doc.9734 manual should be reviewed by all interested parties.

This document Doc.9734 defines the entity's responsibilities for maintaining safe operations, the roles and duties of personnel involved in safety oversight, the procedures for identifying and mitigating safety risks, and the processes for reporting and documenting safety-related incidents. Doc.9734 clearly advocates for a balanced approach to safety surveillance.[87] Supervisory authorities established by the state should refrain from imposing overly strict controls, as well as a completely passive behavior. An excessively rigorous state approach to supervision may cause various difficultied for the controlled entities. Overly meticulous adherence to every norms and standards or prolonged inspections may lead to a decrease in the entity's efficiency, damage its reputation, or even cause bankruptcy. It can also contribute to lowering employee morale and, consequently, aviation standards. On the other hand, apassive state role boils down to merely observing the aviation entities that have assumed responsibility for independent control. In this situation, the reports submitted by them are accepted by the state without any reservations, which means that these entities effectively perform regulatory and supervisory functions. This approach will grant entities substantial freedom of action, and essentially they become self-regulators without any means to verify whether the data they present is accurate and reliable. Neither of these extreme approaches should be accepted. Therefore, in order to optimize the safety oversight function, it is recommended to combine legal provisions with the practical approach of aviation authorities while also considering the broader public interest in the exercise of control functions. ICAO in point 2.4.7 Doc.9734 recommends that the national safety oversight system be effective and include:

86 *Ibidem*, clause.4.5.1.
87 SOM Manual, ICAO 2006, Ed.2, Doc 973 4, paragraph 2.4.

a) the adoption of safety management principles;[88]
b) a wide range of factors of the controlled area (including various conditions affecting the study area);
c) a clearly defined strategy aligned with the holistic goal;
d) a consideration of the human factor;
e) harmonious cooperation and appropriate communication between the state authority and the controlled entity.[89]

The role of the national supervisory authority designated in this manner will contribute to the effective performance of its function and will strengthen regulatory and operational capabilities. In addition, Doc.9734 also outlines procedures for conducting safety audits, inspections, and assessments to verify compliance with regulations and standards. The aim of the Safety Oversight Handbook is to ensure the highest level of safety and thereby protect passengers, flight personnel and the environment.

The second part of ICAO Doc.9734 concerns the establishment of RSOOs. On the one hand, these authorities should exist in each state, either as independent and separate bodies or through the delegation of safety oversight powers to the authorities of the national aviation authority. On the other hand, several countries in the region may form a joint venture (joint institution). Such institutions may be formalized international intergovernmental organizations (e.g. the Pacific Aviation Safety Office – PASO) or less institutionalized forms of cooperation established under the auspices of ICAO (e.g. the Cooperative Development of Operational Safety and Continuing Airworthiness Programme – Southeast Asia – COSCAPSEA). ICAO does not impose a legal form or institutional structure for a regional safety oversight authority on states, leaving the choice to the parties concerned. However, ICAO can act as a facilitator for cooperation if states cannot agree on the legal structure of the future entity. In three cases in the Asia-Pacific region, ICAO has established such forms of cooperation that have been in place for more than 20 years. This option fulfills the requirements for integrating and harmonizing legal and organizational systems in many states.

In different regions of the world, states have established regional institutions, thus creating a system of cooperation between national authorities within a one operational platform. These institutions vary in their degree of competence: from those that adopt regulations and submit them for approval by ICAO and another regional aviation organization (e.g. the South American Regional Safety Oversight Cooperation Scheme – SRVSOP), to those with a wide range of prerogatives in establishing norms and regulations for aviation safety (e.g. the European Union Aviation Safety Agency – EASA).

88 These principles are set out in Annex 19 of the Chicago Convention "Safety Management", which was adopted in 2013.
89 SOM Manual, ICAO 2006, Ed.2, Doc 973 4, paragraph 2.4.7.

The RSOO system refers to a network of aviation safety regulators that work together to ensure the safety and security of air transport in the region. The aim of this system is to promote and coordinate regional cooperation in aviation safety and security, to exchange of information and best practices, and to ensure the implementation of international safety standards and recommended practices. The system contributes to the harmonization of regulations and practices in the region, which helps to ensure a high level of safety for air travelers.

Many such institutions have already been established around the world. They operate within different regions and are listedin Table 2.2. Table 2.2 illustrates all RSOOs across different regions of the world.

Table 2.2 RSOO with division into regions of the world

Continent	*Legal basis/date of establishment*	*Member states*
Africa:		
Regional Unit for Aviation Safety Oversight and Civil Aviation Protection(URSAC)	2019 (previously, in the years 2004–2019, known as: Community Agency for the Supervision of Civil Aviation Safety and Security (ACSAC))	Benin, Burkina Faso, Guinea-Bissau, Ivory Coast, Mali, Niger, Senegal, Togo
Aviation Safety Oversight Agency for Central Africa (ASSA-AC)	Multilateral agreement, 2016	Chad, Cameroon, Congo, Central African Republic, Equatorial Guinea, Gabon
African and Malagasy Civil Aviation Authority (AAMAC)	Multilateral agreement, 2012	Benin, Burkina Faso, Cameroon, Chad, Central African Republic, Congo, Equatorial Guinea, Gabon, Guinea-Bissau, Ivory Coast, Madagascar, Mali, Mauritania, Niger, Senegal, Togo, Union of the Comoros
Banjul Accord Group Aviation Safety Oversight Organization (BAGASOO)	Multilateral agreement, 2009 r.	Cape Verde, Gambia, Ghana, Guinea, Liberia, Nigeria, Sierra Leone
East African Community Civil Aviation Safety and Security Oversight Agency (EAC-CASSOA)	Multilateral agreement, 2009 r.	Burundi, Kenya, Rwanda, South Sudan, Tanzania, Uganda
Interim Aviation Safety Organization of the Southern African Development Community (iSASO)	Multilateral agreement, 2017 r.	Angola, Botswana, Congo, Eswatini, Lesotho, Madagascar, Malawi, Mauritius, Mozambique, Namibia, Seychelles, South Africa, Tanzania, Zambia, Zimbabwe
Latin America:		
Central American Aviation Safety Agency (ACSA)	Multilateral agreement, 2000 r.	Belize, Costa Rica, Guatemala, Honduras, Nicaragua, El Salvador

(*Continued*)

Table 2.2 (Continued)

Continent	*Legal basis/date of establishment*	*Member states*
Caribbean Aviation Safety Security Oversight System (CASSOS)	Multilateral agreement, 2001 r.	Antigua and Barbuda, Barbados, Dominica, Guyana, Haiti, Jamaica, Suriname, Trinidad and Tobago, St. Lucia, St. Kitts and Nevis, St. Vincent and the Grenadines
Regional Safety Oversight Cooperation System (SRVSOP)	Memorandum of Understanding (MoU), 2001 r.	Argentina, Bolivia, Brazil, Chile, Colombia, Colombia, Cuba, Ecuador, Panama, Paraguay, Peru, Uruguay, Venezuela
Asia and the Pacific Region		
Pacific Aviation Safety Office (PASO)	Multilateral agreement, 2004 r.	Cook Islands, Kiribati, Nauru, Niue, Papua New Guinea, Samoa, Solomon Islands, Tonga, Tuvalu, Vanuatu
Interstate Aviation Committee (IAC)	Multilateral agreement, 1991 r.	Azerbaijan, Armenia, Belarus, Kazakhstan, Kyrgyzstan, Moldova, Russian Federation, Tajikistan, Turkmenistan, Uzbekistan
The Cooperative Development of Operational Safety and Continuing Airworthiness–Southeastern Asia (COSCAPSEA)	ICAO programming document, 2001 r.	Brunei, Cambodia, Indonesia, Lao People's Democratic Republic, Malaysia, Myanmar, Papua New Guinea, Philippines, Singapore, Thailand, Timor-Leste, Vietnam
The Cooperative Development of Operational Safety and Continuing Airworthiness – Southern Asia (COSCAP-SA)	ICAO programming document, 1997 r.	Bangladesh, Bhutan, India, Maldives, Nepal, Pakistan, Sri Lanka
The Cooperative Development of Operational Safety and Continuing Airworthiness – Northern Asia (COSCAP-NA)	ICAO programming document, 2003 r.	China, Hong Kong Special Administrative Region (China), Macau Special Administrative Region (China), Democratic People's Republic of Korea, Mongolia, Republic of Korea
Europe		
European Union Aviation Safety Agency (EASA)	Secondary legislation, EU regulation, 2002 r.	Austria, Belgium, Bulgaria, Croatia, Cyprus, Czech Republic, Denmark, Estonia, Finland, France, Germany, Greece, Hungary, Iceland, Ireland, Italy, Latvia, Liechtenstein, Lithuania, Luxembourg, Malta, Netherlands, Norway, Poland, Portugal, Romania, Slovakia, Slovenia, Spain, Sweden, Switzerland

Source: Own elaboration.

Considering the legal character of a future regional safety oversight body, the actual scope of its competencies and organizational structure should be taken into account. Bodies that are established through international agreements (see: CASSOS) or as a result of a secondary legislation of another organization (see: EASA) have a strong mandate and legal empowerment to act. The legal foundation of the act establishing an institution has strong legal force when the new institutional structure is equipped with prerogatives that grant it real and extensive regulatory and supervisory powers. The European institution EASA enjoys far-reaching independence and an extensive set of prerogatives. Thanks to this, it effectively performs its functions and serves as a complementary element of the European Union's activities in the field of aviation safety. On the other hand, Latin American institutions such as SRVSOP or CASSOS, although established through an international agreement (respectively the Memorandum of Understanding and a multilateral agreement), adopt regulations that are not directly binding and must be approved by both LACAC and ICAO. In addition, these institutions do not have extensive powers enshrined in the statutes that establish them, which means that they have less influence on the harmonization of the regional system of aviation law. In the context of regional institutions in Africa, there is a strong desire for greater institutionalization and a faster process of codifying aviation law, a trend observed in recent years. These institutions have recognized a correlation between the level of aviation safety and the uniform regulatory system. Processes of intensification of interdependence and interinstitutional cooperation are underway in various regional safety oversight organizations in Africa. One can note, for example, frequent meetings occur between African authorities and the European authority EASA, which serves as a model for the implementation of a uniform aviation safety system.

The effective implementation of regional safety oversight bodies depends on the political will and commitment of the states wishing to establish them. In the era of internationalization of international relations in various areas, many parts of the world are witnessing the process of unification and standardization of legal regulations affecting the level of safety and the integration of nations within each respective field.

2.5 Codification of aviation safety in the regime of bilateral agreements

The issue of safety is also reflected in the provisions of bilateral air services agreements. The practice of including aviation safety and security clauses has not always been present in such agreements. Initially it is important to clarify the concept of bilateral agreements, their legal scope and their underlying conditions. A bilateral agreement constitutes a formal and legal basis for air operations between the two parties concerned. The parties to an agreement need not be limited solely to states.; they may also be international organizations.

2.5.1 Origins of bilateral agreements

The origin of bilateral agreements on air communication is very long and spans over a hundred years of experience. From the outset, bilateral agreements were concluded between the two states, but the liberalization of legal framework forced faster processes of market opening. Currently, an international organization is also a party to such a bilateral agreement. For example, the EU, which has the competence to regulate air transport under Article 100 of the Treaty on the Functioning of the European Union (TFEU), enters into bilateral agreements with third countries, known as horizontal agreements. The EU concludes a bilateral air transport agreement with a third country that will apply to all member states.[90]This has the advantage that member states do not have to negotiate the provisions of the bilateral agreement separately, which would prolong the legislative process. Thus, the EU negotiates an agreement on behalf of all member states, which results in uniform provisions applicable in every member states, and it also opens the aviation market to all member states with a third country.

After the end of World War I, the importance of civil aviation increased through the adoption of the Paris Convention of 1919 and the regulation of air navigation rules between states in bilateral agreements. It also became clear that bilateral agreements would apply exclusively to civil aviation (referred to as "private", during the interwar period). Currently, the legal basis for concluding bilateral agreements on air communication is the Chicago Convention of 1944. Article 6 of the Convention is generally recognized as the legal basis for such agreements. According to its provisions, the performance of international scheduled air services over the territory of one state may take place only under a special permit granted by that state and in accordance with the conditions specified by it. It should be clearly noted that there is no explicit provision here that mandates the conclusion of bilateral agreements. However, the practice of states has evolved in this manner, as it had already existed before the adoption of the Chicago Convention, so that the regulation of air connections between the two parties is based on bilateral agreements. Hence, this system is often referred to as the Chicago-bilateral system. Valuable considerations regarding the legal conditions and the essence of the Chicago-bilateral system are presented by Joseph Gertler.[91] He believes that although bilateral agreements

90 For example, on December 12, 2006, the Euro-Mediterranean Air Services Agreement between the European Community (i.e. the European Union) and its member states, on the one hand, and the Kingdom of Morocco, on the other. In accordance with the provisions of Article 26 of this Agreement, it replaces the corresponding provisions in the existing bilateral air services agreements between the 20 member states of the EU and Morocco. Since several EU states did not, at that time, have an appropriate bilateral agreement with Morocco at the moment, the provisions of the horizontal agreement apply to all EU countries. The Euro-Mediterranean agreement does not abolish bilateral agreements previously concluded by some of the contracting states, but it takes precedence if those provisions are incompatible with the new horizontal agreement.

91 Gertler Joseph Z., *Bilaterial Air Transport Agreements: Non-Bermuda Reflections*, Journal of Air Law and Commerce, Vol. 42, 1976, pp. 779–824.

contain heterogeneous elements, they simultaneously form an integrated whole that should be recognized as positive element.[92]

2.5.2 *Types and regulations of bilateral agreements*

We can distinguish two types of bilateral agreements:

1. restrictive bilateral agreements (Chicago or Bermuda type);
2. liberal bilateral agreements (open skies).

Restrictive bilateral air services agreements are specific to the Chicago system (often referred to as Bermuda-type agreements). A characteristic feature was the signing of very restrictive bilateral agreements regarding commercial and operational rights, as a result of which carriers had very limited opportunities for development. The provisions in these agreements contained restrictions on the freedom of market access of air carriers and on fair competition. Therefore, in practice, there was a principle of "one state one carrier". This meant limiting the conduct of air operations to one carrier from each party to the agreement. Moreover, in aviation law, the term "Bermuda-type agreement" is still in use. The name and type of the agreement derive from the bilateral agreement concluded between the US and United Kingdom on February 11, 1946, in Bermuda – hence the name.[93]

With the liberalization of the aviation market starting from the early 1990s, bilateral agreements on air communication were expanded to include articles addressing aviation security and safety. This was influenced by two factors. The first was the liberalization of restrictive provisions in bilateral agreements. There was an increasingly vocal criticism of the Chicago (Bermuda) system, which limited the development opportunities of entities and states. Barry Diamond, citing numerous critical voices, emphasizes an important point that Bermuda-type bilateral agreements represent a serious problem for international law, as they become an instrument of economic discrimination.[94] The first symptoms of change began with the deregulation of civil aviation in the US in the mid-1970s. In 1976, the US and the UK announced their intention to modify their mutual air communication agreement in a more liberal direction. In 1977, a new bilateral agreement (known as the Bermuda Agreement II), which replaced the previous one, was signed.[95] In

92 *Ibidem*.

93 Actually, we should say about two types of Bermuda agreements: Bermuda Type 1 and Bermuda type 2. The former concerns restrictive provisions in a bilateral agreement, while type 2 refers to the compact bilateral agreement concluded between the US and the UK in 1977, which contained more liberal provisions. See more: Haanappel P.P.C., *Bilateral Air Transport Agreements – 1913–1980*, The International Trade Law Journal, Vol. 5, 1980, p. 243.

94 Diamond B., *The Bermuda Agreement Revisited: A Look at the Past, Present and Future of Bilateral Air Transport Agreements*, Journal of Air Law and Commerce, Vol. 41, 1975, p. 424.

95 The US and the UK on June 22, 1976, announced the termination of Bermuda Type 1 Agreement of 1946, while simultaneously indicating that a new agreement was forthcoming. A year later, on June

addition, in 1978, a federal law was passed in the form of the Arline Deregulation Act,[96] which liberalized the entire aviation market, by allowing carriers to freely operate services across the country, and, due to the announcement of modifications to bilateral agreements with third countries, a greater number of US carriers would have the opportunity to operate international services.[97]

The second factor influencing the inclusion of aviation safety and security clauses in bilateral agreements was the growing threat of illegal acts directed at the broad concept of civil aviation safety, in the form of numerous terrorist attacks that took place in the 1960s, 1970s, and 1980s. The reaction of the international community was to adopt international agreements that act as a kind of shield against acts of unlawful interference in civil aviation and that regulate the principles of cooperation between states in situations of threat and the occurrence of acts of aviation terrorism.

Nowadays, civil aviation worldwide is largely liberalized. Legal regulations enable the unrestricted development of aviation entities within the state, and the market is open to competition, which contributes to the growth of air traffic globally. However, in many cases, bilateral air services agreements are still the legal basis for air services. Initially, bilateral agreements were very restrictive, as they imposed an excessive role for the state in regulating the aviation market. As a result of such provisions, the aviation market could not develop. With the processes of globalization and economic liberalization in the second half of the 20th century, the aviation sector was gradually exposed to open competition. The then-existing restrictive bilateral air services agreements began to be liberalized or even abandoned. An example is the EU, which, by opening its entire internal market to various economic sectors, replaced the existing bilateral agreements between member states with treaty provisions on a common market. Many statesin the world still have restrictive clauses, such as limitations on transport capacity,[98]

22, 1977, a new agreement was signed, referred to as Bermuda Type 2, which entered into force on July 23, 1977. See Haanappel P.P.C., *Bilateral*..., op. cit., p. 260.

96 Peterson R., *Impacts of Airline Deregulation*, TR NEWS 315, 2018, pp. 10–17.

97 As a result of this deregulation, it was decided to sign new agreements with various states, under which greater rights were granted to American carriers (e.g. the rights of "fifth" freedom). The other party gained little advantage in the form of the ability to operate to two or more locations on US territory. Such an arrangement did not place both sides on equal footing, as the American side held a decisive advantage.

98 In bilateral agreements, states defined the principle that the offered capacity strictly corresponds to the current and reasonably anticipated demand for international carriage on the agreed routes, with a reasonable load factor for the carriage of passengers and cargo. Moreover, a typical provision in many agreements stipulated that the designated carrier of each party would take the interests of the other party into account, so as not to adversely affect thatcarrier. In addition, it was often added to these provisions that the carriage of third-country nationals would only be supplementary.

frequency of operations,[99] mono-designation clauses,[100] route restrictions,[101] or clauses requiring the mandatory approval of tariffs,[102] and flight timetables[103] by aviation authorities. The Cold War polarization and a specific bipolar balance of power necessitated the creation of restrictive agreements to protect national air carriers and to control the situation regarding transport capacity. Such restrictions in agreements became the norm in the period after the World War II for several decades. It was only from the mid-1980s, as a result of the development of air transport and an increased demand for this mode, that states began to liberalize the agreements they have signed. This process proceeded evolutionarily, without abrupt changes.

99 The flight frequency clause meant how often air operations could be carried out on an agreed route. These provisions varied, e.g. two times a week, or during specific days, e.g. on Wednesdays and Saturdays.

100 The monodesignation clause means designating one air carrier from each state to serve a particular air route. In bilateral agreements, each state designated one air carrier to operate the route specified in the agreement. As a result, only two carriers operated between two states on a specific route. This clause did not provide for the possibility of introducing an additional carrier to operate a specific route between the parties concerned. Along with the liberalization of bilateral agreements, this clause was replaced by a multidesignation, meaning that an unlimited number of carriers from each party could be designated to perform operations, in accordance with the provisions of the agreement.

101 In bilateral agreements, provisions were introduced to regulate which points (cities) the designated carrier could serve. Usually it was one point (one city) in each state. Thus, the carrier could operate exclusively from point A in state A to point B in stateB. Very often, a provision was also added that the creation of a new route, other than the one specified in the agreement, would be possible only under a separate intergovernmental agreement. Over time, because of gradual liberalization, the possibility of serving two or even more points was introduced.

102 The tariff approval procedure was extremely restrictive. The number of fares on each route was to be agreed upon by the carriers operating on a given route. In practice, two carriers set the ticket price on a given route, resulting in a lack of pricing freedom and a lack of flexibility to consider various factors. In addition, after the carriers established the fares, these had to be approved by the aviation authorities of each carrier. Moreover, if the carriers were unable to reach an agreement, the aviation authorities would assume the initiative and set the fare for the particular route.

103 Restrictive bilateral agreements obliged the designated carriers to submit for approval the type of services to be performed, the types of aircraft to be used, and the flight schedules. According to the provisions in such agreements, it was forbidden to start air services before the aviation authorities had approved the flight schedule. This procedure was repeated before each new season. In practice, the lack of approval by the aviation authorities meant that the air operations could not be initiated. For example, in 1967, the carrier World Airlines submitted an application to the CAB (the US's central administrative body for civil aviation) to obtain the rights to operate the New York – Los Angeles route. It took six years before the agency issued a negative decision for the carrier due to "obsolescence". As can be seen, the carrier applied to launch a domestic route not an international one, since the latter would have required a political change to the existing bilateral air services agreements with a third country. Zając G., *Dwustronne umowy o komunikacji lotniczej zawierane przez Polskę,* in: "Przegląd Sił Powietrznych", No 4/06, Wyd. Dowództwo Sił Powietrznych RP, Poznań 2006, p. 84–94; *What Prompted Airline Deregulation 20 Years Ago? What were the objectives of that deregulation and how were they achieved?*, 15.09.1998, Vancouver, in: http://corporate.findlaw.com/law-library/what-prompted-airline-deregulation-20-years-ago-what-were-the.html#sthash.I5IhRBGb.dpuf, accessed 23.02.2024.

2.5.3 Safety clauses in bilateral agreements

Bilateral air services agreements usually include safety clauses that define aviation safety requirements, procedures and standards. Aviation safety clauses in bilateral agreements usually cover various aviation safety issues, one of which is certification requirements. This means that states, on the basis of reciprocity, recognize all airworthiness certificates, certificates of competence and personnel licenses issued by the other party, provided that the minimum safety standards established in accordance with the Chicago Convention are met. States retain the right to revoke or limit the issued authorization or operating authorization in the event that the other party does not apply safety standards, in particular with regard to aeronautical equipment, flight crews, the aircraft itself, and its operations. The provisions in bilateral agreements usually require states parties to comply with certain aviation safety standards, such as procedures for passengers and baggage screening, security checks on board aircraft and traffic rules at the airport.

Another issue regulated with regard to safety rules is the requirement for the conduct of safety inspections by the aviation authorities of the states parties to the agreement. Bilateral agreements typically include a clause mandating that the aviation authorities of the states parties carry out regular or ad hoc safety inspections to verify whether airlines and airports comply with the specified standards. These are the so-called ramp inspections. The purpose of ramp inspections is to ascertain the validity of the aircraft's documents and its crew, as well as to assess the visible technical condition of the aircraft and its equipment. The regulations grant each party the right to immediately suspend or modify the operating authorization of the designated carrier of the other party in the event that, as a result of a ramp inspection or lack of access to such inspection, a state determines that it is necessary to take immediate action for the safety of the operations carried out by the carrier concerned.

The provisions of bilateral agreements also include stipulations regarding the sharing of information on aviation safety threats, such as warnings about terrorist attacks or security incidents. Bilateral agreements usually require the exchange of information on aviation safety hazards, or any events that might affect aviation safety.

Contemporary or recently amended bilateral agreements additionally include provisions on aviation security. These provisions relate to the obligations of states parties with respect to civil aviation security to provide each other with every assistance in preventing acts of unlawful seizure of civil aircraft and other unlawful acts directed against the safety of such aircraft, their passengers and crews, airports, and air navigation facilities. In doing so, the states invoke the relevant conventions governing aviation safety and security. This is a broad range of issues covering illegal acts against the safety of aircraft, individuals, airports or other aviation equipment or installations, acts of unlawful seizure of aircraft, or crimes committed on board aircraft. The parties to a bilateral agreement include a provision stating that their obligations relating to civil aviation security form an integral part of the agreement. The provisions also stipulate that states shall comply with the conventions that are part of the Tokyo-Hague-Montreal system, as well as with other provisions regarding the protection of civil aviation against terrorist acts. Bilateral agreements may also include clauses on cooperation in the event of aviation safety incidents, such as air accidents or terrorist threats.

Aviation safety and security clauses in bilateral agreements are designed to ensure aviation safety and to coordinate action between states parties in order to minimize the risk of accidents and safety hazards. It is important that bilateral air services agreements are in line with international aviation safety standards and include provisions allowing for the exchange of information and coordination among states parties in the event of aviation safety threats.

Summing up the considerations concerning the bilateral system, one can recall Gertler's apt conclusion from 1976. Although formulated several decades ago, it can still be considered valid. Gertler emphasizes that the purpose of bilateral agreements should not be limited merely to exchange of routes and traffic rights, but also to establish a wide range of administrative, legal, economic, and operational conditions deemed necessary for the operation of air services. He also stresses that the evolution of this scope and content of the agreements was a logical process based on the accumulated knowledge and experience gained by states on what should be negotiated and agreed upon bilaterally.[104] In the era of liberalization of aviation regulations, contemporary bilateral agreements practically allow the freedom to provide services by air carriers, while leaving the oversight of aviation safety and security to the state.

2.6 Summary

The codification of international civil aviation includes a number of agreements, regulations and standards developed by ICAO which are applied worldwide to ensure the safety of operations. The legal aspects of aviation safety encompass a range of laws and regulations that aim to ensure safety in air traffic. They include among other things:

a) provisions relating to the construction and exploitation of aircraft. All aircraft must comply with the technical and safety requirements specified by the ICAO and national regulations;
b) personnel regulations. Air carriers must recruit and train personnel in accordance with ICAO requirements, regional regulations, and national laws;
c) airport safety regulations. Airports must comply with safety and security requirements such as security screening and protection measures, marking, lighting, etc.;
d) air traffic regulations. States must maintain and control air traffic in accordance with ICAO requirements and national regulations to ensure flight safety;
e) liability for damages resulting from aviation activities. Air carriers and states are liable for damages arising from aviation activities, in accordance with international and national regulations.

104 Gertler J. Z., op. cit., p. 781.

These rules and regulations are necessary to ensure air traffic safety and are regularly updated and improved to provide the best possible protection for passengers and personnel. The chapter presents global legal instruments and an institutional system in the field of aviation safety. A legal analysis of normative acts and a comparative analysis of documents regulating aspects of safety in civil aviation have been conducted. The institutional structure worldwide in this area is presented, including regional aviation safety groups and safety oversight bodies. They constitute an important law-making element affecting the entirety of activities carried out in various regions of the world. An important role in the legislative process at the national level is played by the Global Aviation Safety Plan and the Global Aviation Safety Roadmap, which serve to improve the quality of legislation and set strategic goals for all entities operating in the field of aviation safety.

Bilateral air services agreements, which regulate various aspects of air transport between states, also play an important role. Today, aviation relations are increasingly liberalized, and civil aviation is open to competition and free enterprise. Nevertheless, there are still restrictive agreements that limit the activities of entities, mainly air carriers, with an excessive regulatory function of the state. This causes difficulties in the smooth functioning of civil aviation worldwide. The main international organization ICAO promotes the opening of aviation markets by states, for example through the conclusion of open skies agreements. A significant argument from states limiting the opening of their aviation markets is their aviation policy based on the dominance of a single air carrier recognized as national and favoring its development. Such states express concerns that the full opening of the aviation market and the full liberalization of the legal framework will create uncertainty about the future of such an airline. These states wish to retain influence over the operations of air carriers and guide their development. The global market, as presented in the chapter, is a system of legal, institutional and technological relations, and the function of the state in the modern world should focus on the oversight of safety and foster the development of its own air carriers. The chapter highlights the important role of states and other entities, including international and regional organizations, in the codification of international aviation law. The increase in institutionalization processes contributes to the development of codification in the world and the unification of safety standards, which are the foundation for the development of civil aviation.

3 The regional institutional and legal system for aviation safety

The processes of regionalization and globalization taking place in the contemporary world aim at greater interdependence of states. The development of these connections is a result of the dynamically progressing socio-economic development of nations. Cooperation between states occurs on both bilateral and multilateral levels. The evolution of the latter results in the creation of new institutions that implement the goals of the states that establish them. As part of the regionalization process, many regional institutional structures are being formed, which often operate on the basis of broader cooperation platforms – global international organizations whose scope is not limited to a specific region. Regional institutions and organizational structures strive to exert greater impact on their regions through the unification of regulations aimed at harmonizing standards in a specific field. The same applies to civil aviation. Regional aviation safety institutions perform several important functions:

a) playing the role of regional coordinator of solutions adopted by individual states;
b) establishing key policy aspects aimed at improving aviation safety;
c) codifying and harmonizing of aviation safety rules and standards;
d) acting as a center for the exchange of information and promotion of the best safety practices;
e) performing analyses in the field of air transport safety and assessing the risk of threats.

The process of institutionalizing aviation safety is accompanied by codification in this area. This chapter will discuss the process in individual regions of the world. It will present the process of harmonization of aviation law and the impact of institutions on aviation safety through the creation of uniform legal frameworks in civil aviation. A comparison will also be made of regulations existing in different regions of the world, their level of advancement, and the scope of regulation. International aviation safety standards are the same for all states, although there are often functioning different regulations at the regional level, so it is possible to analyze the legal status in various regions of the world in terms of the implementation of these norms and guidelines. Regional legal solutions that

DOI: 10.4324/9781003557876-4

are specific to a given region will be described. Regions have different approaches to the process of harmonizing areas of civil aviation. The most important thing is drawing conclusions and the willingness of states and institutions to cooperate in order to develop coherent safety standards.

3.1 Legal and institutional system of aviation safety in Europe

The most important regulations concerning aviation safety in Europe are established by several international organizations: the EU, the EU Aviation Safety Agency (EASA), and the European Organization for the Safety of Air Navigation (EUROCONTROL). The European aviation safety system should be understood as a set of legislative, oversight, and operational mechanisms built on a solid foundation of institutional cooperation among states. The formation of uniform legal regulations is related to the emergence and evolution of the process of European integration after World War II. The creation of uniform legal and organizational frameworks is associated with the establishment of the European Economic Community in 1957, which was transformed into the European Community in 1992, and today exists within the EU following the Lisbon Treaty reforms in 2007. Within the European institutional system, EASA operates with a dual international legal character. On one hand, it is an independent international organization with its own legal personality and organizational structures. On the other hand, it is an agency specialized by the EU to pursue its objectives. It was created by an EU legal act and can be dissolved in the same manner. In addition, EUROCONTROL is responsible for unifying safety regulations. It is the oldest intergovernmental organization on the European continent dealing with aviation safety issues.

The safety of European air navigation should be considered from multiple perspectives. The adoption of numerous legal instruments governing aviation safety issues demonstrates the advanced process of the codification of European aviation safety. An important element of the system is also the effectiveness of the implemented regulations thanks to the safety oversight mechanism performed within the EU, EASA, and EUROCONTROL. Despite the existence of several organizations handling safety regulation in air transport, their standards do not conflict with one another, and the institutions cooperate to develop the best solutions to improve and enhance the level of safety in European aviation.

The EU is the primary organization responsible for the regulatory process in the field of civil aviation. However, issues relating to operational safety and technical inspections have been delegated to EASA. Similarly, EUROCONTROL deals with the area of air traffic management safety, although the EU also has this authority. Each of these institutions deals with a different area of safety regulation.

3.1.1 Harmonization of aviation safety regulations at EU level

The main regulatory institution in Europe is the EU. Within the EU, regulations concerning various areas of safety, including airports, air carriers, certification, and airspace management, are adopted. Aviation law in the EU is formulated by Union's institutions, rather than by the member states, due to the implementation of a common transport policy, including a common aviation policy. Although Article 3(1) of the Treaty on the Functioning of the European Union (TFEU) does not list transport policy as an exclusive competence of the Union, but rather as a shared competence between the Eand the member states. Article 90 of the TFEU, however, makes it clear that the objectives of the Treaties are implemented within the framework of the common transport policy. In addition, Article 2(2) of the TFEU provides that in areas of shared competence, member states retain the ability to adopt legislation in a specific field as long as the EU has not already regulated the matter. If the EU decides to regulate an area under shared competence, it may do so in accordance with the principles of subsidiarity and proportionality.[1]

The codification of aviation safety rules is an advanced process that takes place primarily on the basis of the legal and organizational framework of the EU. Uniform regulations are adopted for various aspects of civil aviation, in accordance with the provisions of the TFEU. The EU pursues its air transport policy by establishing a legal framework across all its sectors. Under Article 100(2) of the TFEU, the European Parliament and the Council, acting in accordance with the ordinary legislative procedure, have the prerogative to lay down appropriate rules for air transport. The process of mandatory consultations with the Economic and Social Committee and the Committee of the Regions also play an important role in the legislative procedure.

The current regulations were adopted as part of the amendments to the TFEU introduced by the Lisbon Treaty, although the provisions on the possibility of creating uniform legal regulations throughout the EU (formerly: the Community) existed in the original version of the Treaty (formerly; the Treaty establishing the European Economic Community – EEC) from 1957. However, for a number of years, the Community authorities at that time practically took no action to conduct air transport policy or regulate civil aviation issues, including safety, at a European level. A breakthrough occurred with the 1985 judgment of the Court of Justice of the EU, which ordered the Council (today: the EU Council) to start implementing legal regulations in the area of civil aviation. Shortly thereafter, three legislative packages (with a fourth package adopted more than a decade later) were introduced that regulated and liberalized air transport throughout the Community.[2] The

1 Article 5 of the Treaty on European Union (TEU) in the modified version of the Lisbon Treaty sets out the principles of proportionality and subsidiarity. The principle of subsidiarity means that the Union can act only when, and to the extent that, the objectives of the proposed action cannot be sufficiently achieved by the member states and where the scale or effects of the proposed action make it more effective to achieve at EU level. The principle of proportionality means that the scope and form of action taken by the EU does not go beyond what is necessary to achieve the objectives of the Treaty.

2 The first legislative package was introduced in 1987. It consisted of four legal acts introducing competition between Community carriers. The second package was adopted in 1990, which limited the ability of states to influence the market behavior of airlines and clarified the application of competition rules. The third package, the broadest and to the greatest extent liberalizing air transport, was adopted in 1992. It consisted of three normative acts: Regulation 2407/92, governing common licensing rules for air carriers in the EU; Regulation, 2408/92 guaranteeing the freedom to provide services to EU carriers and replacing existing bilateral air services agreements between member states; and

adoption of the third liberalization package in 1992 and the establishment of the EU under the Treaty on European Union, signed in Maastricht on February 7, 1992 (the Maastricht Treaty), initiated the process of creating and harmonizing aviation law in Europe. The main areas that were regulated in the 1990s focused on economic issues. The process of regulating civil aviation was extremely dynamic, with the main areas of European aviation operations being harmonized, while safety issues were not a primary concern for states at that time.

As a result of the events of September 11, 2001 (the attacks on the World Trade Center in New York, and the Pentagon in Virginia), states began intensively regulating aviation safety. The EU adopted several legislative acts in this area in order to protect itself as much as possible from similar terrorist threats or other acts directed against civil aviation safety in Europe. The EU, which has the competence to regulate air transport at the Union level, decided to establish a separate institutional system to deal with safety issues. It was decided to create EASA in 2002. However, the EU retained the right to continue regulating matters, including security. EASA was intended to be a specialized agency that would support the EU in the area of safety regulation and oversight mechanisms. In addition to the institutional system, the EU comprehensively regulated various areas, including:

a) reporting events threatening aviation safety;[3]
b) establishing an air accident investigation system;[4]
c) regulating unmanned aerial vehicles operations;[5]
d) creating a "blacklist" of air carriers.[6]

Regulation 2409/92 allowing air carriers to set freely the level of charges for services provided within the EU and containing provisions abolishing the institution of government approval of air fares. A decade later, the fourth package was adopted in 2004 and concerned the introduction of a uniform airspace management system in Europe.

3 Regulation 376/2014 of the European Parliament and of the Council of April 3, 2014, addresses the reporting, analysis, and follow-up of occurrences in civil aviation. It amends Regulation 996/2010 of the European Parliament and of the Council and repeals Directive 2003/42/EC of the European Parliament and of the Council, as well as Commission Regulations (EC) No 1321/2007 and (EC) No 1330/2007, OJ EU, *L* 122, 24.4.2014.

4 Regulation 996/2010 of the European Parliament and of the Council of October 20, 2010, on the investigation and prevention of accidents and incidents in civil aviation and repealing Directive 94/56/ *EC*. OJ EU, *L* 295, 12.11.2010.

5 Commission Delegated Regulation (EU) 2019/945 of March 12, 2019, on unmanned aircraft systems and on third country operators of unmanned aircraft systems, OJ EU, *L* 152, 11.6.2019; Commission Implementing Regulation (EU) 2019/947 of May 24, 2019 on the rules and procedures for the operation of unmanned aircraft. OJ EU, *L* 152, 11.6.2019.

6 Regulation (EC) 2111/2005 of the European Parliament and of the Council of December 14, 2005, on the establishment of a Community list of air carriers subject to an operating ban within the Community and on informing air transport passengers of the identity of the operating air carrier and repealing Article 9 of Directive 2004/36/EC. OJ EU, *L* 344, 27.12.2005; Commission Implementing Regulation (EU) 2022/2295 of November 23, 2022, amending Regulation (EC) 474/2006 as regards the list of air carriers banned from operating or subject to operating restrictions within the Union, OJ EU, *L 304 of 24.11.2022.*

Many areas relating to the operational safety and its oversight adopted by the EU have been delegated to EASA. These include issues concerning:

a) the creation of EASA and the definition of its scope of competence;[7]
b) airport safety;[8]
c) safety of flight operations;[9]
d) the certification process for aircraft and flight crews;[10]
e) the establishment of a system for the control of third-country carriers under the SAFA program;[11]
f) air traffic management and airspace control.[12]

The basic issues of aviation safety have been regulated by the EU in Regulation 2018/1139. This Regulation is directly applicable in the member states and does not require transposition into the domestic legal order. It provides the legal basis for the functioning of civil aviation in the EU. Among other things, it lays down the rules for issuing certificates to air operators, aircraft registration, the procedures for granting and issuing authorizations for flight operations, and the oversight of flight safety. The aim of the regulation is to ensure a high level of flight safety and environmental protection by adopting coherent and uniform rules at the European level. In addition, the Regulation aims to:

7 Regulation (EU) 2018/1139 of the European Parliament and of the Council of July 4, 2018, on common rules in the field of civil aviation and establishing a European Union Aviation Safety Agency, and amending Regulations (EC) 2111/2005, (EC) 1008/2008, (EU) 996/2010, and (EU) 376/2014, and Directives 2014/30/EU and 2014/53/EU of the European Parliament and of the Council, and repealing Regulations (EC) 552/2004 and (EC) 216/2008 of the European Parliament and of the Council and Council Regulation (EEC) 3922/91, OJ EU, *L* 212, 22.8.2018.

8 Commission Regulation (EU) 139/2014 of February 12, 2014, laying down requirements and administrative procedures related to aerodromes pursuant to Regulation (EC) 216/2008 of the European Parliament and of the Council, OJ EU, *L* 44, 14.2.2014.

9 Commission Regulation (EU) 965/2012 of October 5, 2012, laying down technical requirements and administrative procedures related to air operations pursuant to Regulation (EC) 216/2008 of the European Parliament and of the Council, OJ EU, *L* 296, 25.10.2012.

10 Commission Regulation (EU) 1178/2011 of November 3, 2011, laying down technical requirements and administrative procedures related to civil aviation aircrew pursuant to Regulation (EC) 216/2008 of the European Parliament and of the Council, OJ EU, *L* 311, 25.11.2011; Commission Regulation (EU) 748/2012 of August 3, 2012, laying down implementing rules for the airworthiness and environmental certification of aircraft and related products, parts and appliances, as well as for the certification of design and production organizations, OJ EU, *L* 224, 21.8.2012; Commission Regulation (EU) 1321/2014 of November 26, 2014, on the continuing airworthiness of aircraft and aeronautical products, parts and appliances, and on the approval of organizations and personnel involved in these tasks, OJ EU, *L* 362, 17.12.2014.

11 Commission Regulation (EU) 965/2012, op. cit.

12 The scope of regulation is covered by the so-called Fourth Liberalization Package (SES I) and the SES II package.

a) establish and maintain a uniform, high level of civil aviation safety and security in the EU;
b) regulate basic issues in the field of civil aviation;
c) support member states in fulfilling their obligations arising from EU law and international obligations governed primarily by the Chicago Convention;
d) promote bilateral and multilateral cooperation;
e) strengthen passengers' trust in safe air transport.

Regulation 2018/1139 also provides the legal basis for the establishment of the EASA. The provisions of the Regulation impose an obligation on member states to ensure the safe conduct of air operations and other aviation activities by all entities operating in the field of civil aviation. It sets forth the principles governing the measures to be implemented by both member states and EASA in achieving the objectives of the Regulation, which include, in particular: incorporating global experience in the field of the current state of knowledge and best practices used in aviation, considering the interdependence between aviation safety, cybersecurity, and other relevant factors, facilitating mutual cooperation in the investigation of air accidents, serious incidents and other incidents infringing aviation safety and security rules, and taking non-binding measures that promote aviation safety principles.

Based on the provisions of the Regulation, instruments for aviation safety management have been established. These include two documents developed at the EU level: the European Aviation Safety Programme,[13] and the European Plan for Aviation Safety,[14] and two analogous documents at the member state level. [15]

The European Aviation Safety Programme was developed by the European Commission in consultation with EASA. It concerns the functioning of the European aviation safety system. It must contain elements related to the obligations of the state in the field of safety management as outlined in Annex 19 to the Chicago Convention, i.e.:

a) state safety policy through the creation of fundamental aviation legislation;
b) risk management through the fulfillment of licensing and certification obligations, the performance of safety oversight functions of aviation entities, the establishment of a process for investigating aviation accidents and incidents, the identification of hazards, and the establishment of a mechanism for resolving safety problems;
c) ensuring safety by conducting effective oversight;
d) promoting safety through robust internal and external communication as well as disseminating reliable safety information.

13 Article 5 of Regulation 2018/1139.
14 Article 6 of Regulation 2018/1139.
15 Article 7 and Article 8 of Regulation 2018/1139.

This document also includes the characteristics of the process of developing, adopting, updating, and implementing the European Plan for Aviation Safety.

The European Plan for Aviation Safety was prepared by EASA in cooperation with member states and other stakeholders. The purpose of this document is to identify the main safety risks to which the European aviation safety system is exposed. The Plan also indicates the actions to be taken to minimize the occurrence of a these risks. Additionally, it also requires the EASA to monitor the implementation of these measures using established safety performance indicators. The European Plan for Aviation Safety is intended to reflect the overall effectiveness of safety efforts across the EU, and is updated annually.

3.1.2 Interinstitutional cooperation on aviation safety

The EU also engages in interinstitutional cooperation in strengthening European safety. International cooperation is in line with the EU policy set out in the 2015 document Aviation Strategy for Europe.[16] Only effective cooperation between member states, EU institutions, and all stakeholders was recognized as key to ensuring the global success of European aviation in the future. The strategy also stressed that, in order to ensure coherence and unity at the international level, the EU should speak with one voice in its relations with other international organizations in the world, including ICAO, which will also contribute to higher safety standards.[17]

The EU cooperates closely with ICAO, the main global aviation organization responsible for the formulating international standards and guidelines. In the field of aviation safety, EU cooperation is facilitated through EASA, which has concluded numerous bilateral agreements with third countries and international organizations. Table 3.1 summarizes the EU's bilateral agreements with third countries.

Cooperation in the field of aviation safety also takes place through partnership programs established by the EU and implemented by EASA with various regions of the world.

Cooperation with other intergovernmental organizations worldwide is also actively pursued, such as ICAO, EUROCONTROL, the European Civil Aviation Conference (ECAC), and regional bodies operating globally. Aviation safety NGOs, including IATA, also play an active role. Moreover, the EU works to raise awareness of safety by organizing various international conferences and symposia that provide rich opportunities for information exchange among participants and contribute to broadening the idea of strengthening safety across a wide range of civil aviation issues.

16 Communication from the Commission to the European Parliament, the Council, the European Economic and Social Committee and the Committee of the Regions, An Aviation Strategy for Europe, COM(2015) 598 final, 7.12.2015.

17 *Ibidem*, point 3.1.

Table 3.1 Overview of EU bilateral agreements with third countries in the field of aviation safety

	Signed	*Entry into force*
United States[1]	June 30, 2008	May 1, 2011
Canada[2]	May 6, 2009	July 26, 2011
Brazil[3]	July 14, 2010	August 27, 2013
People's Republic of China[4]	May 20, 2019	September 1, 2020
Japan[5]	June 22, 2020	June 22, 2020[a]
The UK[6]	December 24, 2020	January 1, 2021

Source: Own elaboration based on EASA data.
[a]The agreement is temporarily applied until it enters into force.

1 Agreement between the United States of America and the European Community on cooperation in the regulation of civil aviation safety, OJ EU, *L* 291, 9.11.2011.
2 Agreement on civil aviation safety between the European Community and Canada, OJ EU, *L* 153, 17.6.2009.
3 Agreement between the European Union and the Government of the Federative Republic of Brazil on civil aviation safety, OJ EU, *L* 273, 19.10.2011.
4 Agreement on civil aviation safety between the European Union and the Government of the People's Republic of China, OJ EU, *L* 240, 24.07.2020.
5 Agreement on civil aviation safety between the European Union and Japan, OJ EU, *L* 229, 16.07.2020.
6 The UK ceased to be a member of the EU on January 31, 2020. The EU commenced negotiations on the conclusion of a new trade agreement with the UK. The official signing of the bilateral trade agreement, Part II of which concerns aviation safety, took place on December 24, 2020.

EASA and ICAO cooperate in various initiatives on aviation safety. So far, several agreements have been signed between the parties. These are:

a) the Memorandum of Cooperation between EASA and ICAO on safety oversight audit and related matters, signed in Montreal on March 21, 2006;[18]
b) the Memorandum of Cooperation between the EU and the ICAO providing a framework for enhanced cooperation, signed on April 28 and May 4, 2011;[19]
c) the Working Agreement on Continuous Monitoring Activities between the EASA and the ICAO, July 30, 2014.

EASA's cooperation with African states within the African Civil Aviation Commission (AFCAC) framework was signed during the meeting in Ezulwini (Eswatini) in 2017. At that time, African states signed the Ezulwini Declaration on Regional Security Oversight Organizations. EASA and ICAO were present at the event, where EASA signed an agreement with AFCAC to cooperate in improving

18 Non-binding act. It was replaced by a working arrangement in 2014 (Working Arrangement on continuous monitoring activities between the EASA and the ICAO).
19 OJ EU, *L* 232, 09.09.2011. The agreement entered into force on March, 2012.

safety oversight in Africa and promote and strengthen the regional integration process.[20]

The EU's cooperation with EUROCONTROL has been taking place since the signing of a memorandum of cooperation dated December 22, 2003. This collaboration focuses on airspace safety management, currently implemented mainly in the framework of the Single European Sky initiative (SES I and SES II). However, years earlier, EUROCONTROL norms and standards in the field of air traffic management were incorporated into EU legislation. In 2004, EU adopted regulations on the SES, developed in cooperation with EUROCONTROL. The cooperation between the two organizations dates back to the 1990s, when Commission Directive 97/15 was implemented adopting EUROCONTROL norms and amending Council Directive 93/65,[21] to establish mandatory standards for air traffic management.

The creation of the Single European Sky legal framework in 2004 was the first step in the implementation of a coordinated system for safe air traffic management. In partnership with EUROCONTROL, the EU adopted a series of air safety regulations that provided the legal basis for the implementation of the EU's SESAR program, co-financed by both the EU and EUROCONTROL.

Although the EU signed an accession protocol to EUROCONTROL,[22] it has not yet entered into force. In December 2012, the EU and EUROCONTROL concluded an agreement establishing a general framework for enhanced cooperation.[23] The Parties agreed to strengthen and consolidate the implementation of the SES framework.

The EU's cooperation with the ECAC is based on the 2012 Agreement on Civil Aviation Security.[24] Together, they fulfill their obligations to European integration in the field of aviation safety through joint efforts related to the drafting of legislation, holding discussions at the European level, and conducting aviation safety and security audits.[25] ECAC supports the EU in implementing international rules.

3.1.3 Legal basis and scope of EASA tasks

An important factor in shaping civil aviation safety in Europe was the creation of a single institution, equipped with a legal framework for the effective implementation of safety-related measures. Following the events of September 11, 2001, states and

20 https://www.easa.europa.eu/en/newsroom-and-events/press-releases/easaicao-forum-results-new-global-framework-regional-aviation, accessed 17.02.2024.

21 OJ *L* 95, 10 April 1997.

22 Protocol on the accession of the European Community to the Eurocontrol International Convention relating to Cooperation for the Safety of Air Navigation of December 13, 1960, as variously amended, and as consolidated by the Protocol of June 27, 1997, OJ EC, *L* 304, 30.09.2004.

23 Agreement between the EU and the EUROCONTROL establishing a general framework for enhanced cooperation, OJ EU, *L* 016, 19.01.2013.

24 Cooperation Arrangement with the Directorate-General for Mobility and Transport of the European Commission (DG MOVE) in the field of civil aviation security, signed on December 13, 2012, in Paris, France.

25 ECAC, ECAC's Strategy for the Future – A Policy Statement, ECAC 2021.

international organizations dealing with civil aviation around the world noticed the lack of broader safety regulations.

In the EU, the first major act addressing aviation security was Regulation No 2320/2002 of 2002, which laid down detailed common security rules. However, due to various issues, this act was replaced in 2008 by a new Regulation 300/2008, which provided states with greater flexibility in adopting security measures and procedures. After 2002, the EU oversight was strengthened and national legislation within the member states was modified and aligned with EU aviation safety and security regulations.

The harmonization of rules and procedures at the EU level in the field of aviation safety and security was also accompanied by the establishment of an institution to carry out tasks related to these responsibilities. In 2002, the European Union Aviation Safety Agency (EASA) was established by Regulation 1592/2002, which is no longer in force.[26] Currently, the legal basis for its operation is Regulation 2018/1139 of 2018 (as amended several times). EASA started its activities in 2004, and its headquarters is located in Cologne, Germany. It brings together 32 states (the 27 EU member states plus Iceland, Liechtenstein, Norway, and Switzerland). EASA plays a key role in coordinating aviation safety and environmental protection across the EU.

The main functions of EASA include:[27]

a) developing draft normative acts within the scope of the Regulation for the European Commission;
b) conducting certification;
c) preparation of technical regulations;
d) ensuring safety oversight, including carrying out inspections and supporting EU member states;
e) promoting international and regional safety standards;
f) working with stakeholders to improve safety in Europe.

EASA has a legal personality and is simultaneously an institution of the EU.[28] It possesseslegal capacity and the ability to perform legal acts. Both the EASA itself and its officials benefit the privileges and immunities of the EU under Protocol No. 7 to the Lizbon Treaty. The EASA has the following organizational structure: the Management Board, the Executive Director, and the Board of Appeal.

The Management Board is composed of representatives from the member states and the European Commission.[29] Each member of the Board has the right to vote.

26 Regulation (EC) 1592/2002 of the European Parliament and of the Council of July 15, 2002, on common rules in the field of civil aviation and establishing a European Aviation Safety Agency. EC L 240, of September 7, 2002 (non-binding).
27 Article 75 of Regulation 2018/1139.
28 Article 94(1) of Regulation 2018/1139
29 Article 99(1) of Regulation 2018/1139.

Each member state is entitled to appoint one member of the Management Board and an alternate, while the European Commission may appoint two Board members and two alternates. Members of the Management Board are appointed for a four-year term with the possibility of re-election (previous regulations provided fora five-year term). From among its members, the Board elects a chairperson and a vice-chairperson, who also have the right to vote. Their term of office is four years, with the possibility of single renewal for an identical period. Meetings of the Management Board are convened by the chairperson at least twice a year. At the request of the Chairperson or at the request of one-third of the Board members, an additional meeting can be convened. The Executive Director may participate in these meeting as an observer, without voting rights. Moreover, any person whose opinion may be deemed necessary for the case under discussionmay also be invited to participate as an observer. Members of the Management Board may be assisted by advisers or experts. The Board takes decisions by a simple majority of votes (in previous regulations, decisions were adopted by a two-thirds majority).

Among the most important tasks of the Management Board are:[30]

a) appointing the Executive Director and the extension of his/her term or removal from office;
b) adopting the annual report on the EASA's activities;
c) approving the annual budget by a two-thirds majority of the representatives entitled to vote;
d) appointing the members of the Board of Appeal;
e) adopting the internal rules and staff regulations;
f) adopting an anti-fraud strategy and ensuring that the findings and recommendations of the audits carried out by the European Anti-Fraud Office (OLAF) are followed;
g) adopting the European Plan for Aviation Safety in accordance with Article 6 of Regulation 2018/1139;
h) giving an opinion on the draft European Aviation Safety Programme in accordance with Article 5 of Regulation 2018/1139.

The Executive Director is appointed and dismissed by the Executive Board on a proposal from the European Commission following an open and transparent selection procedure by a two-thirds majority of its members with voting rights (under previous regulations, the decision to appoint a person was taken by the Management Board by a three-quarters majority of its members). The candidate must demonstrate significant achievements and documented competencies and experience related to civil aviation. Before the appointment, the candidate selected by the Management Board is invited to present a statement before the relevant committee of the European Parliament and answer questions posed by its members.

30 Article 98 of Regulation 2018/1139.

The Board makes its decision by a three-fourths majority vote of its members. The Executive Director's term of office lasts five years, and is renewable once.

The Executive Director has the following functions:[31]

a) manages the entire institution;
b) submits to the European Parliament, at its request, a report on the performance of its duties;
c) implements decisions adopted by the Management Board;
d) makes decisions on investigations, inspections, and other oversight activities specified in the legislation;
e) prepares the annual report on the EASA's activities and submits it to the Management Board for approval;
f) prepares the programming document and, after obtaining the approval from the Management Board, implements it and subsequently reports on its execution;
g) reports to the Management Board on the implementation of the European Plan for Aviation Safety;
h) manages the day-to-day activities of the EASA.

There is also a Board of Appeal within the EASA structure.[32] This body is responsible for reviewing appeals against decisions that are subject to appeal. The term of office of the Boards of Appeal members is five years and is renewable. Additionally, the members of the Board of Appeal are prohibited from holding any other positions within the EASA.

Furthermore, members of the Board of Appeal cannot take part in any appeal proceedings if they have a personal interest in the matter or if they were previously involved as representatives of one of the parties in the proceedings or if they participated in making of decision that is now under appeal. The Board examines the appeals by making a preliminary assessment of whether they are admissible and well founded. If the appeal is determined to be unfounded, the Board can reject the application. However, if the appeal is considered admissible and well founded, the Board forwards the case to the EASA, which can make a new decision considering that takes the Board's findings into account.

3.1.4 Safety regulation system in other European organizations

The study begins with an examination of ECAC. It is the organization on the European continent dedicated to civil aviation. It was established in 1955 as a result of the decision of the states participating at the founding conference in 1954 convened by the Council of Europe in Strasbourg.[33] Five years later, EUROCONTROL was created, and the EU (then in legal form as the European Community), and although

31 Article 104 of Regulation 2018/1139.
32 Articles 105–113 of Regulation 2018/1139.
33 ECAC IN FOCUS: Together for a Stronger European Aviation, ECAC 2021, p. 109.

it had the authority to regulate and unify civil aviation regulations under the Treaty of Rome of 1957, it began the process of codification from the end of the 1980s. ECAC is an international intergovernmental organization that currently brings together 44 states.[34]

ECAC was initially set up as a consultative body within the framework of ICAO. In later years, this institution acquired the characteristics and elements of an international organization. It was endowed with its own system of bodies, including a permanent secretariat, gained independence from the ICAO, and has increased its scope of activities and powers. The ECAC founding act has been extended over time through successive modifications. The latest amendments to the ECAC Constitution were adopted during the 38th ECAC Special Plenary Session on December 10, 2020.[35] Its organizational structure consists of a Plenary Conference (meeting every three years), meetings of the Directors-General of civil aviation from the member states (held three times a year), and a permanent secretariat headed by an Executive Secretary.[36] The ECAC's headquarters are in Paris.

The main areas of ECAC's activity are focused on aviation safety. In parallel with the process of harmonizing aviation regulations by the EU in the late 1980s and early 1990s, ECAC also contributed to the process of regulation and institutionalization of these issues through by creating in 1990 the Joint Aviation Authorities (JAA), an organization responsible for harmonizing safety standards in civil aviation, and being the first safety oversight institution (RSOO) at that time.[37]

At the time of EASA's establishment, which took over the functions previously performed by the JAA, the scope of ECAC's safety-related activities was reduced so that tasks and functions would not duplicate. Currently, ECAC deals with matters of certification, environmental protection, and aviation security and safety. In the latter area, ECAC issues legal regulations, raises awareness by organizing conferences and seminars, publishes safety-related materials, and provides guidelines and recommendations. In the performance of its regulatory function, it focuses mainly on the investigation of aviation accidents and incidents. To this end, the ECAC Expert Group on Air Accident and Incident Investigation (ACC) was set up in 1992. In 2016, an updated version of the Code of Conduct for Cooperation in the field of Air Accidents and Incidents Investigation was adopted.[38] On the operational side, in 2018, ECAC appointed The European Safety

34 As of January 31, 2025, https://www.ecac-ceac.org/about-ecac/member-states, accessed 2.02.2024. ECAC members are: Albania, Armenia, Austria, Azerbaijan, Belgium, Bosnia and Herzegovina, Bulgaria, Croatia, Cyprus, Czechia, Denmark, Estonia, Finland, France, Georgia, Germany, Greece, Hungary, Iceland, Ireland, Italy, Latvia, Lithuania, Luxembourg, Malta, Monaco, Montenegro, Netherlands, North Macedonia, Norway, Poland, Portugal, Republic of Moldova, Romania, San Marino, Serbia, Slovakia, Slovenia, Sweden, Switzerland, Turkiye, Ukraine, and the UK.

35 *ECAC IN FOCUS: Together for a Stronger European Aviation*, ECAC 2021, p. 133.

36 Article 4 of the ECAC Constitution.

37 *ECAC IN FOCUS: Together for a Stronger European Aviation*, ECAC 2021, p. 58.

38 The original version was adopted in 2006. Code of Conduct on Cooperation in the Field of Accident/Incident Investigation. https://www.ecac-ceac.org/activities/safety/air-accident-and-incident-investigations, accessed, 27.02.2024.

and Air Navigation Coordination Group (ESANCG),[39] which aims to coordinate the actions of various international and European institutions, to facilitate dialogue with stakeholders, draw up an action plan and report on its implementation.

As demonstrated, ECAC not only conducts codification activities by regulating aviation safety matters, but also contributes to the institutionalization process. It does so by creating bodies and institutions performing activities related to the investigation of air accidents, as well as supporting and promoting safety in Europe and worldwide through institutional cooperation at the bilateral and multilateral level.

Another important European organization is EUROCONTROL. This organization was founded just five years after the creation of ECAC, in 1960. Under the Convention establishing that organization signed on December 13, 1960,[40] which entered into force on March 1, 1963, its primary mission is to ensure air traffic safety. This organization is of a civil-military nature in accordance with Article 1(2) of the EUROCONTROL Convention. It consists of main bodies such as the Permanent Commission, the Provisional Council, the Director-General and the Secretariat, as well as plenty of consultative bodies, including: the Air Navigation Services Board, the Audit Board and the Civil-Military Stakeholder Committee. The organization's headquarters is based in Brussels.

It cooperates with states in the development, implementation, and modernization of air traffic management system, and supports regional organizations in creating regional safety plans.[41] As part of the airspace management coordination function, EUROCONTROL is responsible for ensuring flight safety throughout Europe. This organization oversees air traffic control systems and takes measures to prevent air accidents. In this regard, it cooperates with other states and organizations to ensure the safety and efficiency of air traffic around the world. EUROCONTROL is also responsible for innovations, conducting research, and developing new technologies that can help ensure the safety and efficiency of European airspace. The organization is actively involved in implementing innovative solutions, such as integrated air traffic management systems. Environmental protection is also a key priority for the organization. It conducts analyses and develops future scenarios for the decarbonization of global aviation. EUROCONTROL supports international initiatives, including the CORSIA system developed by ICAO. The organization proposes solutions to help states and organizations achieve climate policy goals aimed at reducing aviation's impact on climate change.[42]

39 https://www.ecac-ceac.org/index.php/activities/safety/european-safety-and-air-navigation-coordination-group-esancg, accessed 27.02.2024.
40 International Convention on Cooperation in the Interest of Aviation Safety "EUROCONTROL".
41 Article 2 of the EUROCONTROL Convention.
42 Raising the Bar: Building "EUROCONTROL 2030", EUROCONTROL 2023.

3.1.5 Safety oversight system

Regional safety oversight institutions are a mechanism through which a group of states works together to improve safety in the region by establishing and maintaining an appropriate oversight system. In Europe, this function is performed by the EASA. It should be emphasized that this institution acts as a broad platform for cooperation between European states in various areas related to maintaining and supervising aviation safety.

In order to exercise the functions of the regional safety oversight body more effectively, EASA periodically publishes a document called the European Plan for Aviation Safety. The development of this plan is based on Article 6 of Regulation (EU) 2018/1139. The document sets out the objectives, priorities, and measures aimed at ensuring flight safety throughout Europe. Beginning with the 2022 edition, EASA develops plans for a three-year period with an annual update (previously, the plans covered four-year period). In 2022, a plan for 2023–2025 has been developed.[43] It has been divided into three parts.

Part 1 deals with strategic priorities. Considerations include air transport restrictions caused by the COVID-19 pandemic in 2020–2022 and the armed invasion of Ukraine by the Russian Federation in February 2022, which altered the perception of regional and aviation safety, were considered. Five strategic areas are identified:

1. system safety (risk management, protective measures against health threats, actions related to climate change, and its impact on aviation safety);
2. personnel competencies (increasing proficiencyin aviation language and improving the quality of training);
3. operational safety (identifying risk factors in commercial and general aviation operations; assessing risks during aircraft certification or related to air traffic management (ATM); ensuring the safety of equipment used during ATM; and identifying risks in airport operations and ground handling services);
4. safe and sustainable new technologies (streamlining digitalization and automation processes through the implementation of innovative technological solutions that enhance flight safety, such as automatic collision warning systems with the ground or with other aircraft; utilizing artificial intelligence technologies to improve safety and move towards more autonomous flight operations; and establishing rules for the use of unmanned aircraft);
5. environmental protection (striving for decarbonization by reducing CO2 emissions from aircraft; using better quality aviation fuel; and promoting the ICAO CORSIA initiative).

Part 2 sets out concrete actions to mitigate the main threats to aviation safety. The tasks to be carried out are described along with relevant legal regulations.

43 European Plan for Aviation Safety 2023–2025, EASA 2022.

Part 3 identifies the main areas of risk. Pandemic-related conditions after 2020 affecting a number of risks in aviation have been taken into account. In addition, the risks are identified in connection with geopolitical factors, i.e. the Russian-Ukrainian armed conflict after 2022.

In all priorities, it is important to identify risk areas, identify systemic actions, and develop/implement a legal framework in each area. The main objectives of the European Plan for Aviation Safety focus on minimizing threats and reducing risks in aviation, as well as continuously improving aviation safety systems. The horizontal objective set for all priority areas is to ensure the highest level of aviation safety for the entire Europe and, indirectly, for the international community as well. It is therefore important to work with other regulatory bodies around the world to ensure common standards and best practices in aviation safety. The European Plan for Aviation Safety is a document of pan-European significance. EASA continuously updates this plan to incorporate new technologies and address emerging safety challenges.

3.1.6 The role of EASA as a regional aviation safety group

EASA is both the safety oversight authority for the 27 member states of the EU and the three states parties of the European Economic Area – EEA (Iceland, Liechtenstein, and Norway), and Switzerland, and also acts as a Regional Aviation Safety Group (RASG-EUR).

Establishing such bodies is in line with ICAO policy, which encourages member states to strengthen regional forms of cooperation for aviation safety.[44] The plans for creating such an institution were approved by ICAO in General Assembly Resolution A37-4 during the 37th session of the ICAO General Assembly in Montreal from September 28 to October 8, 2010.[45] In Europe, at the meeting of the Directors-General of the Civil Aviation Authorities from the EASA member states on February 15–17, 2011, it was decided to establish a European aviation safety structure RASG-EUR.[46] Finally, at the ICAO Regional Office for Europe in Paris on May 16, 2011, the representatives of the member states took a formal decision to establish the RASG-EUR.[47] The first meeting of the European RASG-EUR group was held on January 23–24, 2012.[48]

44 On October 6, 2009, the ICAO Air Navigation Commission recommended to the Council the establishment of regional aviation safety groups (RASG) worldwide. The aim was to harmonize the activities and legal framework for the implementation of safety regulations and guidelines, in line with ICAO policies and objectives.

45 European Regional Aviation Safety Group (RASG-EUR) Procedural Handbook, First Edition, February 2013, p. 2.

46 Report of the First Meeting of the Middle East Regional Aviation Safety Group, Cairo, Egypt, September 18–19, 2011, RASG-MID/1-REPORT. See https://www.icao.int/MID/Documents/2011/RASG_MID_1/Docs/rasg_mid_1_Final_Report_EN.pdf, accessed 25.01.2024.

47 https://unitingaviation.com/regions/eurnat/european-regional-aviation-safety-group-rasg-eur/, accessed 17.01.2024.

48 https://www.icao.int/EURNAT/Pages/news_articles/20130127-rasg-eu.aspx, accessed 17.01.2024.

It is the only comprehensive forum dedicated to aviation safety in Europe. Like other groups, the purpose of RASG-EUR is to promote coordination and cooperation between all parties interested in improving the level of aviation safety. During RASG-EUR meetings, evaluations of the implementation of international regulations and recommendations are made, as well as it is verified the effectiveness of the implemented legal instruments in accordance with indicators defined by the ICAO. In addition, aviation safety in the member states is assessed in terms of the number of accidents, fatalities, incidents, serious incidents, and any events affecting aviation safety. National safety programs are also reviewed in accordance with the GASP. During the debate, further actions are proposed to accelerate the effective implementation of the rules and recommendations. Finally, the RASG-EUR provides ICAO with information on the progress made in achieving its objectives and tasks.

The structure of RASG-EUR includes:

a) the Chairperson who is elected by the member states from among their own representatives;
b) the Secretary, who is the Director of the ICAO Regional Office EUR/NAT;
c) the Secretariat, which is the ICAO EUR/NAT Regional Office in Paris.

The level of aviation safety in Europe is one of the highest in the world. This is evidenced by the annual safety reports published by EASA which fulfills the functions as the RASG-EUR.[49] Table 3.2 shows the number of accidents over the last decade compared to global figures.

Analyzing the data on the number of accidents in Europe reveals an overall downward trend. Although in the period 2011–2014 the average rate in Europe was slightly higher than the global average, from 2015 to 2020, the number of accidents in Europe was lower than worldwide. The exception is 2021, where this indicator is the highest since 2014. However, it is also necessary to consider the number of accidents involving fatalities in this regard, in the period 2017–2021, no accident in which even one person died was recorded.[50] It can be concluded that in recent years the level of safety in Europe in terms of the number of accidents relative to the global figures has increased, which was certainly influenced by safety procedures and regulations that are effectively implemented and enforced by regional organizations established for this purpose (e.g. EASA) and the relevant authorities from the member states.

3.2 Legal and institutional regulations on the African continent

On the African continent, the process of codifying and institutionalizing of aviation safety has been taking place for several years and is carried out within the

49 EASA, *Annual Safety Review*, 2022.
50 *Ibidem*, p. 36.

Table 3.2 Comparison of accidents per million operations in the European region with the number in the world between 2011 and 2023

Year	*Accident rate per million operations in Europe*	*Accident rate per million operations worldwide*
2011 (base year)	3.6	2.8
2012	3.7	2.1
2013	3.4	2.3
2014	3.9	3.0
2015	2.2	2.6
2016	2.3	2.68
2017	1.1	2.42
2018	1.6	1.75
2019	2.7	3.0
2020	1.8	2.09
2021	2.8	1.93
2022	2.6	2.16
2023	1.41	1.82

Source: EASA, Annual Safety Review, 2005–2024.

framework of the African Civil Aviation Commission (AFCAC). African states are following the example of European legal regulations, anticipating that the process of harmonizing aviation rules will lead to an improved safety. The codification of many areas of civil aviation is carried out with the involvement of most statesin the region, which gives hope for the effective implementation of the implemented legal regulations.

At the outset, it should be noted that the process of institutionalizing civil aviation on the African continent does not have a long history, comparable to that of Europe. It is worth remembering that until 1960, most of the current states in Africa were colonies of European powers. The process of decolonization started with the famous Year of Africa (1960), marked the beginning of these territories gaining dependence, and the so-called "decade of Africa" (the 1960s) witnessed 27 states gaining independence.[51] In the following years, the remaining units also moved toward self-determination. Therefore, the process of African unity and harmonization of standards could only realistically begin in the second half of the 20th century.

Aviation regulations in Africa vary from state to state. In many of them, such as Egypt, South Africa, Tunisia, and Morocco, there are robust and well-functioning agencies regulating flight safety and ensuring compliance with international

51 For more information, see Mazrui Ali A., Independent African states and the struggle for southern Africa, in: *The decolonization of Africa: southern Africa and the Horn of Africa*, UNESCO 1981, pp. 13–24; Smith A. W. M. and Jeppesen Ch. (eds), *Britain, France and the decolonization of Africa: future imperfect?*, London: UCL Press 2017; *Politics and Decolonization in Africa: Theoretical Pointers and a Preamble*, Africa Today, Vol. 67, No. 4, 2021.

standards. In contrast, in states like the Democratic Republic of Congo and Sudan, flight safety remains a more serious concern. Therefore, it is important to verify that the carrier and the flight are fully authorized and meet all required safety standards before departing from such states. The following analysis presents the legal regulations functioning in Africa along with the institutional system that is responsible for developing, implementing, and compliance of aviation safety regulations.

3.2.1 Determinants of aviation safety in Africa

There are many reasons for the poor aviation safety situation in Africa. First of all, it is necessary to start by diagnosing individual factors affecting the level of aviation safety and formulating legal, institutional, and organizational solutions to increase the competitiveness and attractiveness of aviation in Africa. Mutali Kapchangah distinguishes five such causes:

1. a lack of investment in air transport in Africa;
2. a lack of harmonization of safety standards;
3. a poor aviation security;
4. a profit-orientation approach, without taking into account safety and security issues;
5. deep economic and social disparities between developed and developing states in Africa.[52]

In turn, African states identified the following reasons for the poor level of safety in the Ezulwini Declaration of 2017[53]:

a) the slow implementation of national safety oversight systems together with ICAO international safety regulations and recommendations;
b) an insufficient number of qualified personnel for implementing safety regulations;
c) the lack of adequate measures to ensure the proper functioning of institutions responsible for safety and for monitoring of its enforcement in individual states;
d) an inadequate safety culture and its organization;
e) the lack of uniform legal regulations, procedures, or political guidelines applicable across all African states;
f) insufficient guidance and lack of harmonized training mechanisms for implementing the safety rules specified in the ICAO Annexes to the Chicago Convention.

52 Kapchangah M. K., *Africa aviation security: Implications for peace and security*, Institute for Security Studies 2008, p. 2.
53 Ezulwini Declaration on Regional Safety Oversight Organizations adopted in Ezulwini on 24 March 2017 https://ncaa.gov.ng/media/it3gdrxe/afi-min-ezulwini-declaration-rsoo_eng.pdf, accessed 10.01.2024.

In recent years, it can be noted that in order to improve the level of safety, states are increasingly aware of the need to introduce and implement appropriate legal regulations and establish institutions in this regard. Political declarations are also important, which may subsequently influence legally binding decisions. Aviation safety must be a priority for Africa, as much as for other states of the world. There are no simple recipes for creating a safe sky, but each of the factors that contribute to enhanced safety must be taken seriously.

The lack of investment has led to a gradual deterioration of Africa's aviation infrastructure. One of the key factors is the aging fleet. Having machines that are, on average, 20 years old or more poses a direct and real threat to the lives of both passengers and people on the ground. Many of these aircraft still date back to the former USSR, e.g. Antonov and Iliushin models. It is worth pointing out that in 2005, out of 14 registered air accidents in Africa, as many as ten of them involved Antonov aircraft, two involved Iliushin model, one involved a Boeing, and one a DC aircraft.[54] Rejuvenation of the fleet is the first step towards improving this situation. Along with updating machines, it is also necessary to modernize the ground infrastructure, including airports, and air navigation services. Airport safety must be given priority because such an airport serves as a "window" to the world, and a "gateway" to the state.

Harmonization of rules is another crucial factor in boosting the level of safety. Until recently, African states addressed these issues individually and did not respect the international recommendations and standards set by the ICAO. For example, states did not have national aviation security programs in place, and similar programs for airports were also absent.[55] It is worth mentioning that all African countries are members of ICAO and are obliged to comply with the standards created by that organization. Imposing penalties on states that fail to meet their obligations will not yield the desired effect. Instead, cooperation and assistance from other states and organizations are necessary.

A notable example is Nigeria. In 1993, the US suspended flights to Nigeria due to the lack of proper aviation security standards in the latter, while simultaneously helping in streamlining procedures. Cooperation between the authorities of both states resulted in the lifting of the ban on flights to Nigeria in 1999. Together, a high level of safety at Nigerian airports was achieved, and new security regulations were implemented.[56] This is an example of proper cooperation and proof that with the political will and commitment the existing system can be improved.

3.2.2 Codification of aviation safety regulations in Africa

It can be said that in Africa, both the processes of codifying and institutionalizing aviation safety are underway. By creating new regulations, harmonizing standards,

54 *Ibidem*, p. 11.
55 *Ibidem*, p. 14.
56 *Ibidem*, p. 8.

and developing new legal instruments aimed at improving the level of aviation safety, institutions and bodies responsible for enforcing these regulations are also being established across various states. Legal documents in the field of aviation safety in Africa and an assessment of their effectiveness will be discussed in the following section.

The codification of aviation safety regulations in Africa has accelerated in the last decade. There are many legal acts, guidelines, and other programs that have been introduced and contribute to improving the level of safety in air transport. The most important elements of the legal regime and the system of aviation safety in Africa include:

1. the Yamoussoukro Decision of 1999 together with the Yamoussoukro Declaration of 1988;
2. the Abuja Safety Targets (AST) of 2012;
3. the Ezulwini Declaration of 2017.

3.2.2.1 Yamoussoukro Declaration

On October 7, 1988, the Yamoussoukro Declaration (Côte d'Ivoire) on a new African air transport policy was adopted. It was signed by the ministers responsible for aviation from the 40 African statesthat were members of the Organization of African Unity (now the African Union).[57] The Yamoussoukro Declaration represents a vision for the development of civil aviation in Africa, taking into account the liberalization conditions that took place in the world at that time, i.e. the process of deregulation in the US and the beginning of the initiation of a single aviation market in Europe within the European Economic Community (now: the EU). This document aligns with the global trend toward liberalizing civil aviation and harmonizing regulations in order to facilitate safer air transport. The integration process in the field of civil aviation in Africa was divided into three phases, which were to be implemented over eight years.

This document focuses on economic solutions and liberalization of air transport as well as the functioning of the aviation market. The key elements include:

a) plans to merge small and ailing air carriers into larger ones that can compete in an increasingly open aviation market;

57 Yamoussoukro Declaration, 7.10.1988. United Nations Economic and Social Council, E/ECA/TRANS/77A, 17.10.1988, https://repository.uneca.org/ds2/stream/?#/documents/2288a96a-b678-507f-bd22-cd8e539b1baa/page/5. The declaration was signed by: Algeria, Benin, Botswana, Burkina Faso, Burundi, Cameroon, Cape Verde, Chad, Central African Republic, Congo, Democratic Republic of the Congo (d.Zaire), Egypt, Ethiopia, Gabon, Gambia, Ghana, Guinea, Guinea-Bissau, Equatorial Guinea, Ivory Coast, Kenya, Liberia, Libya, Madagascar, Mali, Morocco, Mauritius, Mauritania, Niger, Nigeria, Rwanda, Senegal, Sierra Leone, Somalia, Swaziland, Tanzania, Togo, Tunisia, Uganda, and Zimbabwe.

b) cooperation between carriers in the field of joint insurance, computerized reservation systems, shared market access, and the granting of *en route* rights;
c) implementation of a new air carrier management system.

Although there are no direct references to safety, it nevertheless gave rise to future codification in this area. The Yamoussoukro Declaration is an important political vision for cooperation and integration of air carriers. It is important to remember that, at that time, almost all carriers were state-owned (national) airlines.[58] This meant that operations were centrally managed and focused on political goals rather than on competing with each other in an increasingly open aviation market. Existing bilateral air services agreements limited the development of air traffic in Africa, as states, in protecting their national carriers either did not allow or severely restricted the performance of operations by foreign carriers. Of course, this system maintained the situation in which air transport was expensive, elitist, and uncompetitive, so quality and safety were not the primary features of the African market. The Yamoussoukro Declaration was supposed to change this situation, but in the face of significant reluctance from the signatory states, it failed to achieve its intended goals. However, the rapid liberalization of the aviation market and the dynamic growth of air traffic in Europe and other regions did not gone unnoticed in Africa. African states decided that, considering the existing external conditions, decisive steps should be taken to implement the provisions established in 1988.

3.2.2.2 Yamoussoukro Decision

The next milestone was the adoption of the Yamoussoukro Decision on November 14, 1999.[59] Unlike the Yamoussoukro Declaration from 1988, this act contains provisions specifically addressing aviation safety. In its preamble, it reaffirms the objectives of the CChicago Convention, i.e. the development of safe, regular air transport based on equal rules for all. Under Article 5.1 of the Decision, states confirmed the removal of all frequency and capacity constraints, which would be subject to market-based mechanisms determined by air carriers. In this context, states agreed not to impose any restrictions, except those related to environmental protection, aviation safety, and technical matters.[60]

Article 6.12 of the Yamoussoukro Decision, entitled "Safety and Security", reaffirms the mutual commitment to protect civil aviation from acts of unlawful interference. Furthermore, the Decision obligates each states to comply with the provisions of various aviation safety conventions in accordance with ICAO provisions, in particular Annex 17 of the Chicago Convention. Each state has also

58 Schlumberger Ch. E., *Open Skies for Africa Implementing the Yamoussoukro Decision*, World Bank 2010, p. 5.
59 Decision relating to the implementation of the Yamoussoukro Declaration concerning the liberalization of access to air transport markets in Africa, United Nations Economic And Social Council, ECA/RCID/CM.CIVAV/99/RPT.
60 Article 5.1 of the Yamoussoukro Decision of 1999.

undertaken to consider any request by another state party to the Agreement for the application of special safety measures to counter a specific threat. At the same time, the contracting states reaffirmed their obligation to comply with international standards and practices on civil aviation safety recommended by the ICAO. [61]

The Yamoussoukro Decision entered into force on August 12, 2000, in accordance with Article 12.1.1, i.e. 30 days after the signature was affixed by the President of the Assembly of Heads of State and Government of the African Economic Community.

3.2.2.3 Abuja Safety Targets

Within the framework of AFCAC, all 54 African states adopted a document to enhance safety - the Abuja Safety Targets (AST). This document was adopted by the ministers responsible for civil aviation during the ministerial conference on aviation safety in Africa held on July 16–20, 2012, in Abuja, Nigeria. These targets were adopted in 2012 and later confirmed and updated in 2017.[62]

AST is a set of 16 targets, which are as follows:[63]

1. gradually reduce the accident rate in Africa from 8.6 to 2.5 per million departures by the end of 2022, with a particular focus on controlled flight into terrain (CFIT) and loss of control in-flight (LOCI) events;
2. establish and strengthen civil aviation authorities with independent regulatory oversight, balanced funding sources, and sufficient resources to effectively conduct oversight and regulation of the aviation industry by 2022;
3. commitment of all states to:
   a) identify significant safety concerns (SSCs) by 2018;
   b) identify any new SSCswithin six months from the date of their official publication by ICAO;
4. adhere to deadlines and provide resources for the implementation of national action plans in accordance with ICAO's USOAP (Universal Safety Oversight and Audit Programme), requiring all states to adopt ICAO action plans by 2019 and respect the deadlines as well as the provision of resources for their implementation;
5. Effective Implementation (EI) of national action plans under the ICAO USOAP, in accordance with the adopted principle:
   a) if EI < 60%, achieve 60% by 2020;
   b) if 60% ≤ EI ≤ 70%, achieve 80% by 2022;
   c) if EI 70% < EI, achieve 95% by 2028 r.

61 Article 6.12 of the Yamoussoukro Decision of 1999.

62 The AST were modified during the meeting of the African Union Special Technical Committee in Lome, Togo, on March 13–17, 2017.

63 AFCAC, *Mechanism for Monitoring Implementation of Safety Systems & Initiatives*, June 30, 2018, pp. 93–94.

6. implementation of the State Safety Programme (SSP) and Safety Management Systems (SMS) by all states in accordance with agreed milestones by the end of 2025;
7. certification of all international airports by the end of 2022;
8. obtaining IATA Operational Safety Audit (IOSA) certification for all African air carriers by the end of 2022;
9. establishing an effective and operational Search and Rescue (SAR) organization by the end of 2019;
10. transition from Aeronautical Information Services (AIS) to Aeronautical Information Management (AIM) by the end of 2022;
11. implementation of Performance Based Navigation (PBN) procedures for all instrument runways by the end of 2025;
12. gradually reduce the occurrence of AIRPROX events in managed airspaces by at least 50% annually from the December 2017 baseline, with the goal of achieving and maintaining zero AIRPROX rate by reducing the number of errors in the relevant components by the end of 2020;[64]
13. establishing unified air navigation services in the Africa-Indian Ocean Region (AIF) by the end of 2024 to ensure harmonized air navigation services regarding flight separation, CNS/ATM system interoperability reduction of airspace complexity and achieving seamless operations along major air traffic flows, and harmonization of the various initiatives formulated by the regional economic communities and air navigation service providers in the AIF region;
14. implementation of ASBU B0 modules (Aviation System Block Upgrade) by the end of 2018;[65]
15. development and implementation of national plans to reduce CO2 emissions by the end of 2022;
16. effective participation of the ' Air Navigation Service Providers (ANSPs) of all member states in the mutual evaluation program in Africa until the end of 2022.

3.2.2.4 The Ezulwini Declaration

The document of paramount significance is the Ezulwini Declaration on RSOOs adopted in Ezulwini (Eswatini)[66] on March 24, 2017, by the ministers responsible

64 Airprox in legal definition means a situation in which, in the opinion of the pilot or air traffic control personnel, the distance between aircraft, as well as their relative positions and speed is such that the safety of the aircraft could be compromised – definition in: https://www.lawinsider.com/dictionary/airprox, accessed 15.01.2024.

65 The Aviation System Block Upgrade Framework (ASBU) was first established by ICAO at the 12th Air Navigation Conference on November 19–30, 2012, to outline a strategy for the modernization of the global air navigation system. AN-Conf/12, more information: Global Air Navigation Capacity & Efficiency Plan, 2013–2028, ICAO 2014, Doc.9750.

66 The Kingdom of Eswatini is the new name of the Kingdom of Swaziland, which was introduced in 2018.

for civil aviation in AFCAC.[67] The declaration is vital for African aviation safety as it establishes a strategy for further joint actions, identifies the reasons for inadequate implementation of existing mechanisms, and calls for the adoption of new legal instruments and recommendations. It stresses the importance of regional cooperation to improve aviation safety oversight, which in turn contributes to Africa's economic development. The Ezulwini Declaration sets out a series of commitments by the states to improve aviation safety on the African continent, including:

a) the commitment to finding a sustainable solution to the shortcomings in aviation safety oversight through enhanced political engagement at national, regional, and continental levels;
b) the acceleration of the process of establishing a safety oversight system along with appropriate legal regulations;
c) increasing cooperation between different safety oversight bodies with states and ICAO;
d) ensuring a sufficient number of civil aviation specialists to maintain effective oversight of the implemented safety regulations;
e) approving the implementation of a global strategy and action plan to improve the performance of safety oversight institutions.

3.2.3 Implementation of safety regulations and procedures in Africa

Considering the political directions set forth in the Ezulwini Declaration, as well as the AST, it was decided to monitor the implementation of the adopted legal regulations and state commitments. To that end, within the African civil aviation safety system, a mechanism for monitoring and implementing safety regulations and initiatives has been established.[68] This mechanism also evaluates the AST implementation under AFCAC. It includes the following elements:[69]

a) recommended methods for implementing regional and national safety targets or initiatives;
b) interventions supporting the implementation of regional safety targets by leading intergovernmental international organizations, such as ICAO, AFCAC, EASA, and RSOO,[70] as well as by aviation NGOs such as IATA;
c) integrated and automated safety oversight systems that are capable of collecting and sharing safety data between member states;
d) analysis of safety data collected by IT tools such as ICAO SIMS;
e) reporting on the implementation status of safety initiatives and targets.

67 https://ncaa.gov.ng/media/it3gdrxe/afi-min-ezulwini-declaration-rsoo_eng.pdf, accessed 10.01.2024.
68 AFCAC, *Mechanism for Monitoring Implementation of Safety Systems & Initiatives*, June 30, 2018.
69 *Ibidem*, point 2.5, p. 13.
70 RSOO – Regional Safety Oversight Organizations. It is a collective term referring to a platform of all safety oversight institutions within which annual meetings on global aviation safety issues are organized. https://www.icao.int/safety/Implementation/Pages/COSCAPs-RSOOs-RAIOs.aspx, accessed 20 .21.2024.

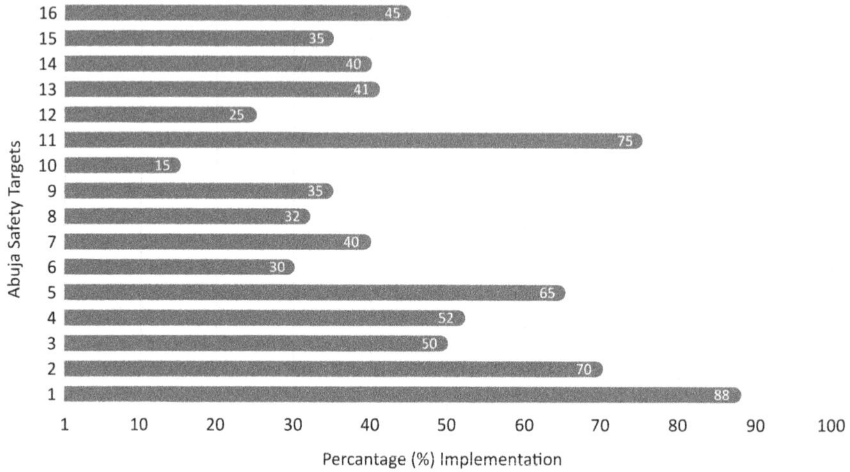

Figure 3.1 AST implementation status in AFCAC countries, as of 2021.

Source: Report of the Twenty-Fifth Meeting of the AFI Planning and Implementation Regional Group (APIRG/25), November 7–11, 2022, ICAO, p. 20.

This mechanism was approved during the 30th plenary session of AFCAC Assembly in Livingstone, Zambia, on December 4–5, 2018.[71] A review of the implemented legal and organizational instruments is carried out annually. The implementation of AST is very poor, with some aspects still at an early stage. Figure 3.1 shows the degree of implementation of AST in 2021, i.e. nine years after their establishment.

Based on the data from Figure 3.1 and based on the analysis of individual records, attention should be paid to the most important one. Achieving the first target of reducing the accident rate in Africa from 8.6 to 2.5 per million departures by the end of 2022 is a key indicator. Table 3.3 shows the achievement of this target from 2012 to 2023.

Analyzing the above indicators, it can be concluded that the accident rate in Africa is much higher than the global air accident rate. Considering the base year 2011 and the implementation of AST in relation to that year, the performance has varied over time. From 2012 to 2019 it was a variable fluctuation, with the number of accidents increasing one year, and decreasing the next. Only in 2020 this rate was relatively low and amounted to 3.64 accidents per million flight operations. This indicator was very close to the target. It is more interesting that in the following year this rate was reduced further to 1.53. The year 2021 was the first year in which the AST target was achieved. However, this is not a reliable indicator. This figure is heavily distorted and does not reflect the real nature of the situation. Both 2020 and 2021 were the years of the COVID-19 pandemic and the

71 AFCAC, *Mechanism for Monitoring…*, op. cit., paragraph 2.6, p. 14.

Table 3.3 AST Goal 1 Achievement Indicator: reducing the accident rate in Africa from 8.6 to 2.5 per million departures by the end of 2023

Year	*Accident rate per million departures in Africa*	*Accident rate per million departures worldwide*
2011 (base year)	8.6	2.8
2012	13.5	2.1
2013	7.3	2.3
2014	11.2	3.0
2015	2.8	2.6
2016	8.23	2.68
2017	7.56	2.42
2018	5.16	1.75
2019	10.34	3.0
2020	3.64	2.09
2021	1.53	0.57
2022	7.01	2.16
2023	3.98	1.82

Source: Own elaboration based on the annual reports of RASG-AFI 2011–2023.

spread of SARS-COV-2 coronavirus, which was associated with the introduction of legal restrictions on flight operations around the world.[72] In Africa, too, states imposed legal bans or restrictions on flights and therefore all carriers experienced the impact. Consequently, the number of flights was exceptionally low and therefore the reduced number of accidents reflects this situation. The same applies to the global accidents rate. In 2021, there was also a much lower number of accidents worldwide, which can be explained by legal restrictions related to the performance of flight operations.

According to the report of the eighth meeting of the Steering Committee of the Regional Aviation Safety Group for Africa and the Indian Ocean (RASG-AFI) in August 2022, most of the AST established in 2012 have become obsolete, either because some of the targets have been met or because many of them have not been achieved. At the same time, aviation safety conditions and global challenges have changed, which must be considered when creating new targets adapted to the changing reality.[73] Restrictions on air transport caused by the COVID-19 pandemic distorted the results for 2020 and 2021. It is expected that in the coming years the targets will be more accurately reflected,as air transport has become to recover from 2022 and most of the existing legal restrictions have been lifted (provided that similar legal and organizational restrictions are not reintroduced as

72 Twenty Fourth Meeting of the Africa-Indian Ocean Planning and Implementation Regional Group (APIRG/24) & Seventh Meeting of the Regional Aviation Safety Group for the AFI Region (RASG-AFI/7), Status of Implementation of the AFI Safety and Air Navigation Targets, AFCAC, 1 and 8 November 2021, Annex A, point 1.

73 Report on the Eighth Meeting of the Steering Committee of the Regional Aviation Safety Group For Africa-Indian Ocean (RASC/8), RASC/8 Report, August 2022, paragraph 5.12.

during the COVID-19 pandemic). The coming years will show whether it is possible to achieve AST or if further measures are necessary. Cautious is warrant against overly optimistic goals that do not reflect the significant legal, political, and economic conditions of individual states. The failure to implement legal regulations, the lack of political will and determination to achieve previous target, and the poor economic condition of many states are the main reasons for the failure to implement ambitious AST.

Poor aviation security refers to insufficient standards and procedures to counteract acts of aviation terrorism. After the attacks on the US on September 11, 2001, both states and international institutions became acutely aware of the serious threat. In Europe, until then, there were no uniform standards in this area, which may surprise on one hand, and on the other hand it can be attributed to the ongoing harmonization of the internal aviation market and liberalization processes within this sector. Integrated standards are equally needed in Africa, where experiences with terrorist acts have been, unfortunately, enormous. Numerous acts of aviation terrorism have taken place on the continent, and many terrorists originate from there. This is largely due to the lack of consistent legal regulations, with many states "give" connivance to this form of action. Assassinations are not uncommon either. A notorious example occurred on April 6, 1994, when a plane carrying the presidents of Rwanda and Burundi was shot down.[74] Both were killed, and the attack formed part of the civil war between the Tutsi and Hutu tribes in Rwanda.

The existing international system, called the Tokyo-Hague-Montreal system, and the standards set out in Annex 17 to the Chicago Convention are the basic mechanisms for countering aviation terrorism. Their effective application and implementation of executive provisions into the national legal order depend heavily on the political will of individual state, a process that have proven weak in many African states. However, it can be positively marked, that recent years have witnessed improvements in this area within the enhanced framework of the Europe-Africa interinstitutional cooperation.

3.2.4 Institutionalization of aviation safety in Africa

Aviation safety standards in Africa are regulated by a regional intergovernmental organization called the African Civil Aviation Commission (AFCAC) and based on ICAO regulations. The purpose of these standards is to ensure a high level of safety and reliability of flights in Africa. These include, among other things, requirements related to aviation equipment and procedures, personnel qualifications, airport security, air traffic control, and regulatory inspections.

The process of codifying and institutionalizing civil aviation began as early as 1969, when an organization called the African Civil Aviation Commission was established. The creation of the Single Aviation Area is considered to be

74 Data from the website: http://news.bbc.co.uk/onthisday/hi/dates/stories/april/6/newsid_2472000/2472195.stm, (accessed 3.02.2024).

the beginning of the Yamoussoukro Declaration of 1988, which was a vision for the development of a safe and common aviation policy for African states. The legal regulations in the field of aviation safety in Africa within the framework of AFCAC are presented in the following section. In addition, there are other aviation safety sub-regional organizations in Africa that can be classified into such groups:

a) RSOO – regional safety oversight organizations;
b) RAIO – regional accident and incident investigation organizations.

Institutionalization in the field of civil aviation in Africa is a necessity. AFCAC performs similar functions to those of a comparable European institution namely EASA, and deals with normative issues in a similar manner. AFCAC is tasked with contributing to the unification of standards in the industry and improving the safety of travelers and other users. At the same time, meetings of AFCAA representatives with EASA in various forums are an important element of the process of institutionalization of aviation safety in Africa leading to the formulation of future normative acts. These meetings have lead to positive regulatory changes in African aviation.

3.2.4.1 Legal regulations and tasks of AFCAC

The African Civil Aviation Commission (AFCAC) was established by the adoption of the Statute of the African Civil Aviation Commission on January 17, 1969, in Addis Ababa in Ethiopia. The statute entered into force on March 15, 1972. However, the new statute adopted in Dakar in Senegal on December 16, 2009, which annulled and replaced the previous one, is currently in force. The AFCAC Statute consists of 26 articles. The preamble refers to several legal acts important for African unity, most notably the Constitution of the African Union of July 11, 2000[75] and the Treaty establishing the African Economic Community of June 3, 1991.

The first sentence of the preamble acknowledges that civil aviation plays an important role in achieving the objectives of the African Union. In that spirit, it is stressed that safe air transport within the African continent and from/to Africa

75 The Constitution of the African Union signed at Lome on July 11, 2000, (Togo). Under Article 33 it replaced the Charter of the Organization of African Unity under Article 33. United Nations Treaty Series, Vol. 2158, I-37733. It was signed by the Assembly of Heads of State and Government of the Organization of African Unity. The Constitution entered into force on May 26, 2001. The African Union was originally established by all 53 OAU countries. South Sudan joined the AU after gaining independence in 2011 and then became a formal member of the organization, as well as the Kingdom of Morocco in 2017. There are currently 55 AU member states. For more information, see Packer C. A. A. and Rukare D., The New African Union and Its Constitutive Act, The American Journal of International Law, Vol. 96, No. 2, 2002, pp. 365–379. Tiyanjana Maluwa, *Ratification of African Union treaties: Law, policy & practice*, Melbourne Journal of International Law, Vol. 13, 2012, pp. 1–49.

can only take place in accordance with the principle set out in the preamble to the Chicago Convention, i.e. "in a reliable and correct manner, and international air transport services can be established on the basis of equal opportunities for all and conducted in an appropriate and economical manner".[76] Following the Yamoussoukro Decision of 1999, the institutional nature of AFCAC as an executive agency was confirmed, a position further endorsed by the Assembly of Heads of State and Government of the African Union on June 27, 2007, in Accra, Ghana.[77] The Statute confirms the need to create a common aviation policy for the whole of Africa. This would be one of the key elements of economic integration that was initially built within the Organization of African Unity and now the African Union. The codification of the areas of civil aviation, including safety, also is in line with the objectives of the 1991 Abuja Treaty.[78]

AFCAC is the main regulatory and operational institution in the field of civil aviation. It fulfills a dual role in terms of international law. On one hand, it is an international organization. Rysińska argues that an international organization is a deliberate, multilateral union of states, established by an agreement among them, and equipped with a system of permanent bodies.[79] On the other hand, AFCAC is a specialized agency of the African Union, i.e. a body (institution) asked with handling civil aviation issues on the African continent. Rysińska emphasizes that the international agency is part of its parent organization that exercises control over it.[80] Thus, the dual role of AFCAC is confirmed by Article 2 of the AFCAC Statute and the decision of the African Union Assembly of Heads of State and Government in 2007. The objectives of AFCAC as outlined in Article 3 of its Statute, and are as follows:

a) coordinating civil aviation affairs in Africa and cooperating with the ICAO and other relevant organizations and institutions working for the promotion and development of civil aviation in Africa;
b) facilitating, coordinating, and ensuring the successful implementation of the Yamoussoukro Decision by overseeing and managing the liberalized air transport sector in Africa;
c) supporting and enforcing appropriate rules and regulations that provide fair and equal opportunities for stakeholders and promote fair competition;
d) promoting mutual understanding on political issues between member states and states in other regions of the world;

76 Preamble to the Chicago Convention, Journal of Laws of 1959, No. 35, item 212.

77 Paragraph 6 of the preamble to the AFCAC Statute.

78 Treaty establishing the African Economic Community (AEC – structure was based on the former European Economic Community – EEC) adopted in Abuja, Nigeria, June 3, 1991. The Treaty entered into force on May 12, 1994.

79 Rysińska I., *Organizacje międzynarodowe. Zarys problematyki*, in: Parzymies Stanisław, Rysińska Irena (ed.), *Polska w organizacja międzynarodowych*, Warsaw 2002, p. 17.

80 For more information: *ibidem*, pp. 11–29.

e) supporting, inter alia, the implementation of ICAO standards and recommended practices on safety, security, environmental protection, and operational regularity in the aviation sector;
f) ensuring compliance with and implementation of the decisions made by the Executive Assembly.

Article 4 outlines the functions of AFCAC. The key safety-related functions include:

a) encouraging and supporting member states to comply with ICAO norms and recommended practices, as well as with regional air navigation plans (Article 4(b));
b) encouraging and supporting the establishment of independent civil aviation institutions (Article 4(d));
c) advising member states on all matters relating to civil aviation (Article 4(h));
d) developing and harmonizing common rules and regulations concerning, among others, aviation safety, aviation security, environmental protection, fair competition, dispute resolution, and consumer protection (Article 4(k));
e) increasing and coordinating synergies in the fields of search and rescue and accident investigation (Article 4(l));
f) coordinating the selection of African states to the ICAO Council and African experts to the Air Navigation Commission after obtaining the consent of the African Union (Article 4 (n));
g) performing other functions as may be entrusted to it by the Executive Council or the Assembly of the African Union in order to pursue its objectives (Article 4(p)).

The main bodies of the organization, in accordance with Article 9 of the Statute, are:

a) The Plenary, as a supreme body;
b) The Bureau, as the executive body;
c) The Secretariat, as the administrative body for handling the day-to-day operations of the organization.

In accordance with Article 10(1), the Plenary is the supreme body of the organization. It is composed of representatives of all member states active in the field of civil aviation. The Plenary meets in ordinary sessions (once every three years) and in extraordinary sessions convened either at the initiative of the Bureau or at the request of two-thirds of all member states to the Bureau (Article 10(3)). Decisions of the Plenary are taken either by consensus or by a two-thirds majority of the member states present and having voting rights, as provided in Article 10(5), subject to Article 21 on withdrawal of membership (the termination of membership in the AFCAC is submitted by the state to the Chairperson of the African Union

Commission, who informs AFCAC thereof, and the withdrawal becomes effective one year after that notification). The functions of the Plenary are defined in Article 11 of the Statute, and include among others:

a) formulating the organization's policy guidelines by adopting resolutions and recommendations;
b) electing the President and Vice-President of the Bureau;
c) approving the organizational structure of AFCAC;
d) approving action plans, business plans, budgets, and other AFCAC regulations.

The Bureau is the executive body and manages the organization. It consists of a President and five Vice-Presidents elected by the Plenary in accordance with the principle of fair geographical representation, as provided for in Article 12(1). The presidency of AFCAC is based on the principle of rotation, i.e. one region holds the presidency for three years. Each of the five Vice-Presidents represents one of Africa's regions. Their term lasts three years with the possibility of re-election. Members of the Presidium must have professional experience in the field of civil aviation. Article 13 defines the functions of the Bureau, which include:

a) convening ordinary and extraordinary plenary sessions, in accordance with the provisions of Article 10 of the Statute;
b) overseeing the implementation of AFCAC's action programs and other Assembly resolutions;
c) supervising and coordinating the activities of the Secretariat;
d) submitting periodic reports on its own activities to the Assembly.

The Secretariat is the main administrative body. It is chaired by a Secretary-General elected by the Plenary on a recommendation from the Bureau as referred to in Article 14. Further provisions of this Article provide that the term of office for the Secretary-General is three years and is renewable. The functions of this body are set out in Article 14(5). The crucial ones are:

a) monitoring and ensuring the implementation of the resolutions, directives, and decisions of the Plenary, the Bureau and the Monitoring Body, in accordance with the AFCAC's rules and regulations;
b) representing the AFCAC and defending its interests in line with the guidelines of the Plenary and the Bureau;
c) promoting AFCAC projects and initiatives;
d) preparing draft budget, action program, strategic aims, and activities of the organization;
e) preparing the financial statements for the past three-year period and the budget for the upcoming three years, to be submitted by the Bureau to the meeting of the Plenary for approval in accordance with the organization's rules;
f) submitting annual reports on AFCAC's activities to the bureau and the Monitoring Body.

Pursuant to Article 17, the AFCAC's budget consists of contributions from the member states in accordance with the rules laid down by the Plenary. The headquarters of the organization is established in Dakar, Senegal, in accordance with Article 8 of the AFCAC Statute. Pursuant to Article 83 of the Chicago Convention, the AFCAC statute is subject to registration with the ICAO Council.

3.2.4.2 The legal nature and functioning of RASG-AFI

The Regional Aviation Safety Group for Africa and the Indian Ocean (RASG-AFI) is a regional aviation safety organization that works to improve aviation safety in the Africa and Indian Ocean region. It was established at the fourth meeting of the Directors-General of the Civil Aviation Authorities of African States in Matsapa, Eswatini, held on November 8–9, 2010.[81] The structure of the RASG-AFI was subsequently approved at its first meeting held on March 26–27, 2012, in Kampala, Uganda.[82] The institution is supported by the ICAO and is composed of representatives of civil aviation authorities, airlines, air navigation service providers, and other aviation entities. The organizational structure of RASG-AFI consists of a Chairperson, three Vice-Chairs (two representatives of member states and one representative of aviation institutions) who are elected for a two-year term, a steering committee, and a Secretariat. The structure is further complemented by four Safety Support Teams (SST):[83]

a) SST for the State Safety Oversight System (SSO–SST);
b) SST for the Operational Safety Issues (OSI–SST);
c) SST for the State Safety Programme (SSP–SST);
d) SST for the Air Navigation Services (ANS–SST).

Within RASG-AFI, a team has also been established to develop annual safety reports (ASRTs). Its tasks include preparing annual reports on the state of aviation safety in Africa, collecting information and identifying the main aviation safety threats in the region, as well as formulating recommendations for the organizations, and developing additional reports for other institutions. The first report was published in 2015.

The main objectives of RASG-AFI are:

1. promoting and enhancing aviation safety in the region by encouraging the exchange of information and best practices;
2. facilitating the development of aviation safety regulations and standards in the region;

81 *Annual Safety Report 2014*, RASG-AFI 2015, p. 4.
82 *Ibidem*.
83 *Annual Safety Report 2021*, RASG-AFI 2022, p. 5. The structure of these bodies was changed in 2022.

3. providing technical assistance and support to member states in their efforts to improve aviation safety;
4. fostering cooperation and coordination between aviation stakeholders in the region.

RASG-AFI meets regularly to discuss safety issues and to develop and implement initiatives aimed at addressing these challenges. The organization also provides training and technical assistance to its member states to help improve their aviation safety capabilities.

3.2.5 Summary

There are many similarities between the development of the European and African aviation systems. Firstly, the process of liberalization of civil aviation and opening up its markets began almost at the same time. In Europe, it was 1987 and in Africa, it was 1988. Secondly, in both regions, this process was divided into three stages, intended to achieve the expected results within a few years. Thirdly, in both regions, a vision of aviation development was defined, which in the following years materialized in the form of the institutionalization and harmonization of aviation regulations, including safety standards. While both regions share many similarities, the process taking place in Africa proceeded more slowly. This was due to the poor economic situation of the states, and political conditions that were not conducive to unity and cooperation due to numerous civil wars in many states, as well as the brutal policies of authoritarian regimes. Despite historical challenges, Africa's aviation sector is steadily advancing toward enhanced safety and regulatory harmonization, propelled by a strong commitment to progress.

3.3 Codification and institutionalization of aviation safety in Latin America

Aviation regulations in Latin America are managed by each state and are based on international and regional flight safety standards. Many states, such as Mexico, Brazil, and Argentina, have well-functioning institutions and laws in the field of aviation safety, that adhere to the safety requirements set by the ICAO. In other states, such as Haiti and Costa Rica, flight safety can be more problematic, which underscores the importance of ensuring that the process of codifying and harmonizing aviation safety proceeds smoothly and effectively, even in those stateswhere current level is unsatisfactory. This section will characterize the process of codification and institutionalization in Latin America, highlighting the regulatory role and tasks of the Latin American Civil Aviation Commission (LACAC) and discussing the main documents and legal regulations in force in this region.

3.3.1 The origin of the aviation legal regulation system and institutionalization in Latin America

The region of Latin America is unique, as there exists a certain community on many levels. Jose C. Bogolasky argues that the states of this region share common traditions, common political and economic problems, and above all, a common history.[84] In the spirit of this unity, the need for integration arose after World War II, leading to establishment of the Organization of American States in 1948 in Bogotá, Colombia. The process of integration and institutionalization among Latin American states in the economic field subsequently expanded over the following years to further areas of activity.

However, the beginnings of the codifying and institutionalizing civil aviation can be traced back even earlier. Awareness of the need to standardize aviation regulations on a broader scale appeared among Latin American states long before the adoption of the Chicago Convention in 1944. In fact, in 1916, the Conference of Pan-American Aeronautics was held in Santiago, Chile. During its sessions, it was recommended that American states harmonize their national aviation legislation in order to establish an International Aviation Code.[85] It was one of the world's first attempts to codify aviation law at a regional level. As a consequence of these proposals, the Permanent American Aeronautical Commission (CAPA) was established during the Inter-American Technical Conference on Aviation in Lima (Peru) in 1931.[86] The Commission proposed the following actions: the codification of international public and private aviation law, cooperation on technical aviation matters and the development of mutual interests in this area, and the creation of a map of inter-American air routes. In addition to their commitment to the multilateral regulation of aviation law, states around the world began to conclude bilateral air services agreements to legally enable air connections between interested parties. The global development of aviation in the third decade of the 20th century provided the impetus for addressing these issues. The first bilateral air services agreement on the American continent was concluded between Argentina and Uruguay in 1922.[87]

84 Bogolasky J. C., Air *transport in Latin America: The expanding role of the Latin American Civil Aviation Commission*, Journal of Air Law and Commerce, Vol. 44, (1978), p. 75.

85 Ibidem, p. 76.

86 The conference was held on September 15–25, 1931. It was attended by 12 states : Argentina, Brazil, Bolivia, Chile, Colombia, Ecuador, Mexico, Panama, Peru, Uruguay, the US, and Venezuela. See more broadly: Pepin, *Un Nouvel Organe Internationale Aeronautique: La Commission Americaine Permanente d'Aeronautique (CAPA)*, 7 Revue Aeronautique Internationale 368 (1937); Jose C. Bogolasky, *Air Transport*..., op. cit., p. 76.

87 Agreement signed on November 18, 1922. See: Jose C. Bogolasky, *Air Transport*..., op. cit., p. 76; See more: York E., *International Air Law in the American Republics*, Journal of Air Law and Commerce, Vol. 3, 1932.

3.3.2 Legal scope and responsibilities of LACAC

After World War II, as integration expanded in various areas, the process of codifying and institutionalizing civil aviation in the Americas gained momentum. As a result of numerous meetings of technical committees from the states concerned[88], an aviation organization was established in 1973 called the Latin American Civil Aviation Commission (in Spanish: Comisión Latinoamericana De Aviación Civil – CLAC; in English: LACAC) was established. CLAC-LACAC was founded on the basis of a statute adopted on December 14, 1973, in Mexico City by representatives of the aviation authorities of various Latin American states. This region includes the South American states and those within the Caribbean basin. The statute of this organization was published in the United Nations Treaty Series, in accordance with relevant international law, after the required number of ratifications was achieved in 1981.[89] One of its important provisions deals with aviation safety.

The CLAC-LACAC statute consists of 34 articles grouped into seven chapters. According to Article 2 of the Statute, a member of the LACAC may be only a state from the Latin American region (Latin America, Central America, and Caribbean). There were 14 founding states, and as of 2025, there are 22 members: Argentina, Aruba, Belize, Bolivia, Brazil, Chile, Colombia, Costa Rica, Cuba, Dominican Republic, Ecuador, Guatemala, Honduras, Jamaica, Mexico, Nicaragua, Panama, Paraguay, Peru, El Salvador, Uruguay, and Venezuela.[90] Unlike AFCAC or EASA, LACAC is a consultative organization. Although it does have a regulatory function, each decision must be approved by the governments of individual countries before it becomes legally binding. The objectives of the institution are set out in Article 5 and are as follows:

a) promoting and supporting cooperation between states to ensure the orderly development and better utilization of air transport to and from the Americas;
b) performing analyses concerning economic issues in the field of air transport;
c) exchanging statistical information between member states and collection and transmitting other statistical information at the regional level;
d) encouraging the application of ICAO standards and recommended practices regarding facilitation and proposing further measures to increase the flow of passengers, freight, and mail in the region;
e) supporting arrangements between states in the region contributing to the better implementation of ICAO regional plans concerning the provision of air navigation equipment and services and the adoption of ICAO standards in airworthiness, maintenance and aircraft operations, personnel licensing, and accident investigation;

88 Between 1959 and 1962, three regional civil aviation conferences were held by the aviation authorities of the states concerned. Between 1960 and 1969, 13 meetings of the Inter-American Air Transport Team (CITA) were organized. Jose C. Bogolasky, *Air Transport...*, op. cit., p. 77.

89 Statute of the Civil Aviation Commission of Latin America, signed at Mexico on December 14, 1973, United Nations Treaty Series, Vol. 1241, No. 20170, 1981.

90 https://clac-lacac.org/us/?lang=en#res-his_eng, accessed 22.01.2024.

f) supporting the training of aviation personnel;
g) supporting collective agreements on technical assistance in Latin America in the field of civil aviation to make the best use of all available resources, in particular those provided under the United Nations Development Programme (UNDP).

At the institutional level, LACAC can cooperate with other organizations in the region and worldwide, including AFCAC and ECAC.[91] Its organizational structure consists of the Assembly, the Executive Committee, and the Secretariat.[92]

The Assembly is the plenary body of the organization and is composed of all member states (Article 9), each with one vote (Article 12). Its meetings are held in ordinary and extraordinary sessions. Ordinary sessions are held at least once every two years (Article 9 of the Statute). The first ordinary session was held in August 1974 in Buenos Aires (Argentina). Extraordinary sessions, may be convened in two ways: either on the Executive Committee's own initiative or at the request of a majority of LACAC member states. As of January 31, 2025, 25 ordinary sessions and seven extraordinary sessions have been held.[93] In Article 12, subject to Articles 12 bis and 25 of the LACAC Statute, the Assembly can adopt the following types of normative acts: conclusions, recommendations, and resolutions. These decisions are adopted by a simple majority.[94] In accordance with Article 13 of the Statute, the Assembly has the following tasks:

a) elects a President and four Vice-Presidents[95] in accordance with the principles of fair geographical representation, rotation, and the contribution of each member state to the development of air transport in the region;[96]
b) approve decisions on the election of members of committees, working groups, or expert groups.

The Executive Committee consists of a President and four Vice-Presidents elected by the Assembly for a two-year term. The Committee coordinates, implements, and oversees the action plan established by the Assembly. In accordance with Article 15 of the Statute, it proposes the establishment of working groups and

91 Article 7 of the Statutes of the LACAC.
92 Article 8 of the LACAC Statute.
93 https://clac-lacac.org/meetings/categories/asembly/?lang=en, accessed 31.01.2024.
94 Due to the SARS-COV-2 pandemic, Article 12bis was introduced into the LACAC Statute. It allows voting by correspondence (without the need for physical presence during the session), if the Executive Committee deems such a measure to be permitted. In such cases, two thirds of the member states will have to agree to this solution. The new provision was introduced in Assembly resolution A4-3. During the period of legal restrictions and related travel bans or limitations on physical contact, as well as in accordance with the rules of social distancing, in order to minimize the spread of COVID-19, such legal measures were taken by various organizations. Virtual meetings also took place in 2020 and 2021.
95 The change was made in the resolution of the A4-1 Assembly.
96 *Ibidem*.

expert groups and staff. The Executive Committee may modify the budget of the organization, after consulting with the member states (Article 20).

The Secretariat manages the day-to-day administrative and organizational work of LACAC. It is headed by a Secretary. The work of the Secretariat are determined by the Executive Committee in accordance with the guidelines of the Assembly (Article 16 of the Statute). Since 2005, the Secretariat has been based in Lima, Peru.

In the light of Article 25, the Statute may be amended by a two-thirds majority vote of the member states. Mexico is the depositary of the international agreement.

3.3.3 Other aviation safety institutions in Latin America

The issue of regional safety is extremely important for Latin American states. Cedro points out that we are currently observing the regionalization of safety, which is related to the historical conditions of the Latin American region, the influence of the US, and that strengthening ties within the continent is the most reasonable strategy to maintain peace and stability in this region.[97] Safety in the Latin American region is relatively high, although there are no uniform regulations across the region. A quick glance at the statistics reveals a low rate of air accidents and a low number of fatalities. Table 3.4 compares the number of accidents in the Latin American region with the global figures between 2008 and 2018. The accident rate has decreased sharply over the decade. In 2008, this rate was 11.07 accidents per 1 million flight operations, while in 2015 it had already fallen to just 1.03 accidents per 1 million flight operations. This figure is much lower than the world average for that year, which was 2.78. In the next two years, the accident rate in the Latin American region was also lower than the global average (in 2016 it was 1.08 compared to the global rate of 2.68, and in 2017 it was 1.64 compared to 2.42). Only in 2018 was this indicator slightly higher than the global average and amounted to 3.17 against the global 1.75. In the following years, the accident rate in the American region and on a global scale have become similar. However, 2020 was a special year, due to the legal restrictions on flight operations due to the spread of the coronavirus and therefore these indicators are not reliable. They are underestimated because there were few flights in 2020 and 2021.

However, there is no horizontal approach to safety procedures and regulations within the LACAC. Fernando Fiallos notes that higher safety standards are associated with an economically sustainable system, that involves creating economic regulations aimed at connecting different parts of the American continent with each other and with the rest of the world (Table 3.4).[98]

97 Cedro P., Latin American concept of security, in: Lisińska M., Beliavska B. (eds), *Latin America in international relations*, Kraków 2015, p. 51.

98 For more information, see Fiallos F., *LACAC and current challenges of civil aviation in Latin America*, in: Mendes De Leon P., Buissing N. (eds), *Behind and Beyond the Chicago Convention: The Evolution of Aerial Sovereignty*, Wolters Kluwer, 2019, pp. 141–158.

Table 3.4 Comparison of the number of accidents in the Latin American region with the number in the world between 2008 and 2023

Year	*Accident rate per million departures in Latin America*	*Accident rate per million departures worldwide*
2008	11.07	4.7
2009	7.55	4.07
2010	5.26	4.27
2011	5.32	2.8
2012	4.09	2.1
2013	3.65	2.3
2014	3.59	3.0
2015	1.03	2.6
2016	1.08	2.68
2017	1.64	2.42
2018	3.17	1.75
2019	3.8	3.0
2020	2.37	2.09
2021	2.77	0.57
2022	3.09	2.16
2023	2.82	1.82

Source: Own elaboration based on data from SAM Region Safety Plan, 2019, Appendix B, and Annual Safety Plan, RASG-PA 2020–2023.

Within CLAC-LACAC, several institutions dealing with aviation safety and security can be identified, which adopt appropriate decisions and issue documents setting out the organization's action plan and strategy for the coming years. Notable among these are:

a) South American Aviation Security and Facilitation Regional Group – SAM AVSEC/FAL/RG;
b) Regional Aviation Safety Group - Pan-America – RASG-PA;
c) Regional Safety Oversight Organisation (RSOO).

3.3.4 Legal scope of LACAC AVSEC/FAL/RG

The Aviation Security and Facilitation Regional Group (AVSEC/FAL/RG) is an institution established as a result of LACAC resolution in 2010 following the adoption of the Joint Declaration on Civil Aviation Security on the American Continent between ICAO and LACAC on February 17, 2010.[99] The first meeting of this organization was held in 2011 and it now takes place annually. During the

99 A Joint Declaration was adopted at ministerial level in Mexico in February 2010 Subsequently, a memorandum of cooperation was signed between ICAO and LACAC on the establishment of a legal framework for enhanced cooperation in Montreal, Canada, on September 27, 2010. This resulted in the adoption by the LACAC Assembly during its 19th ordinary session of Resolution 19-5, Punta Cana (Dominican Republic) on November 1–5, 2010.

Inter-American Conference on the Implementation of the ICAO Global Aviation Safety Plan, held in Panama on July 24–27, 2018, five strategic actions were identified to strengthen aviation safety and security in the face of emerging challenges:[100]

1. increase risk awareness and response. It is crucial to understand the risks in order to optimally create policies and measures, which must be effective, proportionate, and sustainable. It should be emphasized that carrying out a risk assessment makes it possible to identify gaps and weaknesses that can then be eliminated with optimal use of available resources;
2. develop a culture of safety and human capabilities. Developing a safety culture means creating an environment where safety is a priority and an integral part of daily activities and decisions. This involves educating and training employees, creating, establishing and enforcing safety procedures, monitoring and improving safety practices, fostering safety communication and cooperation, and highlighting positive examples of a safety culture. The goal is to create a culture where safety is a natural part of everyday activities, not just an additional obligation. The existence of well-trained, motivated, and professional aviation personnel is a key prerequisite for effective aviation security;
3. improve technological resources and fostering innovation. This involves the use of modern technologies to increase the level of safety. This may include implementing cybersecurity systems, upgrading access control systems, adopting solutions for safety incident tracking and management, and using artificial intelligence and machine learning for early threat detection and prevention. Improving technological resources is key to maintaining safety in the digital age of preventing cyber-attacks on civil aviation, protecting data and assets, and increasing the efficiency and effectiveness of security activities without compromising operational performance;
4. improve safety oversight and quality assurance. Legal regulations and the related quality control and oversight mechanisms at the global, national, and local levels are vital to ensure sustainable effective aviation security;
5. increase international cooperation. This means the cooperation among states, organizations, and institutions to increase safety in the field of civil aviation in the international arena. It may include cooperation in preventing and combating aviation terrorism, information exchange, and conducting joint cybersecurity actions. Strengthening international cooperation is essential because many threats to civil aviation safety are transnational and require the cooperation of multiple states and institutions to mitigate them effectively. Enhanced cooperation will enable key aviation safety objectives to be achieved faster and more effectively.

100 Eighth Meeting of the ICAO/LACAC NAM/CAR and SAM Aviation Security and Facilitation Regional Group, AVSEC/FAL/RG/8, Mexico City, Mexico, August 13–17, 2018, paragraph 8A.

In 2024, 46 countries and territories were members of this Group.[101] Member states elect a Chairperson and Vice-Chairperson of the organization for a term of three years. The Secretariat is located in the ICAO regional offices on the American continent, namely in Lima, Peru (South American, SAM), and in Mexico City, Mexico (North American, Central American and Caribbean, NACC) as well as in the LACAC secretariat (also in Lima). There is no single permanent headquarters; instead, two organizations, ICAO and LACAC, support the work of this institution. The priorities described above are in line with the objectives of the organization, which are as follows:[102]

a) strengthening the safety of air operations, aircraft, aviation personnel, and passengers;
b) reducing the occurrence of illegal acts against aviation safety or other hostile actions directed at civil aviation;
c) assisting member states in updating their legislation and ensuring compliance with aviation security and facilitation in air transport by national aviation safety oversight authorities and assisting state-run international airports in implementing new regulations;
d) developing a regional structure for aviation security and air transport facilitation based on regional cooperation;
e) establishing a regional mechanism for the harmonized implementation of the guidelines contained in ICAO Annexes 9 (Facilitation) and 17 (Security) to the Chicago Convention, subject to the development of a regional policy on the compliance of national standards with international regulations and recommendations on airport security procedures.

3.3.5 Regional Aviation Safety Group – Pan-America (RASG-PA)

The Regional Aviation Safety Group – Pan-America (RASG-PA) was established in 2008. Its creation was proposed by two ICAO regional offices on the American continent: the ICAO Regional Office for North America, Central America, and the Caribbean (ICAO-NACC), and the Regional Office for South America (ICAO-SAM).[103] During a joint meeting held on November 10–14, 2008, the Regional Aviation Safety Group – Pan-America (RASG-PA) was established.

101 Anguilla, Antigua and Barbuda, Argentina, Aruba, Bahamas, Barbados, Belize, Bermuda, Bolivia, Brazil, British Virgin Islands, Canada, Cayman Islands, Chile, Colombia, Costa Rica, Cuba, Curaçao, Dominican Republic, Ecuador, El Salvador, France (for the French Antilles and French Guiana), Grenada, Guatemala, Guyana, Haiti, Honduras, Jamaica, Mexico, Montserrat, Netherlands (for Bonaire, Sint Eustatius, and Saba), Nicaragua, Panama, Paraguay, Peru, Saint Kitts and Nevis, Saint Lucia, Saint Vincent and the Grenadines, Saint Maarten, Suriname, Trinidad and Tobago, Turks and Caicos Islands, the UK, the US, Uruguay, and Venezuela.

102 Eighth Meeting of the ICAO/LACAC NAM/CAR and SAM AVSEC/FAL/RG, paragraph 7.

103 https://www.gov.br/anac/en/topics/international-activities/international-organizations/regional-aviation-safety-group-pan-america-rasg-pa, accessed 5.01.2024

RASG-PA serves as a forum for cooperation between all interested states of the region in building the capacity to deal with safety issues and threats. The organization also supports states and other aviation organizations in developing the best safety standards, striving to harmonize them. It is also an integration platform in the area of civil aviation safety across the American continents. Membership in RASG-PA is not only limited to states, it can also include other entities, such as industry organizations and institutions involved in aviation safety. Currently, the members of this group are:

a) all states on the American continents under the jurisdiction of the ICAO NACC and the ICAO SAM offices (35 statesof the region and 14 dependent territories);
b) international organizations of an intergovernmental and non-governmental nature, both global and regional, as well as public and private entities providing air services (in particular: airports, air carriers, aircraft manufacturers, training organizations, and others);
c) Regional safety organizations such as Regional Safety Oversight Organizations (RSOOs), operational safety and continuous airworthiness program development groups, such as COSCAP, and regional accident and incident investigation organizations (RAIOs).

The organizational structure of RASG-PA consists of:[104]

1. the Executive Steering Committee;[105]
2. the Pan-American Regional Aviation Safety Team (PA-RAST);
3.

RASG-PA publishes annual aviation safety reports. The first such report was released in 2010. The report is an instrument for safety analysis in the Pan-American region. Its primary purpose is to focus on the main areas of aviation safety of the continent and provide the necessary information to implement safety management activities, plans, and programs to reduce the occurrence of risks in the aviation sector as much as possible.

3.3.6 RSOO on the American continents

In Latin America, as in other regions of the world, RSOOs are established in accordance with ICAO regulations (Doc.9734). In the Latin American region, states have also set up such institutions, thereby creating a system of cooperation among national authorities within a single platform for action. These institutions

104 https://www.icao.int/RASGPA/Pages/About.aspx, accessed 4.01.2024.
105 The Executive Steering Committee for 2023–2025 consists of eight states (Argentina, Brazil, Canada, Chile, Guatemala, Colombia, Trinidad and Tobago, and the US) and eight entities (Airbus, ALTA, ATR, Boeing, CANSO, Embraer, Flight Safety Foundation, and IATA).

adopt regulations and submit them for approval by both LACAC and ICAO. This system refers to a network of aviation safety regulatory bodies in Latin America that work together to ensure the safety and security of air transport in the region. In Latin America, there are several aviation safety oversight bodies within the RSOO framework. These are:

a) the Central American Aviation Safety Agency (ACSA) – an institution gathering Central American states;
b) the Caribbean Aviation Safety and Security Oversight System (CASSOS) – an institution bringing together Caribbean countries;
c) the Regional Safety Oversight Cooperation System (SRVSOP) – an institution of South American states.

The rules adopted by these organizations is exemplified by the SRVSOP Statute. Article 4 of the Statute specifies the functions of the institution, which include:[106]

a) regulatory; proposing the establishment of uniform rules and procedures in the field of civil aviation safety which are consistent with the relevant standards and recommended practices contained in the Annexes to the Chicago Convention;
b) coordination and monitoring; establishing and implementing a technical assistance program for safety oversight in participating countries, in cooperation with ICAO, ensuring that new rules and procedures comply with the provisions and obligations set out in the Chicago Convention and related documents, as well as coordinating the development of other regulationsand procedures to be adopted by the organization for implementation by its members, in accordance with the ICAO standards, and subsequently monitoring their compliance;
c) advisory and training; providing comprehensive advisory support, assistance, and training to member states so that they could implement and apply the standards and recommended practices contained in the Annexes to the Chicago Convention and related documents; coordinating the planning and execution of relevant activities as well as offering support and advice for the implementation of any uniform rules and procedures adopted by the organization;
d) guidance; motivating and guiding member states to establish a training program for technical personnel in order to disseminate aviation regulations throughout the region and to implement them in states that adopt or harmonize their own rules accordingly;
e) organizational; planning and conducting certification and oversight process with multinational expert teams, in cooperation with the states concerned; recommending the necessary measures to address safety oversight issuesand assisting in their implementation for states that request such help.

106 https://www.srvsop.aero/site/wp-content/uploads/2017/02/AmmendReglSRVSOPJun2013.pdf, accessed 20.02.2024.

3.3.7 The Latin American Open Skies Agreement and the predictions for regional legal and political cooperation

Aviation regulations in South and Central America are formed by national legal framework, in accordance with international legislation (standards) in this field, mainly based on ICAO instruments. The CLAC-LACAC aviation system is consultative, and the decisions must consequently be approved by the member states to enter into force. This significantly hinders the organization's effective functioning. Nonetheless, the inability to create legal regulations and harmonize rules in this region does not preclude the thesis that the level of aviation safety is relatively high, especially compared to the African. The strategy for the development of civil aviation in Latin America for 2020–2030 indicates that one of the strategic goals of the third decade of the 21st century will be the harmonization and strengthening the coordination of activities among regional entities related to operational safety.[107] Other remaining strategic goals concern:

a) strengthening regional cooperation with national aviation authorities and other entities, including representing the region in ICAO and other international institutions;
b) the further liberalization of air traffic rules;
c) exchanging information between working (technical) groups in order to achieve sustainable development of the aviation sector in Latin America;
d) developing a qualitatively new management model for the organization.

The vision for regulating aviation safety in Latin America is based on cooperation among governments, the aviation industry, and ICAO to ensure the safe and efficient development of air traffic in the region. The aim is to adapt safety standards to the latest technologies and challenges, including the development of civil aviation and the growth of air traffic in the region. This vision also assumes that every state in the region will be capable of implementing and enforcing global aviation safety regulations and standards, while the aviation industry will be able to take full advantage of modern technologies to increase flight safety and efficiency. An important element in the codification of aviation safety is the cooperation between states in the development of national aviation safety systems. In this way, high flight safety throughout the region can be ensured through implemented legal regulations and harmonized aviation law.

An excellent example of the vision for a unified legal system and an aviation market is the multilateral "open skies" agreement from 2010. This legal act was signed during the 19th Ordinary Session of the LACAC Assembly in Santo Domingo

107 Plan estratégico 2020–2030 comisión latinoamericana de aviación civil, CLAC, paragraph 6, A.8. Plan approved at the fourth extraordinary session of the Assembly, September 12–13, 2019, Sao Paolo (Brazil).

(Dominican Republic) on November 4, 2010.[108] In Latin America, this agreement can enable states and aviation entities to develop their activities and promote increased trade and tourism. The agreement also aims to facilitate collaboration between governments and the aviation industry in addressing challenges related to flight safety and efficiency.

In the preamble, the states reaffirmed their commitment to aviation safety and, in this context, considering the facilitation of air transport in the region, this agreement was adopted.

First of all, the main provision in this agreement is the granting by each party of the right to provide air services by any carrier of the other party (the multi-designation clause). This is a very important legal clause, as it allows any carrier registered in a given state to offer services and perform air operations to the state that granted this clause. Its counterpart is the mono-designation clause (when two states concluding a bilateral air services agreement stipulated that only one carrier from each side may provide air services), which was widely used before the process of liberalizing aviation regulations began in the second half of the 20th century. Such restrictions limited the freedom of operation and the development of air transport. The open skies agreement is intended to allow any carrier to provide services, without repeated consent from the interested states, subject to compliance with other safety provisions and regulations.

Article 1 grants air freedom rights (all technical and commercial freedoms – from the fourth to the seventh freedom), including the right of cabotage (the eighth and ninth freedoms). Subsequent articles deregulate carrier designation, authorization, and the right to refuse, revoke, or limit the operating authorization or technical permission. These are standard clauses in every multilateral open skies agreements.

Article 8 contains aviation safety regulations. Pursuant to Article 8(1), any party may request consultations at any time regarding safety standards applied by the other parties on matters relating to aeronautical equipment and services, flight crews, aircraft, and aircraft operations. Such consultations must take place within 30 days of the request. In the light of Article 8(2), if, as a result of such consultations, it is found by either party that another does not maintain and effectively apply the safety standards set out in the Chicago Convention, it must be informed and urged to implement the necessary measures to comply with ICAO standards, with a deadline for the fulfilling of that obligation.

Another provision concerns the possibility of conducting inspections. In accordance with Article 16 of the Chicago Convention, it was agreed that a state

108 Acuerdo Multilateral d e Cielos Abiertos para Los Estados Miembros de La Comision Latinoamericana De Aviacion Civil, https://clac-lacac.org/multilateral-open-skies-agreement-2/?lang=en#eng-am_ta, accessed 4.01.2024. Open skies agreements aim to eliminate government interference in air carriers' commercial decisions on routes, capacity and prices, de facto deregulating the aviation market and allowing carriers to provide services based on market terms. The state regulates only general guidelines for the functioning of entities in civil aviation and supervizes the safety of these operations. Thanks to the liberalization of the rules, air transport becomes more accessible and thus more affordable for consumers.

has the right to inspect any aircraft operated by or on behalf of an air carrier of any party. The purpose of such inspections is to verify the validity of the relevant aircraft documentation, the crew licenses, and the compliance of the aircraft equipment and condition with the applicable standards set out in the Convention. Such inspections must not cause undue delays or disrupt the carrier's operation. Another provision in Article 8(4) of the open skies agreement provides that if it appears that appropriate measures must be taken for the safe operation of an air carrier, any party has the right to suspend or impose conditions on the operating authorization or technical permission of that carrier with immediate effect. The Agreement also stipulates in Article 8(6) an obligation to notify the ICAO Secretary-General if any party fails to comply with the deadline for meeting safety requirements, as well as to report any other related decisions.

Article 9 of the open skies agreement contains provisions on aviation security. States have unequivocally undertaken that any bilateral or multilateral agreement they conclude on the protection of aviation against acts of unlawful interference shall form an integral part of the open skies agreement. The states have also undertaken to comply with the rights and obligations arising from international law on aviation security, in particular, as established under the Tokyo-Hague-Montreal system. Article 9(2) undertakes to provide mutual assistance to prevent terrorist acts referred to in the above-mentioned scheme, as well as any other threats to civil aviation security. It is further agreed in Article 9(3) that the parties will act in their mutual relations in accordance with the international aviation security regulations established by the ICAO and as set forth in the Annexes to the Chicago Convention. The parties require aircraft operators located in their territory to comply with aviation security legislation. According to Article 9(4), states must apply appropriate safety and security measures on their territory for aircraft, passengers, crew, personal belongings, baggage, cargo, and aircraft supplies. Should one state request another to adopt special safety measures to counter a particular threat, such a request will be positively considered.

In Article 9(5), states committed to providing mutual assistance in the event of an accident or threat of unlawful seizure of civil aircraft or other illegal acts against the safety of such aircraft, their passengers and crews, airports, appliances or air navigation services. This provision expresses the solidarity between the states – parties to the agreement and is a manifestation of joint efforts in the fight against threats to aviation security. Article 9(7) establishes a consultation mechanism in case of any suspicion that a party is not complying with its obligations under Article 9 of the open skies agreement. Such consultations may lead either to a positive outcome and termination of the procedure or, in the absence of a response from the state suspected of violating these provisions, or failure to reach an agreement on the matter in question, may give rise to refusal, withdrawal or suspension of the authorizations issued to the entity concerned.

The open skies agreement also regulates the safety of travel documents. In accordance with Article 10, all states must take appropriate measures to ensure that the travel documents (including passports) they issue are adequately secured. Thereupon, controls will be established for the issuance and verification of the lawful use of passports and other travel documents. Moreover, in order to guarantee the highest quality of travel documents and to avoid their misuse, counterfeiting, alteration, or erroneous issue, the parties agreed to establish appropriate security procedures in line with the standards and recommendations set by the ICAO. Maintaining the highest safety standards also requires cooperation between states in exchanging operational information on counterfeit or imitated travel documents, as provided in Article 10(5). This will strengthen resilience against the falsification of travel documents, the use of fake or imitation travel documents, the use of valid travel documents by impersonators, the misuse of authentic travel documents by legitimate holders for criminal purposes, the use of expired, invalidated, or fraudulently obtained travel documents.

In the context of both national and aviation safety, Article 11 contains another very important legal provision. This article regulates the issue related to passengers who are not allowed to cross the border, who do not possess documents or who are deported. In order to enforce this provision effectively, robust border controls have been established. States agreed to apply the standards and recommended practices set out in Annex 9 to the Chicago Convention with respect to missing and undocumented passengers and deported individuals. In this way, the states aim to strengthen cooperation in combating illegal migration.

The multilateral open skies agreement replaces the restrictive bilateral air services agreements that regulated the conduct of air operations between the parties concerned. So far, nine countries have signed the agreement and three of them have ratified it.[109] According to Article 40(1), the Agreement enters into force 30 days after the date of deposit of the third instrument of ratification and thereafter for each state 30 days after the deposit of its instrument of ratification or accession. Since the condition set out in the agreement has been met, the multilateral open skies agreement has already entered into force for those states. The agreement is open for signature by the other American states.

Pursuant to Article 36(1), the CLAC-LACAC is the depositary of the agreement. This institution, designated as the party responsible for the storage of documents and other materials related thereto, is to ensure the safety and integrity of the deposit, making it available to the parties in a timely manner, and supporting all activities arising from the agreement. In fulfillingits functions, the depositary sends certified copies to all parties to the agreement and to those states wishing to accede to it. In addition, pursuant to Article 36(2), upon the entry into force of that Agreement, the depositary transmits a certified copy thereof to the United Nations Secretary-General in accordance with Article 102 of the Charter of the United Nations and to the Secretary-General of the ICAO, in accordance with Article 83 of the Chicago Convention, for registration and publication.

109 The states that have signed the agreement are: Brazil, Chile, Colombia, Dominican Republic, Guatemala, Honduras, Panama, Paraguay and Uruguay – as of January 31, 2024. Three states have ratified it: Brazil, Panama, and Uruguay.

LACAC is the appropriate forum in the Latin American region to discuss and collaborate on key issues of civil aviation, such as:

a) strengthening the level of aviation safety in the region by developing institutionalization in civil aviation and adapting to emerging challenges;
b) harmonizing standards and regulations in the economic field, thus enabling a uniform approach to the development of aviation, thereby increasing the quality and safety of the air services;
c) harmonizing technical and operational rules in the field of aviation safety and security to reduce the risk of potentially illegal acts targeting civil aviation and its users;
d) implementing international and regional legal regulations to accelerate the liberalization of the Latin American aviation market and open it to competition.

3.8 Summary

LACAC is a regional aviation organization that supports and develops flight safety in Latin America. It cooperates with ICAO in this regard. The main tasks of LACAC include providing technical support and training to member states, and supporting efforts aimed at improving and developing safety in the region. It also develops and promotes common flight safety standards in Latin America to ensure safe and efficient air traffic operations.

One may consider the contemporary role of LACAC and whether it is able to meet the challenges of the modern world and evolving safety requirements. Still, in many South American states, the level of safety is far below international standards. Fernando Fiallos indicates that in Peru, a passenger flying on a domestic route can transfer a ticket to another passenger.[110] The process of harmonizing aviation law in Latin America is not satisfactory, as there is still a lack of political will on and insufficient commitment to implementing unified international standards at the regional level. Of course, individual countries respect aviation safety regulations, which reflects in accident and fatality statistics. The Latin American region has relatively low accident rate, but each state has its own regulations and is not conducive to an integrated approach. Fiallos believes it is necessary for LACAC to adopt a comprehensive safety plan, as higher safety standards make the system more attractive to users.[111] Yet, there is a lack of a common, regional, holistic approach to regulating air transport and safety. A uniform regional regulatory framework for safety will contribute to the development of aviation in individual states and, consequently, to broader economic development. Each country will benefit from creating consistent legal frameworks for air transport. In this respect, there must be a faster liberalization process by adopting a multilateral open skies agreement by more states, therebybuilding a new aviation order based on principles such

110 Fiallos Fernando, *LACAC*..., op. cit., pp. 141–158.
111 *Ibidem*.

as equality, community, competitiveness, economic and legal freedom, and high safety standards.

Unlike the European EASA system or the African AFCAC system, the mechanisms adopted by LACAC are not directly binding. They require the consent of the member states to become legally binding. However, the instruments adopted by LACAC can influence the shape of the legislation in Latin America and set the stage for further harmonization and improvement of safety.

3.4 Determinants of the process of institutionalization and codification in Asia and in the Pacific Region

The cultural, political, and economic diversity of the Asia-Pacific states makes it extremely difficult to speak of unity and common interests among the states in this region. The heterogeneity manifests itself on many levels: from fully democratic systems to communist and authoritarian regimes; from liberal and free market economies to centrally planned state economies; and from secular states to extremely religiously governed states (in many countries there are different denominations, both monotheistic and polytheistic). In this region, it is therefore challenging to find unity in many areas, but aviation law seems to be the field with the least divergence. Although there is no single aviation organization in the region which, as in the case of EASA, unites all states,a gradual process of institutionalization and codification of aviation law in the Asia-Pacific region can be observed.

3.4 Legal nature and scope of RASG-APAC

There is also a Regional Aviation Safety Group in Asia and Pacific (RASG-APAC) comprising of states, airlines, and industry, as well as non-governmental organizations acting in the field of aviation.

RASG-APAC was established during the 47th Conference of Directors General of the Asia-Pacific Civil Aviation Authorities in Macau in the People's Republic of China (PRC), which took place on October 25–29, 2010.[112] The first meeting of this institution was held in Noumea, New Caledonia, on October 10–11, 2011.[113] The structure of the RASG-APAC consists of the following bodies: a Chairperson and Vice-Chairperson (elected from among the representatives of the member states for a three-year term) and a Secretary assisted by a Secretariat (the Secretary is the Regional Director of the ICAO Asia and Pacific Office). The headquarters of the organization is located in Bangkok, Thailand.

112 Earlier, in 2009, states in the Asia-Pacific region signed a letter of intent to establish a regional aviation safety organization. On May 25, 2010, during the 4th meeting of 190th session, the ICAO Council approved the establishment of such an institution. More on 47th Conference of Directors General of Civil Aviation Asia and Pacific Regions, Macao, China, October 25–29 2010, DGCA – 47/DP/4/3.

113 First Meeting of the Regional Aviation Safety Group – Asia and Pacific Regions (RASG-APAC/1), Noumea, New Kaledonia, 10–11.10. 2011.

This organization was established to promote aviation safety in Asia and the Pacific Region. It provides a platform for aviation safety regulatory bodies, industry representatives, and other relevant stakeholders in the region to cooperate and exchange information on aviation safety.

RASG-APAC works to improve aviation safety by promoting the implementation of international aviation standards and recommended practices, fostering cooperation and coordination between stakeholders, and facilitating the exchange of information and best practices related to safety. Like other groups worldwide, it supports the implementation of ICAO's GANP and GASR.

The latest priorities for RASG-APAC are as follows:[114]

a) the reduction of operational risk;
b) the improvement of safety oversight;
c) the implementation of coherent, uniform, and transparent SMS and SSPs;
d) the enhancement of the risk management and regulatory oversight;
e) the upgrading of aviation infrastructure.

RASG-APAC also issues annual safety reports. When analyzing accident statistics in Asia and the Pacific Region, these rates are lower than the global average. Table 3.5 shows the number of accidents in the last decade compared to global indicators.

Table 3.5 Comparison of accidents per million operations in Asia Pacific with worldwide between 2009 and 2023

Year	*Accident rate per million operations in Asia and the Pacific Region*	*Accident rate per million operations worldwide*
2009	4.2	4.07
2010	3.66	4.27
2011	2.47	2.8
2012	2.82	2.1
2013	2.47	2.3
2014	2.99	3.0
2015	2.44	2.6
2016	1.69	2.68
2017	1.74	2.42
2018	1.6	1.75
2019	1.34	3.0
2020	1.05	2.09
2021	0.82	1.93
2022	1.38	2.16
2023	1.06	1.82

Source: Own elaboration based on annual report data: Asia Pacific Region Annual Safety Report 2016, 2017, 2018, 2019, 2020, 2021, 2022, and 2023.

114 RASG-APAC Regional Aviation Safety Priorities And Targets, https://www.icao.int/APAC/RASG/RASG%20eDocs/APAC%20Aviation%20Safety%20Priorities%20and%20Targets.pdf, accessed 10.01.2024.

Analyzing accident rates per million operations in the Asia-Pacific region, reveals a downward trend from 2009 to 2023. In 2009, there were 4.2 accidents per million operations, while in 2019 it was 1.34. Of course, the analysis intentionally stops at 2019, as the subsequent years, 2020 and 2021, were affected by the COVID-19 pandemic and legal restrictions related to the performance of flight operations. During those years, states implemented numerous measures to curb the spread of coronavirus significantly impacting the aviation industry. The number of operations decreased sharply, and those performed were subject to strict regulatory conditions. It should therefore be no surprising that accident rates werelow in these two years. The situation was similar in other regions of the world, where these figures were significantly lower than in 2019. However, in the Asia and the Pacific Region, another pattern emerges, since 2013 and continuously through 2021, the accident rates have generally been slightly lower than the global average.

In the diverse Asia and the Pacific Region, which is so diverse and with different political systems, aviation safety issues serve as a basis for integration and building a common space for dialogue. This approach to institutionalizing and codifying aviation law should be noted positively, as it contributes to building a uniform legal framework that is, reflected in a low number of accidents and constant improvements of quality.

3.4.2 Institutional and regulatory system for safety oversight in Asia and the Pacific Region

Within the framework of organizing aviation safety oversight in APAC region, a multilateral mechanism has been established in accordance with the international rules set out in ICAO Doc.9734. There are five safety oversight organizations in the Asia and the Pacific Region:

a) Pacific Aviation Safety Office (PASO), covering 10 states from the Pacific Region: Cook Islands, Kiribati, Nauru, Niue, Papua New Guinea, Samoa, Solomon Islands, Tonga, Tuvalu, and Vanuatu;
b) Interstate Aviation Committee (IAC), covering the 9 states of the former Union of Soviet Socialist Republics (USSR), i.e.: Armenia, Azerbaijan, Belarus, Kazakhstan, Kyrgyzstan, Russian Federation, Tajikistan,Turkmenistan and Uzbekistan;
c) The Cooperative Development of Operational Safety and Continuing Airworthiness Program – Southeast Asia (COSCAP SEA) – covering 12 states: Brunei, Cambodia, Indonesia, Lao People's Democratic Republic, Malaysia, Myanmar, Papua New Guinea, Philippines, Singapore, Thailand, Timor Leste, and Vietnam,
d) The Cooperative Development of Operational Safety and Continuing Airworthiness – South Asia (COSCAP SA) – covering 7 states: Bangladesh, Bhutan, India, Maldives, Nepal, Pakistan, and Sri Lanka.
e) The Cooperative Development of Operational Safety and Continuing Airworthiness – North Asia (COSCAP NA) – covering 4 states and 2 special

administrative territories: PRC, Hong Kong Special Administrative Region (China), Macau Special Administrative Region (China), Democratic People's Republic of Korea, Mongolia, and the Republic of Korea.

The first two institutions (PASO) and (IAC) were established through an international agreement, the other three (COSCAP SEA, COSCAP SA, and COSCAP NA) were created as a result of an ICAO program decision. The Asia and the Pacific Region is the largest in terms of territory and population, which is why several safety oversight institutions have been established. They perform the same function as other similar institutions in the world under international regulations. A peculiar case is the creation of an RSOO in the Pacific. PASO was established in 2007 following a previously signed international treaty, as mentioned later. PASO is an intergovernmental organization responsible for promoting and coordinating civil aviation safety in the Pacific. Its members are Pacific states, and its headquarters are established in Nambatu, Vanuatu.[115]

The basis for the functioning of PASO as an international organization is its founding agreement, the Treaty of Apia (as discussed in this section). This Treaty serves as its statute determining the most important issues related to this organization. The statute defines the organization's goals and tasks, the rights and obligations of its members, the structure of the organization (the individual bodies and their competences), and its headquarters.

PASO works with member states to improve aviation safety by developing and implementing international standards and recommended practices established by the ICAO. Its main objective is to ensure a safe and efficient aviation system in the Pacific region by promoting compliance with ICAO standards and promoting best practices in aviation safety management. The core tasks related to aviation safety of the region and the oversight of its proper functioning are issues related to certification and airworthiness, personnel licenses, and investigating air accidents in accordance with the provisions of Annex 13 to the Chicago Convention.[116] Inspections are carried out basing on the regulations set out in international rules by its own qualified inspectors, or by personnel from other states, such as Australia, Fiji, New Zealand, and Papua New Guinea.[117]

PASO, acting as a regional safety oversight authority, is supported by agreements with numerous industry organizations, institutions of a similar nature from other states, as well as financial organizations, namely:[118]

a) air carriers: Airways New Zealand;
b) banking institutions: the Asian Development Bank (ADB) and the World Bank (International Bank for Reconstruction and Recovery – IBRD);

115 _https://paso.aero/about/paso/, accessed 20.01.2024.
116 https://www.atc-network.com/atc-organisations/paso-pacific-aviation-safety-office-vanuatu, accessed 28.01.2024.
117 https://paso.aero/our-work/audits-and-inspections/, accessed 28.01.2024.
118 https://paso.aero/about/paso/, accessed 20.01.2024.

c) non-governmental organizations in the field of civil aviation: the Association of South Pacific Airlines (ASPA);
d) aviation authorities performing safety oversight functions: Civil Aviation Safety Authority of Australia (CASA), Civil Aviation Authority of New Zealand (CAANZ), and US Federal Aviation Administration (FAA);
e) governments supporting the organization: the Government of Australia, the Government of New Zealand, and the Government of Vanuatu;
f) international intergovernmental organizations: ICAO;
g) other institutions: the Pacific Islands Forum (PIF)[119] and the Pacific Tourism Organization (SPTO).[120]

Unlike other regions of the world, the Pacific states have decided to strengthen their safety through a multilateral agreement. It is worth noting the Pacific Islands Civil Aviation Safety and Security Treaty (PICASST), adopted by the Pacific states, signed on August 7, 2004, in Apia, Samoa, known as the Apia Treaty. It was initially signed by four states (Kiribati, Papua New Guinea, Samoa, and Vanuatu) and according to the provisions of Article 12(1), it could come into force 30 days after it was signed by five countries. It was only after this condition was fulfilled did the Treaty enter into force on June 11, 2005.[121] There are currently ten member states: Cook Islands, Kiribati, Nauru, Niue, Papua New Guinea, Samoa, the Solomon Islands, Tonga, Tuvalu, and Vanuatu. Australia, Fiji, and New Zealand have the status of associated states.

The Treaty confirms the full and exclusive jurisdiction of states over their airspace, which is consistent with the principle of sovereignty as set out in Article 1 of the Chicago Convention. Therefore, each state has a responsibility to implement legislation and relevant procedures related to aviation safety oversight and security. The legal scope of these obligations is clarified in Article 3 of the Treaty. In the light of these provisions, and without replacing the rules established globally under international aviation law, the parties agreed that this oversight would be exercised within the framework of regional cooperation in areas such as airworthiness, air

119 The organization was established on 27 October 2005 in Port Moresby, Papua New Guinea, under an international agreement signed by 16 states of the Pacific region. According to Article 2 of the Agreement, its objective is to strengthen regional cooperation and integration in the areas of economic growth, sustainable development, good governance and safety. See more: https://www.forumsec.org/who-we-arepacific-islands-forum/, accessed 30.01.2024.

120 The organization was established on October 18, 1999, in Apia, Samoa, by the Constitution of the South Pacific Tourism Organization (SPTO) in 1983. The name was changed in 2019 to the current one. SPTO has 21 member states from the Asia-Pacific region. According to Article 2(2), its aim is to pursue the sustainable tourism development in the region, strengthen regional cooperation in the development of tourism, promote the region and protect natural resources. Read more: STPO constitution: http://www.paclii.org/pits/en/treaty_database/1999/1.html, accessed 30.01.2024.

121 Three statessigned the treaty on August 7, 2004, (Kiribati, Samoa, and Tonga). The fourth was Vanuatu, which signed the treaty on August 9, 2004, and the fifth was Solomon Islands, which signed on May 12, 2005.

operations, aerodromes, aviation protection against acts of unlawful interference, and personnel licensing.

The parties also agreed on the cooperation mechanism in the areas covered by the international agreement. Pursuant to Article 4(1), the states parties established PASO to perform the role defined in the Treaty. The main task of PASO is to provide advisory and technical support related to the regulatory oversight of civil aviation safety and security against illegal and unlawful acts. PASO has the legal personality necessary for the performance of its functions.[122] The obligations of states are regulated by Article 5 of the Apia Treaty. These include:

a) maintaining at all times the readiness to fulfill the tasks related to ensuring the safety and security of aviation within their territory;
b) participating in the PASO Council;
c) paying annual membership fees determined by the PASO Council;
d) establishing and maintaining a harmonized and coherent legislative framework for aviation safety and security;
e) performing all tasks entrusted by PASO, based on submitted recommendations or reports, thus fulfilling international obligations;
f) ensuring timely reimbursement of any fees charged by PASO to recover the costs of services rendered;
g) providing timely information and data upon request by any of the PASO bodies;
h) informing the PASO Council and the member states of any change in the level of services provided.

The structure of PASO consists of a Council of Directors and a General Manager. The Council of Directors is composed of representatives of each member state, in accordance with Article 6(1) of the Treaty. The Council elects a chairperson from among its members for a term of one year.[123] The functions of the Council are outlined in Article 6(3) and are as follows:

a) appointing the General Manager of the PASO;
b) formulating policy and strategic goals of the organization;
c) overseeing compliance with the statute of the organization and introducing modifications to it;
d) adopting the financial procedures and rules concerning the payment of annual contributions by member states and any other administrative arrangements deemed appropriate;
e) approving the annual budget, work program, fees, and administrative structure of PASO;

122 Article 4(3) of the Treaty of Apia.
123 Article 6(4) of the Treaty of Apia.

f) conducting the debate and publishing the annual reports of the General Manager of the PASO;
g) appointing financial auditors, supervising their work, and accepting their annual financial report.

The Council meets in ordinary session once a year, and extraordinary sessions may be convened at the request of at least half the number of member states of the organization.[124] The manner in which decisions are made in the Council is laid down in Article 6(6). According to its provisions, decisions are made by consensus. If this is not achieved, the matter in question is put to the vote and approved by a two-thirds majority of the states present and voting.

The PASO has its seat in Nambatu in Vanuatu. The Office is headed by the General Manager.[125] Article 7(1) of the Apia Treaty defines the tasks of the Office, which include:

a) conducting the current administrative activities of the organization;
b) providing technical support related to the implementation of legislation on aviation safety and security;
c) developing an annual action plan;
d) preparing the annual report and draft budget;
e) archiving all documentation related to aviation safety and security;
f) providing support and advice to each member state related to the activities of the organization.

Regarding the personnel of the PASO, the Treaty defines the role of inspectors, who are entrusted with carrying out supervision within the organization.[126] The inspectors perform their duties on behalf of the member state. They also enjoy international privileges and immunities in carrying out their responsibilities, in accordance with Article 4(3), subject to Article 8 of the Treaty.[127] The document also provides legal protection for inspectors against any relevant legal proceedings arising from the proper performance of their duties.[128]

The settlement of disputes between the parties is covered in Article 9 of the Treaty. In the event of any discrepancy or doubt as to the interpretation or

124 Article 6(5) of the Treaty of Apia.
125 Article 6(3a) of the Treaty of Apia.
126 Article 8(1) of the Treaty of Apia.
127 Diplomatic privileges and immunities are granted to states in accordance with the Vienna Convention on Diplomatic Relations, done at Vienna on April 18, 1961, as well as to the United Nations under the Convention on the Privileges and Immunities of the United Nations, approved by the General Assembly of the United Nations on February 13, 1946, and to specialized organizations under the Convention on the Privileges and Immunities of Specialized Agencies adopted by United Nations General Assembly, November 21, 1947. Each international organization therefore has the legal power to regulate the diplomatic privileges and immunities of its international officials.
128 Article 8(3) of the Apia Treaty.

application of the treaty, the dispute should first be resolved through negotiation, mediation, or other peaceful means of international dispute resolution.[129] However, if the dispute cannot be resolved in this way, each party has the right to turn to the PASO Council of Directors for assistance in resolving the case. The decision of the Council is final and binding on the parties to the dispute in accordance with Article 9(2) of the Treaty.

The final provisions of the treaty includ a withdrawal clause. Every member state has the right to leave the organization by withdrawing from the Treaty. The resignation takes effect 12 months after the denunciation of the depositary state of the Treaty. Such notice may be withdrawn at any time, but before the end of the one-year notice period.[130] According to Article 15, the function of depositary of the Treaty has been entrusted to the Secretary-General of the Pacific Islands Forum.

One of the PASO activities is the publication of a report on aviation safety in the region.[131] The first such report was issued in 2016. These reports describe the current activities of PASO, as well as plans for the coming years, present the achievements of the organization for the previous reporting year, and also identify problems and challenges facing the region in terms of safety oversight.

The institutional mechanism for oversight of civil aviation safety established under the Apia Treaty is part of the international guidelines and procedures defined by the ICAO and developed in all regions of the world. It is worth emphasizing that the Pacific states cover an extensive geographical area, and their geopolitical location requires a broad platform for cooperation, as individually they are not capable of carrying out all regulatory activities. Therefore, in this context, other states in the region, such as Australia and New Zealand, with broad institutional and legal structures, support the Pacific states in fulfilling their regulatory and functional roles in ensuring aviation safety and security.

3.5 Institutionalization and codification of aviation safety in the MENA region

Improving safety in civil aviation is a priority for every state and organization dealing with air transport. In the Middle East region, many important declarations on aviation safety have been adopted, which serve as both the strategic framework for the action of the statesin the region and the foundations for further harmonization of aviation regulations. It is worth recalling, in this context, the Riyadh Declaration of 20176[132] The states underlined the importance of air transport in the economic development of states, in particular its impact on economic growth and job crea-

129 The settlement of international disputes by peaceful means is provided for in international law, Chapter VI of the Charter of the United Nations, Articles 33 to 38.

130 Article 14 of the Apia Treaty.

131 Pacific aviation safety reports can be viewed: https://paso.aero/publications/#annualreports, accessed 27.01.2024.

132 The Riyadh Declaration on Aviation Safety and Facilitation, adopted by the Arab Civil Aviation Commission on August 31, 2016, in Riyadh, Saudi Arabia. https://docplayer.net/84035733-Inter-

tion, as well as the importance of aviation security and facilitation measures contributing to the development of air transport worldwide, especially in the Middle East and North Africa. The Declaration underlined the fundamental role of ICAO and the regional organization ACAC. It also expressed concern over emerging terrorist attacks, highlighted the threats and risks facing international civil aviation, as well as stressed the continuous need to enhance states; capacities to deal with new and emerging threats. The Declaration called on states to urgently implement legislation on critical elements of the aviation safety oversight system, in accordance with the ICAO international regulations contained in Annex 9 (Facilitation) and Annex 17 (Security) to the Chicago Convention and to implement remedial action plans for individual states. Taking into account the above considerations, the following actions were undertaken:[133]

a) providing political support for the implementation of legal solutions at the national, sub-regional, and regional levels;
b) accelerating the establishment of national bodies responsible for regulatory oversight of aviation safety and security;
c) supporting states in their regulatory functions in implementing national laws, consistent with international standards;
d) supporting and coordinating regulatory activities regarding aviation security, including taking all steps towards the ratification of international agreements on aviation security and facilitation.

The Riyadh Declaration was signed by 21 states.[134] It is a clear signal from a broad group of states, emphasizing that aviation terrorism poses a serious threat to the safety of citizens and states. At the same time it calls for increased efforts to adopt international legal regulations that will serve as the foundation for the global aviation security system. The Middle East region, which has been affected by numerous conflicts and terrorist attacks by the still-active Islamic State, bears witness to the fight against this phenomenon and that terrorist organization. The states of the region have made further commitments, demonstrating their commitment to building a better future for their societies and showing the world a safe region where there is no place for aviation terrorism.

The process of codifying aviation safety is dynamic and constantly evolving, but in general it involves setting and enforcing aviation safety standards to ensure

national-civil-aviation-organization-aviation-security-and-facilitation-plan-development-group .html, accessed 15.01.2024.

133 The Riyadh Declaration: https://docplayer.net/84035733-International-civil-aviation-organization -aviation-security-and-facilitation-plan-development-group.html, accessed 25.01.2024.

134 The states that have signed the Riyadh Declaration are: Algeria, Bahrain, Comoros, Djibouti, Egypt, Iraq, Jordan, Kuwait, Libya, Lebanon, Mauritania, Morocco, Oman, Palestinian Authority, Qatar, Saudi Arabia, Somalia, Sudan, Tunisia, United Arab Emirates, and Yemen. See https://docplayer.net/84035733-International-civil-aviation-organization-aviation-security-and-facilitation -plan-development-group.html, accessed 25.01.2024.

the safety of passengers and crew and to minimize the risk of air accidents. In the Middle East, this process is carried out by intergovernmental organizations working in the field of aviation safety, such as:

a) the Arab Civil Aviation Organization (ACAO) – a regional organization responsible for the comprehensive regulation of civil aviation;
b) the Middle East and North Africa Regional Safety Oversight Organization (MENA RSOO) – an organization dedicated to safety oversight;
c) the Regional Aviation Safety Group - Middle East (RASG-MID) – a regional institution responsible for aviation safety matters.

In the Middle East, the process of codification of aviation safety is continuously being improved and adapted to the changing needs and requirements of the aviation industry to ensure the best possible safety for passengers and crew.

3.5.1 Organization of the aviation safety system in the Middle East region

It is evident that in the Middle East, states are strengthening cooperation in the field of regional institutions, thus fulfilling the obligations of international aviation law, while harmonizing regulations. This effort seeks to foster a uniform approach to the problems and challenges of aviation safety in this volatile region. The institutionalization of civil aviation in the Middle East is developing mainly due to the creation of ACAO and subsequent organizations in the field of civil aviation.

3.5.2 Arab Civil Aviation Organization (ACAO)

The Arab Civil Aviation Organization (ACAO) is an organization of Arab states to coordinate activities related to civil aviation, including regulations and standards of flight safety. It is an affiliate of the League of Arab States (LAS). This organization has undergone various legal forms. The origin of its creation dates back to November 6, 1967, when the LAS decided to create the Arab Civil Aviation Council. It was to serve as a specialized agency of the LAS. It ceased its activities in 1989 because of the transformation of this body into the Arab Civil Aviation Committee. However, this structure was later changed to the Arab Civil Aviation Commission in 1996, which continues to operate to this day, although under a different name, that was modified in 2007 to the Arab Civil Aviation Organization[135] There are currently 22 member states: Algeria, Bahrain, Comoros, Djibouti, Egypt, Iraq, Jordan, Kuwait, Libya, Lebanon, Mauritania, Morocco, Oman, Palestinian Authority, Qatar, Saudi Arabia, Somalia, Sudan, Syria, Tunisia, United Arab Emirates, and Yemen. The headquarters of ACAO was established in Rabat, Morocco.

135 https://uia.org/s/or/en/1100052983, accessed 18.01.2024.

The ACAO has the following tasks:[136]

a) coordinating activities related to civil aviation in Arab states;
b) establishing flight safety standards and operating procedures to ensure the safety of passengers, crew, and other users;
c) facilitating air traffic flow between member states and promoting the development of air transport in the Arab region;
d) promoting training and education in the field of civil aviation;
e) cooperating with other international organizations related to aviation, such as ICAO;
f) dealing with environmental and sustainable development issues in the aviation sector;
g) maintaining a database and monitoring statistics related to civil aviation in Arab countries.

The organizational structure of ACAO consists of the following bodies: the General Assembly, the Executive Council, the General Directorate, and five technical committees.

The General Assembly, as a plenary body, is composed of the heads of civil aviation authorities of the member states. Regular sessions of the Assembly are held every two years, during which action plans for the next period are adopted, and the organization's budget is approved. The Assembly makes its decisions in the form of resolutions.[137]

The Executive Council is an executive body. It is composed of nine members elected by the General Assembly from among the heads of civil aviation authorities of the member states for a two-year term. Meetings of the Council are held at least twice a year. Its main task is to study the civil aviation matters in Arab states, work on the development of this sector and propose actions, prepare the budget of the organization, and implement and monitor the resolutions of the General Assembly.[138]

The General Directorateis the administrative body of the organization. It is headed by a Director-General, who is elected by the General Assembly for a four-year term, renewable once. The primary task of the Director-General is to execute the recommendations and resolutions issued by the General Assembly and the Executive Council, while developing projects and overseeing the day-to-day administrative activities of the organization.[139]

ACAO also has five technical committees composed of qualified experts from the member states. These committees address issues which are referred to them. These are as follows:

136 https://acao.org.ma/site/en/page10.php?idem=2&pgi=12&cat=1, accessed 18.01.2024.
137 https://acao.org.ma/site/en/page10.php?idem=20&pgi=24&cat=333, accessed 18.01.2024.
138 https://acao.org.ma/site/en/page10.php?idem=2&pgi=26&cat=2, accessed 18.01.2024.
139 https://acao.org.ma/site/en/page10.php?idem=2&pgi=12&cat=1, accessed 18.01.2024.

1. the Air Safety Committee;
2. the Aviation Security Committee;
3. the Air Transport Committee;
4. the Environment Committee;
5. the Air Navigation Commission.

Each committee is composed of nine qualified experts representing the member states and meets at least twice a year. They may set up subcommittees or task groups to carry out their work.[140]

ACAO has signed numerous bilateral cooperation agreements in the form of a Memorandum of Understanding with many similar organizations worldwide and third countries. It is worth mentioning them here:

a) with the following states: Iran, France, South Korea, Singapore, the US, the UK, the United Arab Emirates;
b) with organizations: ICAO, Arab Information and Communication Technologies Organization (AICTO), Arab Air Sports Federation, ECAC, AFCAC, LACAC, EUROCONTROL, Arab Tourism Organization;
c) with air carriers: Kuwait Airways.

3.5.3 Legal scope of an open skies agreement in the Middle East

In the Arab states, restrictions related to the operation of air services between states are gradually being lifted. One legal means of liberalizing air transport is through open skies agreements. These agreements are intended to amend existing bilateral air services agreements containing restrictive clauses and provisions limiting or even preventing the development of aviation among the states concerned by opening their markets to competition, eliminating restrictions on air capacity and government approval of fares, as well as by introducing multi-designation clauses for carriers. The states of the Middle East region have also gradually concluded such agreements.[141]

Another approach to liberalization is to modify existing bilateral air services agreements. However, given the numerous regulatory changes in aviation and the increasing competition, the old bilateral agreements would have to be completely overhauled, making it more effective to conclude new open skies agreements. Another legal instrument that could also be employed is the establishment of a comprehensive multilateral agreement between member states that would cover all deregulatory issues and replace the existing restrictive bilateral agreements. This is exactly the route taken by the states of the Middle East. On December 19, 2004 in

140 *Ibidem.*

141 Schlumberger Ch. E., Weisskopf N., *Is the Arab take-off imminent? Opportunities for the development of the North African air transport sector following the Arab Spring*, Annals of Air and Space Law, Vol. XXXVII, p. 253.

Damascus, Syria, under the aegis of ACAO, an agreement on the liberalization of air transport (more broadly referred to as the open skies agreement) was concluded between 12 members of the organization: Bahrain, Egypt, Iraq, Yemen, Jordan, Lebanon, Oman, Palestine, Somalia, Sudan, Syria, and Tunisia.[142]

The Damascus Agreement is a legal framework regulating the execution of air transport services between states parties in a free manner, without any restrictions. It replaces existing bilateral agreements between these states.[143] As part of traffic rights, it grants all seven air freedoms in accordance with the principles of free market, with the exception of cabotage rights (eighth freedom).[144] Domestic transport remains at the disposal of the carrier's state of registration. Multi-designation clause included in the Agreement,[145] grants each state the right to designate an unlimited number of carriers from each state to carry out operations between states parties of the Agreement. This provision meets the expectations of the aviation industry, which seeks to expand and develop its potential. The remaining regulatory provisions are similar to other typical open skies agreements concluded around the world, as already discussed in the study. Such provisions in the Damascus agreement include the right of the carrier to determine freely the capacity and the number of flights at its discretion (Article 7), the replacement of tariff approval by governments with notification (Article 8), the mutual recognition of certificates and airworthiness (Article 10), and the granting carriers broad commercial rights, including the freedom to choose their own ground handling service providers (Article 12). Schlumberger and Weisskopf point out that the Damascus Agreement on open skies offers more opportunities than the Yamoussoukro Decision of 1999. They argue that, in addition to the deregulatory measures for the aviation market, it also contains competition rules and a procedure for resolving conflicts.[146] In this context, the provisions of Article 19 prohibiting the granting of state aid by governments to designated air carriers, as this would be contrary to the principles of fair and equal competition, are of particular importance. In exceptional circumstances, such assistance may be provided, but on a transparent and temporary basis. Under the agreement, the states undertook to comply with safety rules (Article 22) and international conventions and standards on aviation security (Article 23) against acts of illegal aggression against the safety of aircraft, their crews and passengers, airports, and to act in accordance with appropriate procedures.

The open skies agreement contributes to building a safer region based on uniform rules and procedures, a harmonized approach to aviation safety and security matters, and further deepening the process of regional unity.

142 *Ibidem*, p.254.
143 Article 2 paragraph 3 of the open skies agreement.
144 Article 4 (3) of the open skies agreement.
145 Article 5 of the open skies agreement.
146 Schlumberger Ch. E., Weisskopf N., op. cit., p. 254.

3.5.4 Safety oversight system in the Middle East

The experience gained from the existing safety oversight bodies around the world indicate that this is an effective and sustainable regional solution to strengthen member states' safety oversight capabilities. These institutions effectively extend the scope of cooperation, not only between member states, but also by maintaining regular relations with similar institutions worldwide. This leads to greater integration in the field of aviation safety, an exchange of experience and proactive action towards the harmonization of aviation regulations.

For many years, ICAO has been promoting and cooperating with states in the establishment and implementation of regional safety oversight institutions. Together with ACAC, they contributed to the creation of the Regional Safety Oversight Organization for the Middle East and North Africa (MENA RSOO). Nine states from the region (Bahrain, Egypt, Jordan, Qatar, Kuwait, Marocco, Oman, Saudi Arabia, and Sudan) brought this institution into existence based on the 2018 Memorandum of Understanding (MOA).[147] The organization has the following functions:[148]

a) conducting safety audits and inspections in the areas of personnel licensing, air operations, airworthiness, airports and air navigation services;
b) promoting the harmonization of aviation regulations in the region and developing guidelines;
c) organizing and cnducting training, in accordance with the arrangements of the member states;
d) providing support in the implementation of the national safety program;
e) advising on the implementation of the sustainable development policy of aviation and assisting member states in planning and implementing environmental protection measures, including the legal CORSIA mechanism[149] adopted by ICAO in 2016.

147 This document is not an international agreement. In the legal context, it is a form of declaration of states that can later be transformed into a more formalized legal act, e.g. an international agreement. Based on: ICAO, Agenda Item 29: Aviation Safety and Air Navigation Regional Implementation Coordination Mechanisms.

148 http://icscc.org.cn/upload/file/20221215/20221215160026_47549.pdf, accessed 25.01.2023.

149 The Carbon Offsetting and Reduction Scheme for International Aviation (CORSIA) is a program adopted by ICAO in 2016 and is an initiative developed by ICAO to offset greenhouse gas emissions from international flights. The main objective of CORSIA is to stabilize the growth of CO2 emissions from international aviation at the 2020 level and, in the longer term, to reduce emissions to sustainable levels. CORSIA mechanism is market-based, which means that it allows emissions to be offset through the purchase of certificates from emission reduction projects. Airlines that exceed their emissions targets will be required to purchase these certificates to compensate for their excess emissions. Certifications will come from certified emission reduction projects (CERs), such as renewable energy initiatives and energy efficiency activities. The implementation of CORSIA is voluntary in the first phase (2021-2023), and participating countries will choose to participate. Between 2024 and 2026, CORSIA will become mandatory for all international flights departing from ICAO member states that agree to participate in the program. In the third phase,

MENA RSOO meetings are held in Riyadh, Saudi Arabia, where the organization is based. The first meeting of this institution took place on October 1, 2018 in Riyadh. The next meeting was scheduled for March 9, 2020, but due to the COVID-19 pandemic, it was postponed by two years to February 13, 2022.[150] The work of MENA RSOO is led by a steering committee consisting of all member states and two institutions as observers: ICAO and ACAO. Its main tasks are: managing the organization, formulating its policies, and making both organizational and financial decisions. At its second meeting in 2022, decisions were taken on the extension of the structure with new institutional bodies, and the necessary staff to carry out these functions. Other states in the Middle East region were also invited to participate in this form of cooperation. It is worth noting that this is an institution in the process of formation, the structures have not been fully developed. One of the reasons is certainly the impact of the COVID-19 pandemic and the legal restrictions resulting from this fact. MENA RSOO is an integral element of the regional integration process.

3.5.5 Nature and scope of responsibilities of RASG-MID

The Regional Aviation Safety Group for the Middle East (RASG-MID) was established in 2011. Its members are: Bahrain, Egypt, Iraq, Iran, Yemen, Jordan, Kuwait, Libya, Lebanon, Oman, Qatar, Saudi Arabia, Sudan, Syria, and United Arab Emirates. The first meeting took place in Cairo, Egypt, on September 18–19, 2011. During these deliberations, it was stressed that the establishment of the RASG-MID meets the expectations and recommendations formulated by the ICAO.[151] According to Mohamed Khonji, the ICAO Director-General responsible for the Middle East, the establishment of RASG-MID marks the beginning of a new era in safety risk management that requires close cooperation between all parties.[152] RASG-MID is a regional institution created to promote aviation safety in the Middle East region in the broadest sense.

The tasks of the institution focus on issues such as:

a) supporting the implementation of the GANP and achieving the safety objectives set out in the Middle East Safety Strategy;
b) identifying hazards and the main areas of aviation safety risk;
c) publishing prompt and transparent information on safety in the region.

from 2027 onwards, this mechanism will be mandatory for all international flights. See https://aviationbenefits.org/environmental-efficiency/climate-action/offsetting-emissions-corsia/corsia/corsia-explained/, accessed 29.01.2024.

150 MIDANPIRG/19 & RASG-MID/9-WP/9, Outcomes of the 2nd MENA RSOO Technical Meeting, Riyadh, Saudi Arabia, February 14–17, 2022.

151 Report of the First Meeting of the Middle East Regional Aviation Safety Group, Cairo, Egypt, September 18–19, 2011, RASG-MID/1-REPORT. See https://www.icao.int/MID/Documents/2011/RASG_MID_1/Docs/rasg_mid_1_Final_Report_EN.pdf, accessed 25.01.2024.

152 *Ibidem*.

The tasks assigned tothis institution are important not only for member states or intergovernmental and non-governmental aviation organizations, but also for airlines and the industry environment, in particular tourism. First of all, because they show the image of the current state of the safety level based on the statistics and data analysis. All stakeholders can identify the areas of risk, threats, and challenges in the region. In addition, these insights can guide future actions and policies of individual entities in relation to the states of the region. By highlighting the factors determining the level of safety and risk, it is possible to determine the level of attractiveness of the state (or parts of it), which may, in turn, lead to increased tourism or investments.

The RASG-MID plays a key role in ensuring the highest level of aviation safety in the Middle East and works closely with other regional and international organizations to achieve its goals. By 2028, the goal is for all states to fully implement safety oversight systems and predictive risk management.[153]

RASG-MID also presents the state of safety and the number of air accidents in the region by publishing annual reports. The first report was produced in 2012. In the light of the 2021 report, the accident rate in the region in 2016–2020 was slightly higher than the global average, at 0.73 (global indicator: 0.43). The report highlights that no fatalities were reported in 2017 and 2019.[154] Table 3.6 shows the accident rate per million flight operations in the Middle East region compared to the global rate.

The number of accidents in the Middle East region was the highest between 2009 and 2010, with rates three times higher than the global average during that period. Since 2011, a downward trend in the number of accidents has been observed in the region, with the exception of 2014 where several serious air accidents occurred, resulting in a higher rate. However, during the years of 2021 and 2023, there were no accidents reported per million operations in the Middle East region.

It is worth noting that despite the reduced number of operations performed in 2020 due to restrictions related to the COVID-19 pandemic, an exceptionally high number of accidents were recorded that year (four in total, resulting in the death of 176 people). This pushed the accident rate up to 5.76, the highest among all world regions.[155] In 2020, 22.47 million operations were performed, representing a 42% decrease compared to 2019 (38.4 million).[156]

Given the adverse aviation safety effects of the Middle East crisis, including heightened accident rates and increased fatalities during periods of instability, it is critical to consider the impact of regional conflicts and economic challenges on aviation safety. These factors contribute to increased risks, which are compounded by reduced operational capacities and the strain on regulatory oversight and

153 Report of the Sixth Meeting of the Regional Aviation Safety Group – Middle East, RASG-MID/6, Bahrain, September 26–28, 2017, p. 112.

154 RASG-MID Annual Safety Report 2016–2020, Ed.10, 2021, p.5.

155 *Ibidem*, p.13.

156 *Ibidem*, p.9.

Table 3.6 Comparison of the number of accidents per million operations in the Middle East region with the number in the world between 2009 and 2023

Year	*Accident rate per million operations in the Middle East*	*Accident rate per million operations worldwide*
2009	14.8	4.07
2010	11.78	4.27
2011	4.9	2.8
2012	1.9	2.1
2013	2.8	2.3
2014	4.3	3.0
2015	2.5	2.6
2016	2.3	2.68
2017	1.5	2.42
2018	2.3	1.75
2019	1.5	3.0
2020	5.76	2.09
2021	0.0	1.93
2022	1.72	2.16
2023	0.0	1.82

Source: Own elaboration based on the data of annual reports: RASG-MID Annual Safety Report 2012, 2014, 2015, 2016, 2017, 2018, 2019, 2020, 2021, and 2022.

infrastructure. The crisis has underscored the need for strengthened safety standards and international cooperation to address these challenges effectively.

3.5.6 Outline of the Middle East and North Africa aviation legal system

The Arab community organized within ACAO annually celebrates the Civil Aviation Day on February 7, in order to commemorate the establishment of the Arab Civil Aviation Organization.[157] The previously mentioned situation of aviation safety in the Middle East and North Africa illustrates the legal conditions and describes the institutional system. The process of institution-building in the Middle East and North Africa is not yet well advanced. Although the main institution of the region, ACAO, was established in 1996 with roots dating back to the 1960s, the process of harmonization of aviation law and the implemention of international regulations began to take real forms of action in the second decade of 21st century. This institution is the axis around which the activities of the states of the region in the field of aviation safety are focused.

The numerous meetings within the framework of safety oversight authorities and the regional aviation safety group are commendable, as they aim to foster greater involvement of the states of the region in building a common level of

157 In the rest of the world, International Civil Aviation Day is celebrated annually on December 7. This holiday was established by ICAO in 1994 and aims to increase public awareness of the role of aviation in economic, cultural and social development.

safety. The statistics on the number of accidents are not very encouraging. Factors such as the technical condition of aircraft or the lack of compliance with safety procedures are some of the reasons for the poor level of safety, even during the COVID-19 pandemic, where the number of flights was almost half of what it was before its outbreak. Undoubtedly, 2020 and 2021 were challenging years for the entire aviation sector, as evidenced by the Middle East region where the number of meetings of various bodies was postponed, which also has an impact on the speed and dynamics of changes in civil aviation. Optimistic assumptions for the third decade with the decline in the number of accidents and the strengthening of the legal and organizational framework for aviation safety can be achieved with consistent and coherent implementation of international standards and recommendations, as well as through an effective execution of legal instruments in this regard.

The cooperation between the Arab states and other regions should be assessed positively, as it results in greater coordination between individual institutions and authorities in legislative matters and the acquisition of experience towards the harmonization of aviation safety standards. The region must confront major challenges and security threats by proactively meeting its international obligations.

3.6 Summary

The process of institutionalizing regional aviation safety takes place in different ways around the world. International regulations form the core and guidelines defining the goal of developing uniform standards in the region. These forms of cooperation created globally on one hand respond to the international aviation law requirements, and, on the other, exhibit unique characteristics and specific conditions of each region. Both safety oversight bodies and regional aviation safety groups are an element that integrates and strengthens interdependencies in the era of globalization of international relations. The forms of regional institutionalization presented in this chapter are an example of building responsibility for the process of unification and standardization of aviation law. This contributes to the increase in the level of safety, and has a positive impact on the development of international aviation tourism and fosters economic and investment growth of the region.

4 Impact of the COVID-19 pandemic on air transport safety regulations

4.1 The COVID-19 pandemic and its socio-economic implications

The COVID-19 pandemic was caused by the new coronavirus SARS-CoV-2, first detected in Wuhan, China in December 2019. Soon after, the disease began to spread rapidly, and in early 2020, the pandemic became a global problem. Within months of the first cases in China, the virus had spread around the world. The WHO declared COVID-19 a pandemic on March 11, 2020, when the number of cases and deaths worldwide was rising rapidly.[1] Initially, the pandemic was mainly concentrated in Asia, but quickly spread around the world. In March 2020, Europe became the new epicenter of the pandemic, with the number of infections and deaths starting to rise dramatically in countries such as Italy and Spain.[2]

The COVID-19 pandemic has affected the lives of people around the world. Hughes shows social effects in the form of increased boredom during the pandemic. He believes that social distancing measures have caused both a widespread loss of meaning and a significant disruption of the temporal experience.[3] Other social effects include an increase in drug use and drug overdoses. Ali Moghtaderi *et al.* link these phenomena to the social disruption resulting from the COVID-19 pandemic.[4] Many scientists observe the impact of the pandemic on psychological changes in people. Shu-Hui Lee and Kuan-Te Lee, describing the negative consequences of the pandemic on mental health, highlight the impact of pandemic-related stress on prejudices and anxieties.[5]

1 Cucinotta D., Vanelli M., *WHO declares COVID-19 a pandemic*, Acta Biomedica, Vol. 91, No. 1, 19 March 2020, pp. 157–160. doi: 10.23750/abm.v91i1.9397. PMID: 32191675; PMCID: PMC7569573. Maxmen A., *Wuhan market was epicentre of pandemic's start, studies suggest*, Nature Magazine, Vol. 603, 27 February 2022, pp. 15–16. *doi.org/10.1038/d41586-022-00584-8.*

2 ESPON STUDY, *Geography of COVID-19 outbreak and first policy answers in European regions and cities*, Luxembourg 2020, pp. 9–11.

3 Hughes E., *Meaninglessness and monotony in pandemic boredom*, Phenomenology and the Cognitive Sciences, Springer Nature, 2023, doi.org/10.1007/s11097-023-09888-0.

4 Moghtaderi A., Zocchi M. S., Pines J. M., Venkat A., Black B., *Estimating the Uncertain Effect of the COVID Pandemic on Drug Overdoses*, 2023, doi.org/10.1101/2023.01.19.23284772.

5 Shu-Hui L., Kuan-Te L., *The impact of pandemic-related stress on attentional bias and anxiety in alexithymia during the COVID-19 pandemic*, 2022, doi.org/10.21203/rs.3.rs-2410934/v1.

DOI: 10.4324/9781003557876-5

Many countries introduced restrictive measures, such as closing schools, shops, and businesses, to prevent the spread of the virus. Many sectors of the economy, including tourism and air transport, were severely affected by the pandemic. Within months of the outbreak of the pandemic, many countries put in place a number of measures to contain the spread of the virus. The introduction of legal restrictions, such as lockdowns (2020 and 2021) or the subsequent vaccination process in 2021 and 2022, contributed to a decrease in the number of infections and deaths.[6]

The COVID-19 pandemic significantly affected air transport around the world. Air transport was the most affected mode of transport by the COVID-19 pandemic.[7] The legal restrictions imposed in connection with the continuation of this pandemic were a considerable difficulty, but also a challenge for the aviation industry. Aviation was most affected by the state restrictions. As Tikhonov and Sazonov note, the pandemic devastated air transport, e.g. cancellations for many months, which led the industry into serious financial problems.[8] Various determinants of the COVID-19 pandemic for aviation can be identified, particularly legal, political, economic, and social.

4.2 Global and regional legal instruments related to the state of the COVID-19 pandemic and safety in air transport

Analyzing the issues of changes in aviation law and aviation procedures, the COVID-19 pandemic resulted in the introduction of a number of modifications, both by individual countries in their internal legislation and by international organizations. At this point, it is necessary to point out the most important revisions in aviation regulations related to the pandemic and regarding safe travel, which were introduced at that time.

4.2.1 Regulations in Europe

In Europe, the process of regulation related to the COVID-19 pandemic was introduced by the EU, as well as by other intergovernmental aviation organizations (ECAC, Eurocontrol, and EASA, which is affiliated with the EU). Since the beginning of introducing the state of pandemic by the WHO on March 11, 2020, numerous legal documents and guidelines for member states on the procedures to be used have been issued. The Commission communication “Temporary framework

6 Coccia M., *COVID-19 pandemic over 2020 (with lockdowns) and 2021 (with vaccinations): similar effects for seasonality and environmental factors*, Environmental Research, Vol. 208 (2022) 112711, pp. 1–11, doi: 10.1016/j.envres.2022.112711. Epub 2022 Jan 13. PMID: 35033552; PMCID: PMC8757643.

7 Chunli Z., Jianping W., Mingyu L., Linyang W., Duowei L., Kouvelas A., *Recovery preparedness of global air transport influenced by COVID-19 pandemic: Policy intervention analysis*, Transport Policy 106 (2021), p. 60.

8 Tikhonov, A. and Sazonov, A., *Major trends in aviation industry during COVID-19*, Journal of Applied Engineering Science, Vol. 20. No. 4, 2022, p. 1094.

for state aid measures to support the economy in the current COVID-19 outbreak" of March 20, 2020, should be recalled here.[9] The Commission encouraged countries to provide public support to companies facing financial difficulties during the COVID-19 crisis. The Commission thus gave broad approval to the use of state aid in the light of the provisions of Article 107 TFEU. Aksamovic and Simunovic pointed out that the state aid scheme for the aviation sector had become more flexible and that the aid granted to individual undertakings had become faster and less formal.[10]

The EU Temporary Framework instrument was applied from March 19, 2020, to June 30, 2022. The European Commission didn't decide to extend it for another period.[11] European Commission Vice-President Margrethe Vestager, Commissioner for Competition, underlined that the instrument had issued a number of horizontal rules that had helped businesses during the COVID-19 pandemic. Vestager concluded that more than 1,300 pandemic-related decisions had been issued, and more than 950 national countermeasures related to the granting of state aid totaling €3.2 trillion had been approved. Of this amount, more than €750 billion was actually spent between March 2020 and June 2021.[12] However, a reservation was made that the investment support instrument could be continued until December 31, 2022 (with an option to convert and restructure until June 30, 2023), and the Solvency Support Instrument could be continued until December 31, 2023.[13] Among air carriers and airports in Europe, the following received aid, for instance: Lufthansa Group (a German carrier; recapitalization from the German government in the amount of €6 billion and loans of €3 billion),[14] LOT (a Polish carrier, €600 million in the form of loans and €250 million in the form of recapitalization),[15] Berlin Brandenburg Airport (Germany; €1.7 billion recapitalization from the German government),[16] Air France-KLM (a carrier of the Dutch-French group; €1 billion recapitalization from the Dutch government and an equal amount from the French government).[17]

9 OJ *C 91I, 20.3.2020.*

10 Dubravka A., Simunovic L., *The EU scheme for the state aid rules in the air transport sector during the Covid-19 crisis*, Juridical Tribune, Vol. 12, No. 1, March 2022, p. 54.

11 European Commission – Statement, State aid: Commission will phase out State aid COVID Temporary Framework, Brussels, 12 May 2022.

12 *Ibidem.*

13 *Ibidem.*

14 European Commission press release, *State aid: Commission approves €6 billion German measure to recapitalise Lufthansa*, 25.06.2020.

15 LOT Polish Airlines, https://www.lot.com/pl/en/corporate/state-aid, accessed 27.01.2024.

16 Petrauskaite G., *Berlin Brandenburg airport to receive €1.7 billion state aid*, 2.02.2022, https://www.aerotime.aero/articles/30122-eu-commission-approves-aid-to-brandenburg-airport, accessed 27.01.2024.

17 OECD, *State Support to the Air Transport Sector: Monitoring developments related to the Covid-19 crisis*, 21.04.2021, pp. 44, 64.

4.2.2 Regulations in the US

In the US, the system of state aid for air transport safety was very broad. The aid was granted on the basis of a number of legal instruments, including the three most important ones: the CARES Act, the Consolidated Appropriations Act (CAA), and the American Rescue Plan Act.

Safety issues in air transport were addressedas legal solutions in the US. The Coronavirus Aid, Relief, and Economic Safety Act (CARES) was passed by the US Congress on March 25, 2020, and signed into law by US President Donald Trump on March 27, 2020.[18] This wasa very important piece of legislation. It provided economic assistance to individuals and businesses affected by the COVID-19 pandemic. One of the provisions of the CARES Act was a program to support employees in the aviation industry.

The CARES Act provided financial assistance to airlines and contractors in the aviation industry. This was aimed at stabilizing the economic situation, which had been drastically and dramatically threatened by legal restrictions imposed on air transport. Based on these provisions, a legal instrument was activated in the form of bank loans and guarantees granted to airlines to provide liquidity that had been directly affected and had suffered losses due to the COVID-19 outbreak. Under the program, $50 billion was allocated to subsidies to airlines operating passenger services, including traditional air carriers and low-cost, regional carriers, for the sole purpose of continuing to pay salaries, wages, and employee benefits.[19] In addition, the CARES Act provided for $8 billion in subsidies to cargo air carriers.[20]

This program was designed to help the aviation industry that had been affected by the COVID-19 pandemic. Many airlines experienced a significant drop in demand for air travel, resulting in reduced revenue and layoffs.

The CARES Act was intended to help keep the airline industry profitable and preserve jobs. The measures envisaged under the scheme were conditional on air carriers and other entities refraining from laying off employees or reducing wage rates and employee benefits until September 30, 2020. The CARES Act also required airlines to maintain certain levels of air service for the communities they served before the pandemic outbreak. Regulations adopted in a crisis situation were associated with a risk on the part of the government providing such substantial financial assistance to enterprises. Therefore, special provisions were made for the financial protection of the government. The regulations stipulated that the federal government should be adequately compensated for the risks associated with lending and loan guarantees. The instrument guaranteeing the financial protection fromthe federal government was to be a special trust fund for airports and air carriers, established on the provisions of section 9502 of the Tax Code.[21] Entities that received special government financial support were required to share a portion

18 PUBLIC LAW 116–136 — MARCH 27, 2020 134 STAT 281.
19 Sec.3102 (b) (1) of CARES Act.
20 Sec.3102 (b) (2) of CARES Act.
21 26 US Code, Sec.9502, Airport and Airway Trust Fund, Public Law 117–328.

of the profits with the federal government under the terms of the CARES Act. Once the US Secretary of Transportation signed an agreement on behalf of the federal government with an interested party, the US government acquired the right to share in the profits of that entity. In addition, under Sec.3104 of the CARES Act, the Secretary of Transportation could provide for the air carrier to receive relief from legal arrangements to operate a scheduled air transport service without interruption. The purpose of such regulations was to consider the interests of small and remote (peripheral) communities that relied on air transport. In addition, the CARES Act included provisions for the suspension of certain taxes and air charges.[22].The non-call period for the payment of excise duty for kerosene lasted from the entry into force of the CARES Act until December 31, 2020. It wasalso stipulated that no other tax specified in separate federal regulations would be imposed during this period.[23]

Overall, the CARES Act played a vital role in helping to keep the US aviation industry alive and preventing further job losses during the COVID-19 pandemic.

Another important piece of legislation to ensure the safety of the aviation sector was the Consolidated Appropriations Ac It was another regulation, following the CARES Act that addressed the safe operation of air transport during the COVID-19 pandemic.

The Consolidated Appropriations Act, 2021 (CAA) was an expenditure act that was passed by the US Congress on December 21, 2020, and signed into law by US President Donald Trump on December 27, 2020.[24] The Act contained several provisions concerning the aviation industry. One of the most important provisions of the CAA for the aviation industry was the continuation of the Payroll Support Program (PSP), which was first established under the CARES Act. The PSP provided financial assistance to air carriers operating passenger operations, including large airlines and regional carriers, and their contractors, enabling them to continue paying salaries, wages, and employee benefits. The CAA granted an additional $1.5 billion to fund the PSP, allowing the program to continue and support the aviation industry and its employees.[25]

The CAA regulation also provided for the financing of investments in airport infrastructure and improvements in safety. The bill had allocated $2 billion in grants for capital investment in airports and $45 million to improve safety at smaller airports.[26]

22 Sec.3201 of CARES Act.

23 26 US Code, Sec.4261: Imposition of tax, Public law 117–328.

24 H.R.133 – Consolidated Appropriations Act, 2021, Public Law 116–260.

25 United States Government Accountability Office, COVID19 PANDEMIC Preliminary Observations on Efforts toward and Factors Affecting the Aviation Industry's Recovery, 2.03.2021, GAO-21-412T, p. 4.

26 NBAA, *Provisions of Interest to Business Aviation in the Consolidated Appropriations Act of 2021*, 11.01.2021, https://nbaa.org/aircraft-operations/safety/coronavirus/provisions-of-interest-to-business-aviation-in-the-consolidated-appropriations-act-of-2021/, accessed 30.01.2024.

In addition, the CAA provided funding to the Federal Aviation Administration (FAA) and other aviation-related agencies. The bill allocated $1.75 billion to the FAA to support its operations, including modernizing the country's air traffic control system.[27]

Overall, the Consolidated Appropriations Act, 2021 provided important support and funding for the aviation industry in the US. It enabled the continuation of the wage support program and the financing of investments in airport infrastructure and FAA operations.

In the context of aviation safety regulations during the COVID-19 pandemic, it is also worth mentioning the American Rescue Plan Act (ARPA). The American Rescue Plan provided nearly $10 billion for states, territories, and tribes to provide relief for the country's most vulnerable homeowners.

ARPA was the Support and Financial Assistance Act, signed into law by the newly elected US President, Joe Biden on March 11, 2021,[28] which contained many provisions for various sectors of the economy, including the aviation industry. It was commonly called the anti-covid stimulus package.

Under the ARPA, airlines received additional funding to maintain employment and pay salaries to employees. The bill provided for $14 billion in aid to airlines, including major carriers, regional carriers, and their subcontractors. These funds were to be used to pay salaries and other employee benefits and to maintain employment in the aviation industry.[29]

ARPA also envisaged financing investments in airport infrastructure and improving flight safety. The bill provided $8 billion in aid to airports, including funding for infrastructure investments and upgrades to facilities such as lighting systems, runways, and terminals. In addition, the ARPA's provisions stipulated that the Federal Aviation Administration (FAA) would be responsible for distributing the awarded funds. This institution was also to finance projects related to aviation safety, including the modernization of the air traffic control system in the country and scientific research related to flight safety.[30]

In this way, the provisions of the American Rescue Plan Act provided important support and funding for the aviation industry in the US, which allowed it to maintain employment and develop airport infrastructure. The funds received under this instrument offered economic assistance to the heavily affected aviation industry as a result of the COVID-19 pandemic and allowed it to safely maintain and continue its activities.

27 FAA, *Airport Improvement Program (AIP) 2021–2023 Supplemental Appropriation*, https://www.faa.gov/airports/aip/aip_supplemental_appropriation/2021, accessed 29.01.2024.

28 H.R.1319 - American Rescue Plan Act, Public Law 117–2.

29 U.S. Airlines, *Aviation Contractors to Receive Additional $15 Billion Under American Rescue Plan Act*, 3/16/2021, https://www.jdsupra.com/legalnews/u-s-airlines-aviation-contractors-to-2900824/, accessed 3.02.2024.

30 FAA, *Airport Rescue Grants*, https://www.faa.gov/airports/airport_rescue_grants, accessed 30.01.2024.

The COVID-19 pandemic affected air transport worldwide, not just in selected countries. In each, adequate support was introduced to limit as much as possible the negative effects of this serious health crisis. The aid package ran from the early months of 2020 to 2022, and sometimes with the extension of certain legislative acts until 2023. The support provided as part of the fight against the socio-economic consequences of the COVID-19 pandemic has been fundamental for air transport safety. The crucial thing was that the safety of flight operations was not restricted, all users could safely use air transportation, and service providers could perform services with legal safety guarantees.

4.3 Consequences of legal regulations and procedures related to the COVID-19 pandemic on air transport

The effects of legal restrictions on air transport were enormous. They were not only related to legal changes but also had consequences for the state's economy. Many problems arose in managing the COVID-19 pandemic. It is crucial to mention four legal conditions regarding civil aviation safety in the context of this pandemic.

The first is border closures and travel restrictions. Many countries have introduced travel restrictions, including border closures and the requirement to be tested for COVID-19 before departure and/or upon arrival. These requirements varied from country to country, but typically included PCR tests or rapid antigen tests. This forced airlines to change flight routes and adapt to the new regulations.

The second is sanitary restrictions. In order to prevent the spread of the virus, numerous legal sanitary restrictions were introduced, such as wearing masks at airports and onboard aircraft, disinfecting surfaces, restricting access to airport terminals, and maintaining social distancing. These restrictions have increased costs and forced airlines to introduce new procedures.

The third is difficulties in doing business. The COVID-19 pandemic caused many difficulties for airlines and manufacturers of aircraft and other aviation parts in running their business. Tikhonov and Sazonov point out that the American aircraft manufacturer Boeing had to stop production and reduce jobs due to low demand.[31] Other manufacturers experienced similar setbacks, which becamecommon practice during that time. The two largest aircraft manufacturers, Boeing and Airbus, were hit hard by a drastic reduction of orders. Airbus recorded only 383 aircraft orders in 2020, compared to 1,131 orders in 2019. Simultaneously, Airbus delivered 566 aircraft in 2020, 36% less than in the previous year. Boeing recorded an even greater decline, namely, it commissioned 157 aircraft in 2020, which is 59% less than in the previous year and 81% less than in 2018 (when 806 machines were put into service).[32] Many air carriers had to change their strategies and adapt to new regulations and restrictions, which adversely affected their profitability.

31 Tikhonov, A. and Sazonov, A., op. cit., p. 1095.

32 Kalic M., Babic D., Dozic S., Kuljanin J., Mijovic N., *Impact of Covid-19 on the aviation industry: an overview of global and some local effects*, p. 1107. Anali Pravnog fakulteta u Beogradu 2022, Vol. 70, No. 4, s.1079–1127. Doi:10.51204/Anali_PFBU_22405A.

The fourth is the introduction of specific procedures. In order to prevent the spread of the virus, a number of specific procedures were introduced, such as limiting the number of passengers on board, the requirement to present a COVID-19 test result before the flight, as well as mandatory quarantines for passengers arriving from abroad. Initially, in the first months of the COVID-19 pandemic in the first half of 2020, many air carriers blocked middle seats on board aircraft in order to maintain social distancing. These procedures were reviewed after a few months, and some carriers abandoned them, and some continued to maintain these rules for the subsequent months.[33] For instance, American Airlines and United Airlines lifted the middle seat lockdown policy on July 1, 2020, while low-cost carrier Southwest Airlines kept the middle seat empty until October 31, 2020.[34] However, another US carrier, Delta, kept the middle seat empty until May 1, 2021.[35] The policy of each carrier was different because there were no "hard" ICAO requirements or other legal regulations regarding middle seat occupancy. In Europe, on the other hand, many European carriers demanded that the European Commission, on behalf of the EU, should not introduce any legal mandates for blocking middle seats on board aircraft, arguing that such measures had no proven health benefits, and only limited carriers' revenue potential.[36] The head of European low-cost giant Ryanair, Michael O'Leary, called the concept of social distancing on board the aircraft "idiotic", adding that his company would not resume flights if such a law waspassed.[37] Ultimately, the European Commission didnot pass such a regulation.

The introduction of detailed COVID-19 procedures was arduous for passengers, as it was necessary to appear at check-in much earlier than before. It was necessary to present various documents before boarding, in addition to boarding pass and travel documents such as a passport or identity document, they also needed to provide a COVID-19 test certificate with a negative result taken within 48 hours (or even 24 hours) before departure. There were testing points at airports , but these tests were relatively expensive. Before traveling, if a passenger did not have such a certificate, they were forced to perform such a test at the airport. A similar situation also awaited the passengers after landing at the destination. In many countries, legal regulations were introduced requiringthat passengers either present tests specified by national law upon arrival or have them performed at the airport. The whole procedure was time-consuming, which negatively affected the aviation industry. Many people pointed out that carriers and airports would need

33 White A., 63% of U.S. consumers are willing to pay more to have seats blocked – here are the airline policies on this, Select, 2.12.2020, https://www.cnbc.com/select/coronavirus-airline-crowded-flight-policies/, accessed 20.01.2024.

34 *Ibidem.*

35 Griff Z., *How I secure empty middle seats — even if an airline isn't blocking them*, 18.04.2021, https://thepointsguy.com/news/tips-for-empty-middle-seat/, accessed 1.02.2024.

36 Morgan S., *EU circles around aircraft middle-seat issue in virus travel plans*, 13.05.2020, https://www.euractiv.com/section/aviation/news/eu-circles-around-aircraft-middle-seat-issue-in-virus-travel-plans/, accessed 30.01.2024.

37 *Ibidem.*

to take many steps towards enhanced cleanliness and hygiene in future to increase passengers' confidence in air travel or raise safety standards. Such a view is reflected, for instance, in the work of Kalic, Babic, Dozic, Kuljanin, and Mijovic.[38]

From today's standpoint, as strict pandemic restrictions and regulations from 2020–2022/2023 are being lifted, it is evident that these scenarios did not materialize. Of course, hygiene and cleanliness remain important elements of service quality. Passengers desire to fly and their safety has long been safeguarded by numerous regulations introduced well before the onset of COVID-19 pandemic. Air transport has retained the trust of passengers, who did not lost confidence in it, however, they were simply restricted from flying due to external circumstances. The statistics showed a significant increase in the number of passengers in 2023, and 2024 became the first year in which passenger figures surpassed those recorded in 2019. Therefore, the focus now should not be on restoring passengers' trust in the aviation industry in connection with the pandemic, but rather on reopening the possibility of air travel.

The safety regulations to be met by carriers and airports were sufficient in most regions of the world, as demonstrated in this monograph. Compliance with those regulations proved adequate, and in regions where standards were weaker, existing mechanisms and legal instruments were implemented to ensure the highest safety standards for all users. Passengers' confidence in aviation was based on the fact, that it is the safest means of transport. The lower number of passengers in 2020 and 2021 was solely the result of legal restrictions on flight operations, not due to any loss of trust or concerns about the functioning of procedures related to the pandemic. ICAO emphasized that passengers trusted they could fly safely (i.e. all safety regulations for aircraft, and flight crew had been met), operators relied on efficient safety systems to ensure safe operations, and states placed their trust in ICAO, as a platform for unified international standards contributing to the safe operation of air transport.[39] Therefore, it can be concluded that trust resides in a well-functioning passenger-operator-state-ICAO system. The adoption of international air transport safety regulations and their effective implementation, as well as compliance, was the key to ensuring civil aviation safety at a practical level.

Another issue was the mandatory quarantine upon arrival in a country. Many passengers, although they met other regulations (e.g. regarding vaccination), were still quarantined in some countries due to internal regulations (with quarantine duration and location varying from country to country).[40] Quarantine after crossing the border was imposed in the period 2020–2022 by most countries in the world.

38 Kalic M., et al., op.cit., p. 1112.

39 International Aviation Trust Framework (IATF), https://www.icao.int/airnavigation/Pages/IATF.aspx, accessed 5.02.2024.

40 For example, in Poland, from March 2020 to February 2022, the quarantine period was 10 days after crossing the border, either at one's residence or in a special center designated by the sanitary and epidemiological services. From February to March 2022, the quarantine period was reduced to seven days, and from March 28, 2022, it was completely lifted upon arrival in Poland.

In the EU, a Council Recommendation was issued (repeatedly amended during the COVID-19 pandemic) setting out travel rules.[41]

Fifth, the introduction of financial assistance. Many countries introduced special financial assistance programs for airlines affected by the COVID-19 pandemic. Under these programs, airlines received subsidies and loans to cover costs related to the pandemic. It is worth noting that not all airlines received the same level of assistance. Irish carrier Ryanair filed 16 lawsuits against the European Commission in 2020 and 2021, alleging discrimination on the grounds of nationality, as many countries supported their traditional "national" carriers, while excluding other operators, and the European Commission approved such aid.[42] Although, in its rulings, the Court of Justice dismissed these actions, finding that the aid provided by France,[43] Finland,[44] Germany,[45] and Sweden[46] was in line with EU state aid law and did not constitute discrimination, Ryanair has so far won two cases: one concerning aid to KLM[47] (in combination with the Netherlands and France) and another from Portugal[48] in the case of aid to TAP Portugal.

Sixth, mention should be made of the development of technology. In response to the COVID-19 pandemic, many technologies related to air transport were developed, including contactless payment solutions, automated check-in and security checks, and air purification systems in aircraft.

Seventh, international regulations. International aviation institutions such as ICAO and EASA introduced new aviation regulations to combat the spread of the virus.

4.4 Legal instruments on state aid to the aviation industry affected by the COVID-19 outbreak

The outbreak of the pandemic caused huge perturbations in air transport, which is why it was necessary to introduce state aid to counteract these negative effects. Numerous legal regulations were introduced worldwide enabling states to help companies involved in air transport. The legal instruments were designed to allow the state to lawfully transfer funds to help the aviation sector, in order to prevent massive job cuts and bankruptcy of many entities. This was also linked to the state's imposition of restrictions on aviation activities, which obliged the state to provide such support to entities affected by these restrictions. State aid was intended to ensure financial stability for airlines and to prevent bankruptcies and job losses.

41 Council Recommendation (EU) 2020/1475 of 13 October 2020 on a coordinated approach to restrictions on free movement in response to the COVID-19 pandemic. *L* 337, 14.10.2020, pp. 3–9.
42 Dubravka A., Lidija S., op. cit., p. 63.
43 Case: T-259/20 Ryanair/Commission.
44 Case: T-657/20 Ryanair/Commission.
45 Case: T-577/20 Ryanair/Commission.
46 Case: T-238/20 Ryanair/Commission.
47 Case: T-643/20 Ryanair/Commission.
48 Case: T-465/20 Ryanair/Commission.

The forms of public support for the aviation industry during the pandemic varied by country and could include the following instruments:

1. government loans and guarantees – many countries provided loans or guarantees on loans to airlines, helping to ensure their financial stability;
2. subsidies and non-refundable subsidies – some countries provided airlines with subsidies or non-refundable subsidies to cover operating costs and ensure business continuity;
3. deferrals of payments – governments deferred the payment of taxes or airport service charges to help airlines maintain financial liquidity;
4. abolition or reduction of charges – some countries lowered or completely abolished airport charges, which helped reduce costs for airlines;
5. competition sanctions – in some cases, governments applied competition sanctions to help the national airline maintain its position in the market.

Legal solutions in Europe were noteworthy. It should be stated at the outset that in the EU, state aid to entities engaged in economic activity was, in principle, incompatible with EU law, as provided for in Article 107(1) of the TFEU – Lisbon Treaty. EU treaty law regulated the granting of state aid to all entities in accordance with the principles of free competition and non-distortion of the internal market. State aid, in light of the provisions of the Treaty, had to be notified to the European Commission.[49] However, there were a few exceptions. Considering the general content of the competition rules in the TFEU, aid was compatible with treaty law, if one of the following applied:

a) aid of a social character granted to individual consumers (Article 107(2)(a) TFEU);
b) aid to repair the damage caused by natural disasters or emergencies (Article 107(2)(b) TFEU);
c) aid granted to the eastern regions of the Federal Republic of Germany (Article 107(2)(c) TFEU).

The notification procedure consisted of the European Commission examining whether the proposed state aid measure did not affect competition and the internal market. In the event of a positive agreement, the member state could grant the measure under the conditions laid down in the Commission's decision. The decision was legally binding. Any aid other than that referred to in Article 107(2) had to be notified, subject to other rules provided in the next paragraph.

The crisis situation related to the COVID-19 pandemic necessitated a horizontal approach, as individual actions would have significantly extended the consent period. In the first days following the declaration of the pandemic, the European

49 Article 108(3) TFEU.

Commission issued a communication that set out the rules of conduct in a coherent and general manner for everyone.[50] According to the Commission, the situation caused by the pandemic was classified as a "state of emergency". Therefore, the provision of support to aviation companies affected by the COVID-19 outbreak was considered compatible aid under Article 107(2)(b). TFEU. In other cases, it was necessary to notify the Commission to seek its approval for the application of a support measure to the undertaking. Under Article 108(3)(b), aid could be granted where "a serious disturbance in the economy of a member state was being remedied". This situation, in principle, required a notification procedure. However, the Commission clearly stated that the COVID-19 pandemic affected entire countries, significantly impeded the functioning of state economies, and that the restrictions introduced prevented companies from operating normally. In this context, it was considered that state aid was justified and could be granted to an entity under Article 108(3)(b) until the liquidity problems caused by pandemic restrictions were resolved. This position was consistent with the case law of the Court of Justice in this regard.[51]

An exception to the notification procedure was state aid in one of three areas:

1. group exclusions;
2. service of general interest;
3. *de minimis* aid.

The first exception was when the state designed aid measures in accordance with the General Block Exemption Regulation.[52] The EU regulation defined a broad scope of horizontal aid granted to airlines. This included social assistance for passenger air transport in peripheral regions, which occurred when the carrier ensured the continuity of connections for residents living in remote regions and reduced their transport costs.[53]

The second legal exception was the provision of services of general interest (PSO). The legal basis for the imposition of public service obligations was found in Articles 16 to 18 of Regulation 1008/2008.[54] Public service obligation could be

50 Communication from the Commission on the Temporary Framework for State aid measures to support the economy in the context of the ongoing COVID-19 outbreak. *C* 911, 20.3.2020.

51 Joined Cases T-132/96 and T-143/96 Freistaat Sachsen, Volkswagen AG and Volkswagen Sachsen GmbH v Commission, ECLI:EU:T:1999:326, paragraph 167. Judgment upheld on appeal of September 30, 2003, C:2003:510.

52 Commission Regulation (EU) No. 651/2014 of 17 June 2014 declaring certain categories of aid compatible with the internal market in application of Articles 107 and 108 of the Treaty, OJ EU, *L* 187, 26.6.2014.

53 Recital 70 of Commission Regulation No 651/2014. This aid is always granted per air route. According to Article 51(3) of Commission Regulation No 651/2014, it is a route connecting an airport located in a remote (peripheral) region and any other airport located in the European Economic Area.

54 Regulation (EC) No 1008/2008 of the European Parliament and of the Council of 24 September 2008 on common rules for the operation of air services in the *Community*, OJ EC, *L* 293, 31.10.2008.

imposed on both the carrier and the airport, under certain conditions. As far as air carriers were concerned, PSOs were imposed on air routes. The imposition of a PSO on a specific route constituted support provided by the state to outermost regions, which, due to their disadvantaged location, could not fully develop economically. No carrier had previously been interested in serving such regions due to a lack of profitability (low frequency, low number of passengers). In the case of an airport, however, it had to be assessed whether part of its activities could be regarded as activities of general economic interest. According to the interpretation of the European Commission, every activity of an airport was considered an economic activity.[55] However, some of these activities could be classified by the state authorities as being of general economic interest. To this end, the state authorities could impose a public service obligation on the airport operator. In such a situation, the operator could obtain compensation for the provision of such services. It was also possible to consider the management of the airport as a whole as a service of general economic interest. In line with the Commission's position expressed in point 34 in conjunction with point 53(iv) of the 2005 guidelines, the management of such an airport could not include activities not directly linked to its principal activity and commercial operations (e.g. leasing of space). However, this action was rare.

The 2003 Altmark judgment of the Court of Justice of the EU (*Altmark* case) was helpful in clarifying whether public service compensation constituted state aid under Article 107 TFEU.[56] According to the Court, if the following four cumulative conditions were met, the compensation to the airport in this respect would not constitute state aid and would not be subject to the provisions of the TFEU. Firstly, an airport had to be obliged to provide a public service based on clearly defined rules. Secondly, the parameters for granting compensation had to be precisely defined based on objective criteria. Third, the amount of compensation could not exceed what was necessary to cover all or part of the costs associated with the performance of the public service, taking into account a reasonable profit resulting from the performance of those obligations. Fourth, the public service provider had to be selected through a public procurement procedure and deliver the service at the most advantageous price. In the event that other method was chosen, the level of compensation should be determined based on an analysis of the costs that a medium-sized, well-managed undertaking would incur, considering the revenue and reasonable profit resulting from the performance of the specific task. If all four conditions were met, the state could grant compensation to an airport that was not considered state aid under Articles 107 TFEU and 108 TFEU. On the other hand, failure to meet even one of these criteria resulted in the compensation being classified as state aid within the meaning of Article 107 TFEU.

55 See Point 34 of the Community guidelines on airport financing and start-up aid to undertakings departing from regional airports, OJ EC, *C* 312, 9.12.2005.

56 Case C-280/00, judgment of 24 July 2003 in *Altmark Trans and Regierungspresidium Magdeburg* [2003] ECR I-7747.

PSO compensation that qualifies as state aid (if at least one of the Altmark criteria wasnot met) could also have been exempted from the notification procedure, provided that it fulfilled the conditions laid down in the decision regarding services of general interests.[57] This applied to both air carriers and airports. One condition concerned air connections with islands where the average annual air traffic during the two financial years preceding the year in which the service of general economic interest was entrusted did not exceed 300,000 passengers.[58] The second condition concerned airports where the volume of traffic in the same period did not exceed 200,000 passengers.[59]

However, the third exception was the application of *de minimis* aid. *De minimis* aid referred to state aid of a small amount that did not exceed certain limits set by the EU. It was not considered state aid if the conditions laid down in Regulation 1407/2013 were fulfilled.[60] According to provisions of Article 3(2) of this Regulation, as part of *de minimis* aid, an airline could receive financial assistance of up to €200,000 over a period of three years.[61] *De minimis* aid could be granted in various forms, such as tax exemptions, tax reliefs, grants, preferential loans, and guarantees.

On the other hand, countries could not immediately react to the crisis in the aviation industry caused by the COVID-19 pandemic. There was a risk that companies would lay off employees or reduce operations, which would cause huge socio-economic disruptions. To counteract this, the EU issued a number of legal regulations and guidelines.

Many countries continued to provide public aid to the aviation industry to help with post-pandemic recovery. However, as the pandemic situation improved, governments began to gradually phase out this support.

4.5 Legal and economic consequences of the COVID-19 pandemic on global air transport

The effects of restrictions in the area of regulation and their impact on the economies of countries were on an unprecedented scale. As a result of the introduction of legal restrictions during the pandemic in 2020–2022, many legal and economic consequences could be mentioned.

57 Commission Decision of 20 December 2011 on the application of Article 106(2) of the Treaty on the Functioning of the European Union to State aid in the form of public service compensation granted to undertakings entrusted with the operation of services of general economic interest, OJ EU, *L* 7 of 11.1.2012.

58 *Ibidem*, Article 2(1)(d).

59 *Ibidem*, Article 2(1)(e).

60 Commission Regulation (EU) No 1407/2013 of 18 December 2013 on the application of Articles 107 and 108 of the Treaty on the Functioning of the European Union to *de minimis aid*, OJ EU, *L 352* of 24.12.2013.

61 This restriction aims to prevent state aid from having an excessive impact on the internal competition of the EU market.

Table 4.1 Summary of data on the impact of the COVID-19 pandemic on international air traffic globally in 2020

Region	*Market share (%)*	*Air traffic in passenger-kilometers (RPK) (%)*	*Number of seats offered in terms of place/kilometer factor (ASK) (%)*	*Aircraft load factor (%)*
World regions	100.0	−65.9	−56.5	64.80
Africa	1.9	−68.8	−61.0	57.4
Asia and the Pacific	38.6	−61.9	−53.9	67.5
Europe	23.6	−69.9	−62.1	67.8
Latin America	5.7	−62.1	−58.3	74.9
Middle East	7.4	−72.2	−63.3	57.6
North America	22.7	−65.2	−50.2	59.2

Source: 2020 Worst Year in History for Air Travel Demand, IATA Press Release, February 3, 2021, https://www.iata.org/en/pressroom/pressroom-archive/2021-releases/2021-02-03-02/, accessed January 30, 2024.

First of all, it was necessary to point out the decrease in the number of passengers and revenues. As a result of the COVID-19 pandemic, the number of passengers, and consequently revenues from the sale of airline tickets, decreased significantly. Many people decided to cancel their air travel. Adewuya's reflections, which analyzed the decline in air traffic during the 2020–2021 pandemic in Nigeria and Africa in general, were valuable.[62] In many cases, airlines were forced to cancel flights, depriving them of the opportunity to earn revenue. The number of passengers decreased significantly as a result of the legal restrictions imposed. Tikhonov and Sazonov showed how noticeably the number of seats offered on board aircraft, the number of passengers transported, and the potential loss of revenue by air carriers decreased compared to 2019 (before the COVID-19 pandemic).[63] Tables 4.1, 4.2, 4.3–4.4 present IATA's statistics on international air traffic and domestic traffic of the main countries in 2020 and 2021, compared to the base year 2019.

The year 2020 turned out to be the worst, with the former Director General of IATA, Alexandre de Juniac, describing it as a disaster. According to de Juniac, the situation deteriorated dramatically at the end of the 2020 holiday season as stricter travel restrictions were introduced in the face of new COVID-19 variants.[64] According to IATA data, passenger demand in international traffic in 2020 was 75.6% lower than in 2019. Equally, a similar decrease occurred in 2021. In international traffic, the number of available seats on board aircraft decreased by 68.1% in 2020, and by 65.3% in 2021. The load factor fell to 62.8% in 2020, and to 58%

62 Akinrinade S. A., *The Impact of COVID-19 Pandemic on the Global Aviation Industry: Nigeria's Experience*, October 2022, DOI: 10.13140/RG.2.2.20810.44485.

63 Tikhonov, A. and Sazonov, A., op. cit., p. 1096.

64 *2020 Worst Year in History for Air Travel Demand, IATA Press Release, 3.02.2021,* https://www.iata.org/en/pressroom/pressroom-archive/2021-releases/2021-02-03-02/, accessed 30.01.2024.

Table 4.2 Summary of data on the impact of the COVID-19 pandemic on domestic air traffic of countries with the largest share of the domestic market in 2020

Region	*Market share (%)*	*Air traffic in passenger-kilometers (RPK) (%)*	*Number of seats offered in terms of place/kilometer factor (ASK) (%)*	*Aircraft load factor (%)*
Domestic market	54.3	−48.8	−35.7	66.6
Australia	0.7	−69.5	−62.8	66.1
Brazil	1.6	−49.0	−47.4	80.3
People's Republic of China	19.9	−30.8	−19.7	72.9
India	2.1	−55.6	−48.0	74.6
Japan	1.4	−53.6	−32.7	50.9
Russian Federation	3.4	−23.5	−12.6	72.9
USA	16.6	−59.6	−41.4	58.8

Source: 2020 Worst Year in History for Air Travel Demand, IATA Press Release, February 2, 2021, https://www.iata.org/en/pressroom/pressroom-archive/2021-releases/2021-02-03-02/, accessed January 31, 2024.

Table 4.3 Summary of data on the impact of the COVID-19 pandemic on international air traffic globally in 2021

Region	*Market share (%)*	*Air traffic in passenger-kilometers (RPK) (%)*	*Number of seats offered in terms of seat/kilometer factor (ASK) (%)*	*Aircraft load factor (%)*
World regions	100	−58.4	−48.8	67.2
Africa	1.9	−62.8	−55.1	59.5
Asia and the Pacific	27.5	−66.9	−56.7	62.6
Europe	24.9	−61.3	−51.9	68.6
Latin America	6.5	−47.4	−43.9	77.3
Middle East	6.5	−69.9	−55.5	51.5
North America	32.6	−39.0	−29.9	73.8

Source: Passenger Demand Recovery Continued in 2021 but Omicron Having Impact, IATA Press Release No. 5, January 25, 2022, https://www.iata.org/en/pressroom/2022-releases/2022-01-25-02/, accessed January 30, 2024.

in 2021. In domestic air traffic, the decreases were slightly smaller, but they were most noticeable in 2020. The demand was 48.8% lower in 2020 and 28.2% lower in 2021 compared to 2019. The number of seats on offer shrank by 35.7% in 2020 and by 19.2% in 2021, while the load factor decreased to 66.6% in 2020 and 74.3% in 2021 (all the above data compared to 2019, the year before the COVID-19 pandemic). Analyzing domestic traffic, it is worth noting that Russia was the only country to record an increase in air traffic in domestic transport. In contrast to other countries where the declines were significant, the number of operations performed in the Russian Federation increased, and its share in the global market rose to 4.5%.

Table 4.4 Summary of data on the impact of the COVID-19 pandemic on domestic air traffic of countries with the largest share of the domestic market in 2021

Region	*Market share (%)*	*Air traffic in passenger-kilometers (RPK) (%)*	*Number of seats offered in terms of seat/kilometer factor (ASK) (%)*	*Aircraft load factor (%)*
Domestic market	62.4	−28.2	−19.2	74.3
Australia	0.7	−62.4	−50.4	61.2
Brazil	1.9	−27.2	−25.1	80.4
People's Republic of China	17.8	−24.4	−8.9	70.2
India	2.2	−41.8	−28.8	71.4
Japan	1.1	−57.9	−38.3	50.4
Russian Federation	4.5	24.2	19.4	86.5
USA	25.6	−23.8	−16.7	78.0

Source: Passenger Demand Recovery Continued in 2021 but Omicron Having Impact, IATA Press Release No. 5, January 25, 2022, https://www.iata.org/en/pressroom/2022-releases/2022-01-25-02/, accessed January 30, 2024.

Table 4.5 Summary of data on the impact of the COVID-19 pandemic on international air traffic globally in 2022

Region	*Market share (%)*	*Air traffic in passenger-kilometers (RPK) (%)*	*Number of seats offered in terms of seat/kilometer factor (ASK) (%)*	*Aircraft load factor (%)*
World regions	100	64.4	39.8	11.8
Africa	2.1	84.9	51.8	12.9
Asia and the Pacific	22.4	34.0	16.8	9.2
Europe	30.4	100.2	66.8	13.5
Latin America	6.4	62.7	54.6	4.0
Middle East	9.8	144.4	67.0	23.9
North America	28.8	45.5	28.5	9.8

Source: Passenger Demand Recovery Continued in December 2022 & for the Full Year, IATA Press Release No. 4, February 6, 2023, https://www.iata.org/en/pressroom/2023-releases/2023-02-06-02/, accessed January 30, 2024.

This could be explained by the lack of such restrictive regulations on air transport, unlike those in many other countries around the world.

The situation improved in 2022. It was a year with restrictions still in place, but they were gradually lifted around the middle of the year. Tables 4.5 and 4.6 show an upward trend, although the levels are still smaller than in 2019.

Another element was the increase in costs. The introduction of additional safety and health procedures, such as aircraft disinfection and mask-wearing requirements, increased costs for airlines. Many air carriers also had to raise costs associated with the storage of aircraft as a result of flight cancellations,

Table 4.6 Summary of data on the impact of the COVID-19 pandemic on domestic air traffic of countries with the largest share of the domestic market in 2022

Region	*Market share (%)*	*Air traffic in passenger-kilometers (RPK) (%)*	*Number of seats offered in terms of seat/kilometer factor (ASK) (%)*	*Aircraft load factor (%)*
Domestic market	42.0	10.9	4.3	4.7
Australia	1.0	111.7	63.1	18.3
Brazil	1.5	29.9	31.8	−1.2
People's Republic of China	6.5	−39.8	−35.2	−5.0
India	2.0	48.8	30.1	10.2
Japan	1.2	75.9	43.4	11.4
USA	19.2	23.7	14.0	6.7

Source: Passenger Demand Recovery Continued in December 2022 and for the Full Year, IATA Press Release No. 4, February 6, 2023, https://www.iata.org/en/pressroom/2023-releases/2023-02-06-02/, accessed January 30, 2024.

which consequently burdened their budgets. State aid became necessary in this situation.

A significant effect of the COVID-19 pandemic on the air transport sector was the reduction of employment. Due to the decline in passenger numbers and revenues, many airlines had to lay off employees, which negatively impacted their costs and ability to provide services. With the inability to perform flight operations, aircraft were grounded. The lack of air traffic, or its drastic reduction, especially in the first months of 2020, resulted in huge costs for carriers. In order to avoid bankruptcy, other temporary measures were applied, such as those by the Irish carrier Aer Lingus: layoffs of employees or salary reductions.[65] Another Asian carrier, AirAsia Group, suspended all its flights for several weeks starting in March 2020, during which time the company's management and senior staff had their salaries reduced by 15% to 100%.[66] Similar difficulties were faced by the Canadian carrier Air Canada, which, for a period of several months starting on April 1, 2020, had to lay off 16,500 employees (out of a total staff of 30,000) and reduce its route network by up to 90% in April 2020.[67]

The process of limiting losses by reducing employees and cutting wages was temporary. Since mid-2022, carriers have recorded an increase in air traffic.

65 Daly, A., *Aer Lingus to cut wages by 50% as airline reduces working hours for month of April*, The Journal.ie, 19.03.2020, https://www.thejournal.ie/aer-lingus-coronavirus-staff-wages-forsa-5051915-Mar2020/, accessed 1.02.2024.

66 Syahirah S. J., *AirAsia, AirAsia X suspend flights, ground most planes; pay cut for top executives*, The Edge Markets, 26.03.2020.

67 Pillar W., *Air Canada to cut 16,500 workers*, Flight Global, 30.03.2020, https://www.flightglobal.com/strategy/air-canada-to-cut-16500-workers/137622.article, accessed 30.01.2024.

However, there was a problem with handling this increasing volume of passengers. With reduced staff, carriers and airports were unable to manage the growing number of passengers effectively. On the one hand, it was welcomed that the situation in air transport was returning to its pre-pandemic state and that more people were using the services of air carriers. On the other hand, this recovery caused difficulties in service. It was not so easy to recruit a large number of employees suddenly as this required completing appropriate security procedures. The recruitment process was quite lengthy, and the holidays of 2022 turned into a nightmare at many airports. The number of airport service and carrier staff was too small to meet the high demand, a direct result of dismissals during the COVID-19 pandemic.[68] The lack of security personnel was particularly acute, as evidenced at many airports, particularly in Europe. Long queues of passengers formed outside the airport, and the waiting time for check-in stretched to several hours.[69]

In Europe, the situation was even more critical, as carriers had to reduce their network of connections or operate "empty" aircraft to avoid losing their takeoff and landing rights (slots) at certain airports. Existing EU aviation rules on slots required carriers to operate during the current season to retain their rights for the following season, following the principle "use it or lose it". Although the European Commission amended these regulations in 2020 and 2021, lowering the thresholds to as little as 50% of operations required to maintain a slot, this situation did not improve. Casrten Spohr, the CEO of the German carrier Lufthansa Group, stated that his airline might be forced to operate 18,000 "additional, unnecessary flights".[70] Between January and March 2021, only 45% of flight operations were completed. Lufthansa noted that, if they had not faced the risk of losing slots at certain airports, they would have canceled these flights or combined them with others.[71] This highlighted how certain aviation regulations conflicted with measures aimed to reduce aviation's impact on climate change.

Another effect the airline industry experienced during the pandemic was a wave of bankruptcies, liquidations, and mergers. Several traditional and charter air carriers were forced to declare bankruptcy as they were unable to withstand the financial pressures caused by the pandemic.[72] Bankruptcy primarily affected smaller

68 The case of Canadian airports is typical of the problem that prevailed around the world during the 2022 holidays. See: *Airport nightmares won't end this summer, experts say*, CBS, 7.07.2022, https://www.cbc.ca/radio/thecurrent/the-current-for-july-6-2022-1.6511574/airport-nightmares-won-t-end-this-summer-experts-say-1.6512232, accessed 30.01.2024.

69 Charlotte E., *Half of all European flights were delayed last summer. Which airports were the worst – and best?* Euronews, 17.01.2023, https://www.euronews.com/travel/2023/01/16/half-of-all-european-flights-were-delayed-last-summer-which-airports-were-the-worst-and-be, accessed 30.01.2024.

70 Nelsen A., *Airlines flying near-empty 'ghost flights' to retain EU airport slots*, The Guardian, 26.01.2022, https://www.theguardian.com/environment/2022/jan/26/airlines-flying-near-empty-ghost-flights-to-retain-eu-airport-slots, accessed 30.01.2024.

71 *Ibidem.*

72 Dube K., *Emerging from the COVID-19 Pandemic: Aviation Recovery*, Challenges, and Opportunities, Aerospace, 2022, doi:10.20944/preprints202212.0198.v2.

carriers that could not compete with larger ones in the market. Their fixed monthly costs, in the absence of air operations, were disproportionate to their lack of income during the period, despite receiving public aid from the state. One example was the American carrier ExpressJet Airlines, which declared bankruptcy in August 2022.[73] It should also be noted that, due to the decline in demand for flights, the value of aircraft decreased, posing a significant threat to airlines. They were forced to bear the cost of repaying loans for the purchase of aircraft whose value had diminished. If the carrier had leased aircraft, it had to pay monthly installments, which amounted to approximately $1 million per aircraft.[74] In a situation like that of the Hungarian low-cost carrier Wizz Air, which leases 100% of its fleet, these lease payments represent a significant cost, particularly during the grounding of aircraft and limitations on operational capacity that occurred during the COVID-19 pandemic.[75] The situation was less acute forcarriers that owned aircraft, such as Lufthansa, which owned 80% of its fleet.[76]

A further consequence of a pandemic was a change in travelers' preferences. The COVID-19 pandemic caused a shift in travelers' preferences, with many passengers increasingly opting for cars or rail transport over flights. This was due to the lack of available flights or restrictions on carriers' policies regarding security measures. These changes also affected airline operating costs. A 2022 study in the UK by Opinium Research found that two-thirds of respondents preferred to travel by train rather than by plane.[77] However, as the availability of air travel was restored, the desire to use air transport began to increase, resulting in rising demand following the lifting of legal restrictions. Of course, the impact of transportation on climate change wasalso important. For many people, an ecological approach wascrucial, which is why they preferred rail. Although newer aircraft emitted less and less harmful substances into the atmosphere and manufacturers adopted more advanced technical solutions, concerns about sustainability remained significant.

Currently, global air transport accounts for 2.5% of worldwide carbon dioxide emissions, which is not a large figure. However, with air traffic expected to increase, there is concern that the impact of aviation on climate change will grow. Therefore,

73 ExpressJet Airlines was a small regional US carrier that had one of the world's largest aircraft fleets before 2020. Almost all of them were leased from the large carrier United Airlines, with which ExpressJet had a contract. As a result of problems related to air transport restrictions due to the COVID-19 pandemic, in 2020, United Airlines terminated the contract and ExpressJet had to return all leased aircraft. Despite attempts to salvage, in the first seven months of 2021, ExpressJet's revenue was only $5.5 million and expenses were more than $23 million. In this situation, the carrier declared bankruptcy in August 2022. See: Hill, Jeremy, *ExpressJet airlines goes bankrupt in wake of split from United*, Bloomberg, 23.08.2022, https://www.bloomberg.com/news/articles/2022-08-23/expressjet-airlines-goes-bankrupt-in-wake-of-split-from-united, accessed 15.01.2024.

74 Cieśluk K., *How Aircraft Leasing Works & Why Airlines Do It?*, Simple Flying, 12.04.2020.

75 Based on Wizzair financial statements: *Annual report and accounts* 2022, Wizzair 2022.

76 Cieśluk K., op. cit.

77 Robinson E., *Survey reveals popularity of train vs plane for business travel*, Global Railway Review, 6.04.2022, https://www.globalrailwayreview.com/news/133334/survey-reveals-popularity-train-plane-business-travel/, accessed 30.01.2024.

manufacturers, together with regulators in various countries and international organizations, are striving to achieve zero carbon emissions by 2050.[78] The increase in demand for air travel clearly shows that passengers want to travel by aircraft, and the temporary shutdown of air transport operations forced by the COVID-19 pandemic was a break from the global upward trend.

Finally, as a further consequence of the pandemic, it should be noted that it was necessary to revamp the operating policy and strategy of air carriers in order to adapt to the new environment, including the introduction of new safety and health procedures, cost reductions, and increased efficiency. This was achieved by temporarily laying off employees, suspending orders for new aircraft, and renegotiating leasing and insurance contracts. New safety procedures introduced during the COVID-19 pandemic, such as the limitation of the number of seats on board planes or the requirement to wear masks, practically no longer exist and have become a relic of the past.

Carriers have a legal obligation to ensure technical and operational safety, in accordance with international regulations, which they continue to adhere to regardless of the period in which they operate. These regulations clearly specify the conditions for the release to service of aircraft, strictly define the conditions for obtaining and maintaining airworthiness certification, and maintaining flight crew licenses. In terms of check-in procedures at airports, they remain unchanged from before the COVID-19 pandemic. Compliance with these regulations by the relevant entities and their supervision by the safety oversight organizations in each country ensures that the industry is perceived as a safe and valuable system.

4.6 Summary

In conclusion, the COVID-19 pandemic has had a significant impact on air transport, but the sector is gradually recovering and adapting to new legal and socio-economic conditions. Changes are being made to meet the new challenges and expectations of passengers. The relatively rapid recovery has been facilitated by the development of vaccines against COVID-19, which were primarily aimed at reducing the transmission of the SARS-COV-2 coronavirus in its various mutations. The observed decrease in the number of deaths caused by COVID-19 and the lower number of hospitalizations led to the gradual lifting of restrictions. Although vaccination began on a global scale in December 2020, the entire next year 2021 and the first half of 2022 were marked by numerous restrictions. It was only from mid-2022 that legal and social restrictions on travel and all air transport were lifted. The number of passengers began to gradually increase, which now gives hope for the future of the aviation industry. Nevertheless, the process can be

78 Ellerbeck S., *The aviation sector wants to reach net zero by 2050. How will it do it?*, World Economic Forum, 9.12.2022, https://www.weforum.org/agenda/2022/12/aviation-net-zero-emissions/, accessed 31.01.2024.

slow and lengthy, and the aviation industry will have to make changes and adapt to new requirements to regain travelers' trust and succeed in the future.

The year 2023 was the first year where various restrictions were only sporadic and insignificant. On January 16, 2023 ICAO issued guidance to countries on managing risks related to COVID-19.[79] ICAO Secretary-General Juan Carlos Salazar said at the time that as COVID-19 cross-border restrictions on air travel are lifted, it is important to increase the number of air connections. He emphasized that restrictions should only be introduced using evidence-based risk management principles and based on strict recommendations from the World Health Organization (WHO) and ICAO. According to him, such an approach would result in an increase in air travel, tourism, and trade.[80] The recommendations, introduced in January 2023 stated that before imposing further restrictions on air travel, states should consider the following factors:[81]

1. consultation with competent national authorities, in line with national law;
2. risk tolerance levels of individual countries and other relevant national factors;
3. the varying objectives and circumstances of each country, with solutions tailored accordingly, rather than blindly duplicated;
4. evaluation of the effectiveness of each measure or legal instrument before implementing additional travel restrictions;
5. a comprehensive risk assessment that includes health resources in both the country of departure and the country of destination, using comparable indicators;
6. informing all relevant stakeholders about any newly introduced travel restrictions;
7. a systematic review of ICAO and WHO guidelines to ensure they remain relevant and up-to-date in managing COVID-19 risks.

It was vital that borders between countries remain open and air connections maintained. Legal restrictions caused numerous disruptions and perturbations on many levels, and removing these effects may not be easy. The economic impact is also difficult to estimate. Akinrinade highlights that calculating these losses is particularly complex, as the crisis caused by the COVID-19 pandemic did not affect only one country, and in both the economy and theair transport, there are trade and financial links associated with globalization.[82] Therefore, the overall costs can only be estimated in broad terms. It is challenging to predict the potential

79 Risk Assessment prior to Introduction of COVID-19 Air Travel Requirements, 16 January 2023, Electronic Bulletin, EB 2023/6.

80 ICAO recommendations on COVID-19 risk management for international air travel, 18.01.2023, https://www.icao.int/Newsroom/Pages/New-ICAO-recommendations-issued-on-COVID-risk-assessment-and-mitigation-for-international-air-travel.aspx, accessed 30.01.2024.

81 Risk Assessment prior to Introduction of COVID-19 Air Travel Requirements, 16 January 2023, Electronic Bulletin, EB 2023/6.

82 Akinrinade S. A., op. cit.

growth in air traffic that might have occurred, if the COVID-19 pandemic had not emerged. Additionally, restoring the pre-pandemic state may prove impossible, as the collapse of an air carrier or its acquisition by another entity could make such recovery unrealistic.

It seemed appropriate to follow ICAO's approach that all decisions should be guided by common sense and calm. Air transport had the potential to recover to the pre-pandemic levels. Forecasts from various international organizations clearly indicated an upward trend in air traffic. According to Eurocontrol, air traffic in 2023 was expected to reach 95% of 2019 levels.[83] ICAO, on the other hand, forecast that passenger traffic in 2024 would be 4% higher than in 2019.[84] Similarly, the non-governmental organization IATA pointed out that the passenger traffic in 2024 would be 3% higher than in 2019.[85] Thus, based on the projections of 2022 and 2023, it was evident that air traffic compared to 2019 would be higher from 2024 onwards. In the absence of other similar legal restrictions on air transport, a stable growth of the aviation industry could be observed.

The only country that required strict regulations regarding the entry of people from other countries into its territory was the US. According to its internal regulations, traveling to the US required proof of full vaccination with two doses of a vaccine recognized in the US, or a single dose from Johnson and Johnson. Proclamations[86] by the President of the US regarding the Department of Homeland Security (DHS) actions in response to the COVID-19 threat and the protection of US interests led to a series of emergency amendments to existing legislation, extending the entry restrictions until April 13, 2023.[87]

All these aviation safety conditions in the era of the SARS-COV-2 COVID-19 pandemic were introduced as temporary solutions for the duration of this pandemic, i.e. from 2020 to 2022. The legal changes and procedures implemented during this period aimed at increasing the safety of passengers and employees of the aviation sector. The COVID-19 pandemic has shown that aviation regulations can change quickly in response to evolving conditions and require adaptation from the aviation industry.

83 Data from forecasts from December 18, 2022 https://www.eurocontrol.int/news/eurocontrol-predicts-growth-aviation-traffic-over-next-8-months, accessed 30.01.2024.

84 Data is from February 8, 2024, https://www.eurocontrol.int/news/eurocontrol-predicts-growth-aviation-traffic-over-next-8-months, accessed 12.02.2024.

85 Data is from March 1, 2024 https://www.iata.org/en/pressroom/2022-releases/2022-03-01-01/, accessed 14.02.2024.

86 Proclamations of the President of the US are ceremonial, they have no legal effect, although they have a specific value for the legal order in the US.

87 DHS TSA, Requirements for Proof of Being Fully Vaccinated Against COVID-19, EA 1546-21-02B.

Conclusion

The approach mentioned in this book to present normative aspects of safety in international aviation law is a compendium of knowledge necessary to develop and expand the discussed research area. International aviation law is a dynamic, complex area that requires a holistic approach. This study presents a fundamental part of this law by focusing on the legal basis for the functioning of global aviation policy in the context of safety considerations. It is this issue that is crucial for undertaking an in-depth analysis of other areas of international aviation law, such as economics, environmental protection, management in terms of objects and subjects, and many other areas. However, the most important aspect is understanding the normative regulations on the basis of which civil aviation operates in the world.

Theoretical aviation safety issues are used to understand individual phenomena and processes in a holistic way. The term is related to the broader issue of international safety, which has different dimensions and is accompanied by many safety paradigms, such as regional, sub-regional, and local. The aviation safety paradigm is discussed by analyzing it from a realistic, liberal, and constructivist approach. By clarifying theoretical assumptions, entities such as states and international aviation organizations can create improved legal regulations and better address challenges or mitigate threats.

There are dependencies and interactions of many areas in international aviation relations, with legal regulations created by international institutions serving as the common denominator and an incentive to develop safety in this area. In this context, the process of codification and harmonization of international aviation law is essential. Within the framework of the global legal system, it is necessary to point to the rules and standards found in the multilateral and bilateral regimes. At the same time, an institutional system is being developed, that is responsible for enacting legislation, implementing adopted standards, and effectively supervising their compliance.

The regional institutional and legal system of aviation safety is developing more and more dynamically. This system performs an important regulatory, organizational, and control function. In recent years, there has been an increase in the activity of regional organizations and institutions that support the process of codification of international aviation law and shape aviation safety regulations in the region. They are responsible not only for promoting, supporting, and monitoring the implementation of international regulations at the regional level, created mainly within the framework of the ICAO system, but also for creating their own normative regulations, taking into account the specificity of the region, while remaining consistent with ICAO acts and other international agreements with global scope.

Recent years have been marked by the COVID-19 pandemic, which has hit international aviation in a severe and long-lasting way. In the first few months after the COVID-19 pandemic was declared in the world, i.e. in March 2020, aviation was paralyzed, and almost all air operations in the vast majority of countries in the world were suspended. The massive legal restrictions imposed on civil aviation have been very slowly lifted since the third quarter of 2020, although it was not until mid-2022 that the normal functioning of air transport was restored. The COVID-19 pandemic has led to a number of changes in aviation law and procedures, with a view to safety, especially that of passengers. The safety regulations to be met by carriers and airports were intended to guarantee the highest safety standards for all users. The lower number of passengers in 2020 and 2021 was caused by legal restrictions related to the operation of flights. States were obliged to support aviation operators as they were threatened with bankruptcy and faced significant social consequences, such as increased unemployment due to redundancies. Although it was not possible to fully protect against these effects, public aid in many countries contributed to stabilizing the situation and averting serious perturbations.

The analysis of the research confirms the correctness of the hypothesis, which was that the process of codification of aviation law contributes to the coherence of regulations and is important for increasing safety, and the process of regional institutionalization being advanced expandsits scope of impact in terms of personnel and norm-setting, and develops cooperation between states and other participants. The consolidation of safety rules brings many benefits, including improved safety in the aviation sector, and common safety standards allow access to a larger market, which in turn increases competitiveness and contributes to improving the quality of services offered. However, the process of harmonization requires the adaptation of internal legislation in different countries with different legal cultures. This requires multilateral institutional cooperation and coordination between states at a regional level. However, civil aviation is an area of supra-political influence, which is particularly evident by the fact that ICAO, with its 193 countries and territories, is the largest intergovernmental organization in the world after the United Nations, and its regulations are adopted by individual states and aviation organizations in every region of the world. Thanks to the uniform legal framework, it is possible to create facilitations in aviation, in particular in the area of the recognition of airworthiness certificates or flight crew licenses. The regionally advanced process of institutionalizing aviation safety affects a wide range of entities in the area, from intergovernmental states and regional organizations to non-governmental organizational structures working to promote common safety standards. Thanks to the participation of a wide range of entities interested in developing integration and interconnections, it is possible to develop the best aviation safety practices and safeguard the interests of all participants.

The aim of the work, which was to show the normative aspects of safety in international aviation law, both in terms of theoretical considerations regarding aviation safety theory and the practical application of the adopted legal regulations, has been achieved.

The research problem presented in this monograph is an important study of the interaction between contemporary aviation relations and aviation law. The safety status, measured by the number of accidents or incidents, reveals which elements have not been implemented, which do not function properly, and which factors have been omitted. The broader the platform for common, harmonized legislation, the easier it will be to control the overall level of safety in operational terms. The study touches on an important contemporary issue. The ongoing processes of codification of international aviation law are intrinsically linked to the development of the process of institutionalization of regional safety. The expansion of the regulatory function of safety institutions in individual regions of the world is clearly visible.

The present study should serve as research material for in-depth analysis in the field of normative regulation of civil aviation safety. The current research results bring a new approach to the issues of law in the contemporary conditions of international civil aviation. Considering the research results, several important conclusions should be drawn. Firstly, international rules are not the only means of ensuring aviation safety worldwide. They constitute only a legal framework, a certain legal framework that requires the interaction of other factors. The codification process itself should be assessed favorably, in view of the increasing number of threats and challenges facing international aviation. Secondly, greater cooperation between states and international and regional organizations is needed in order to build and maintain a high standard of safety. These legal entities play a significant role in shaping aviation governance and relations. Thirdly, the involvement of the sector of aviation NGOs should be strengthened, which can contribute to building normative coherence and developing new qualitative regulations adapted to dynamically changing international conditions. International rules should be implemented more effectively at a lower level, and regulatory unity and consistency should be promoted.

Literature

Legal acts and documents

26 US Code, Sec.4261: Imposition of tax, Public law 117–328.
26 US Code, Sec.9502, Airport and Airway Trust Fund, Public Law 117–328.
47th Conference of Directors General of Civil Aviation Asia and Pacific Regions, Macao, China, 25 – 29 October 2010, DGCA – 47/DP/4/3.
Additional Protocol for the Suppression of Unlawful Acts of Violence at Airports Serving International Civil Aviation, signed at Montreal on 24 February 1988 (Montreal Protocol).
AFCAC, *Mechanism for monitoring implementation of safety systems & initiatives*, AFCAC, 30.6.2018.
Agreement between the European Union and the European Organisation for the Safety of Air Navigation establishing a general framework for enhanced cooperation, *OJ EU, L* 016, 19.01.2013.
Agreement between the European Union and the Government of the Federative Republic of Brazil on civil aviation safety, OJ EU, *L* 273, 19.10.2011.
Agreement between the United States of America and the European Community on cooperation in the regulation of civil aviation safety, OJ EU, *L* 291, 9.11.2011.
Agreement on civil aviation safety between the European Community and Canada, OJ EU, *L* 153, 17.6.2009.
Agreement on civil aviation safety between the European Union and the Government of the People's Republic of China. OJ EU, *L* 240, 24.07.2020.
Agreement on civil aviation safety between the European Union and Japan, OJ EU, *L* 229, 16.07.2020.
Annex 1 to the Chicago Convention (Personnel Licensing).
Annex 2 to the Chicago Convention (Rules of the Air).
Annex 6 to the Chicago Convention (Operation of Aircraft; Volume 1: International commercial air transport – Aeroplanes; Volume 2: International General Aviation – Aeroplanes; Volume 3: International operations – helicopters).
Annex 8 to the Chicago Convention (Airworthiness of aircraft).
Annex 9 to the Chicago Convention (Facilitation).
Annex 12 to the Chicago Convention (Search and Rescue).
Annex 13 to the Chicago Convention (Aircraft Accident and Incident Investigation).
Annex 14 to the Chicago Convention (Aerodromes; Volume 1: Aerodrome Design; Volume 2: Heliports).
Annex 16 to the Chicago Convention (Environmental Protection; Volume 4: Carbon Offsetting and Reduction Scheme for International Aviation (CORSIA).
Annex 17 to the Chicago Convention (Security: Safeguarding International Civil Aviation Against Acts of Unlawful Interference).
Annex 18 to the Chicago Convention (Safe Transport of Dangerous Goods by Air).
Annex 19 to the Chicago Convention (safety management).
Annual Safety Report 2014, RASG-AFI 2015.

Annual Safety Report 2021, RASG-AFI 2022.
Charter of the United Nations, ICC Legal Tools Database, No 19341.
Commission Decision of 20 December 2011 on the application of Article 106(2) of the Treaty on the Functioning of the European Union to State aid in the form of public service compensation granted to undertakings entrusted with the operation of services of general economic interest, OJ EU, *L* 7 of 11.1.2012.
Commission Delegated Regulation (EU) 2019/945 of 12 March 2019 on unmanned aircraft systems and third country operators of unmanned aircraft *systems, OJ EU, L* 152, 11.6.2019.
Commission Delegated Regulation (EU) 2023/660 of 2 December 2022 laying down detailed rules on the list of air carriers subject to an operating ban or operating restrictions in the Union referred to in Chapter II of Regulation (EC) No 2111/2005 of the European Parliament and of *the Council, OJ EU, L* 83, 22.3.2023.
Commission Implementing Regulation (EU) 2019/947 of 24 May 2019 on rules and procedures for the operation of unmanned aircraft, OJ EU, *L* 152, 11.6.2019.
Commission Implementing Regulation (EU) 2022/2295 of 23 November 2022 amending Regulation (EC) No 474/2006 as regards the list of air carriers subject to operating bans or operating restrictions within the Union, OJ EU, *L* 304 of 24.11.2022.
Commission Regulation (EU) No 139/2014 of 12 February 2014 laying down aerodrome requirements and administrative procedures pursuant to Regulation (EC) No 216/2008 of the European Parliament and of *the Council, OJ EU, L* 44, 14.2.2014.
Commission Regulation (EU) No 651/2014 of 17 June 2014 declaring certain categories of aid compatible with the internal market in application of Articles 107 and 108 of the Treaty, *OJ EU, L* 187, 26.6.2014.
Commission Regulation (EU) No 748/2012 of 3 August 2012 laying down implementing rules for the airworthiness and environmental certification of aircraft and related products, parts and appliances, and for the certification of design and production organizations, *OJ EU, L* 224, 21.8.2012.
Commission Regulation (EU) No 965/2012 of 5 October 2012 laying down technical requirements and administrative procedures related to air operations pursuant to Regulation (EC) No 216/2008 of the European Parliament and of the Council, OJ EU, *L* 296, 25.10.2012.
Commission Regulation (EU) No 1178/2011 of 3 November 2011 laying down technical requirements and administrative procedures related to civil aviation aircrew pursuant to Regulation (EC) No 216/2008 of the European Parliament and of *the Council, OJ EU, L* 311, 25.11.2011.
Commission Regulation (EC) No 1330/2007 of 24 September 2007, implementing rules for the dissemination to interested parties of information on civil aviation occurrences. *OJ EU, L* 122, 24.4.2014.
Commission Regulation (EC) No 1321/2007 of 12 November 2007 laying down implementing rules for the integration into a central repository of information on civil aviation occurrences exchanged in accordance with Directive 2003/42/EC of the European Parliament and of the Council (no longer in force), *OJ L 294,* 13.11.2007.
Commission Regulation (EU) No 1321/2014 of 26 November 2014 on the continuing airworthiness of aircraft and aeronautical products, parts and appliances, and on the approval of organisations and personnel involved in such tasks. OJ EU, *L* 362, 17.12.2014.
Commission Regulation (EU) No 1407/2013 of 18 December 2013 on the application of Articles 107 and 108 of the Treaty on the Functioning of the European Union to de minimis *aid, OJ EU, L* 352 of 24.12.2013.
Communication from the Commission to the European Parliament, the Council, the European Economic and Social Committee and the Committee of the Regions, An Aviation Strategy for Europe, COM (2015) 598 final, 7.12.2015.

Communication from the Commission on the Temporary Framework for State aid measures to Support the economy in the Context of the Ongoing COVID-19 outbreak, *C* 91I, 20.3.2020.
Community guidelines on airport financing and start-up aid to undertakings departing from regional airports, *OJ EC, C* 312, 9.12.2005.
Consolidated versions of the Treaty on European Union and the Treaty on the Functioning of the European Union, *OJ EU, C* 326, 26.10.2012.
The Constitution of the African Union signed on 11 July 2000 in Lome (Togo).
Convention on Compensation for Damage Caused by Aircraft to Third Parties signed in Montreal on 2 May 2009.
Convention on Compensation for Damage to Third Parties Resulting from Unlawful Acts Involving Aircraft, signed in Montreal on 2 May 2009.
Convention for the Suppression of Unlawful Acts against the Safety of Civil Aviation, signed at Montreal on 23 September 1971 (Montreal Convention).
Convention for the Suppression of Unlawful Seizure of Aircraft, signed at The Hague on 16 December 1970 (Hague Convention).
Convention for the Unification of Certain Rules for International Carriage by Air, signed in Warsaw on 12 October 1929 (the Warsaw Convention).
Convention for the Unification of Certain Rules Relating to International Carriage by Air, signed in Montreal on 28 May 1999 (the Montreal Convention).
Convention on International Civil Aviation (Chicago Convention), signed at Chicago, December 7, 1944, Journal of Laws of 1959, No. 35, item 212.
Convention on Offences and Certain Other Acts Committed on Board Aircraft, signed at Tokyo on 14 September 1963 (Tokyo Convention).
Convention Relating to the Regulation of Aerial Navigation, signed at Paris on 13 October 1919, The American Journal of International Law, Vol. 17, No. 4, Supplement: Official Documents, October, 1923.
Cooperation Agreement with the Directorate-General for Mobility and Transport of the European Commission (DG MOVE) in the field of civil aviation security, signed on 13 December 2012 in Paris, France.
Council Regulation (EEC) No 3922/91 of 16 December 1991 on the harmonisation of technical requirements and administrative procedures in the field of civil aviation, OJ EU, *L* 212, 22.8.2018.
Council Regulation (EEC) No 2407/92 of 23 July 1992 on licensing of air carriers (no longer in force).
Council Regulation (EEC) No 2408/92 of 23 July 1992 on access for Community air carriers to intra-Community air routes (no longer in force).
Council Recommendation (EU) 2020/1475 of 13 October 2020 on a coordinated approach to restrictions on free movement in response to the COVID-19 pandemic, OJ EU, *L* 337, 14.10.2020.
Court of Justice of the European Union (CJEU), Case: T-238/20 Ryanair/Commission.
Court of Justice of the European Union (CJEU), Case: T-259/20 Ryanair/Commission.
Court of Justice of the European Union (CJEU), Case: T-465/20 Ryanair/Commission.
Court of Justice of the European Union (CJEU), Case: T-643/20 Ryanair/Commission.
Court of Justice of the European Union (CJEU), Case: T-577/20 Ryanair/Commission.
Court of Justice of the European Union (CJEU), Case: T-657/20 Ryanair/Commission.
Court of Justice of the European Union (CJEU), Case C-280/00, judgment of 24 July 2003 in *Altmark Trans and Regierungspresidium Magdeburg* [2003] ECR I-7747.
Decision relating to the implementation of the Yamoussoukro Declaration concerning the liberalisation of access to air transport markets in Africa, United Nations Economic And Social Council, ECA/RCID/CM.CIVAV/99/RPT.
DHS TSA, Requirements for Proof of Being Fully Vaccinated Against COVID-19, EA 1546-21-02B.

Directive 2003/42/EC of the European Parliament and of the Council and Commission Regulations (EC) No 1321/2007 and (EC) No 1330/2007, *OJ EU, L* 122, 24.4.2014.
Directive 2014/30/EU of the European Parliament and of the Council of 26 February 2014 on the harmonization of the laws of the Member States relating in electromagnetic compatibility, OJ EU, L 96, 29.03.2014.
Directive 2014/53/EU of the European Parliament and of the Council of 16 April 2014 on the harmonization of the laws of the Member States relating to the making available on the market of radio equipment.
EASA, *Annual Safety Review*, 2022.
ECAC, *ECAC's Strategy for the Future - A Policy Statement*, ECAC 2021.
ECAC IN FOCUS: Together for a Stronger European Aviation, ECAC 2021.
Eighth Meeting of the ICAO/LACAC NAM/CAR and SAM AVSEC/FAL/RG.
Eighth Meeting of the ICAO/LACAC NAM/CAR and SAM Aviation Security and Facilitation Regional Group, AVSEC/FAL/RG/8, Mexico City, Mexico, 13–17 August 2018.
Eurocontrol International Convention relating to Co-operation for the Safety of Air Navigation of 13 December 1960.
Euro-Mediterranean aviation agreement between the European Community and its Member States, of the one part and the Kingdom of Morocco, of the other part, signed on 12 December 2006, *OJ L* 386, 29.12.2006.
European Commission – Statement, *State aid: Commission will phase out state aid COVID temporary framework*, Brussels, 12 May 2022.
European Commission press release, *State aid: Commission approves €6 billion German measure to recapitalise Lufthansa*, 25.06.2020.
European Regional Aviation Safety Group (RASG-EUR) Procedural Handbook, 1st Edition, February 2013.
European Plan for Aviation Safety 2023–2025, EASA 2022.
Ezulwini Declaration on Regional Safety Oversight Organisations adopted in Ezulwini on 24 March 2017.
First Meeting of the Regional Aviation Safety Group – Asia and Pacific Regions (RASG-APAC/1), Noumea, New Kaledonia, 10–11.10. 2011.
Global Air Navigation Capacity & Efficiency Plan, 2013–2028, ICAO 2014, DOC 9750.
Global Aviation Safety Plan 2023–2025, Doc 10004, ICAO 2022.
Global Aviation Safety Roadmap, 2023–2025, ICAO Doc.10161.
Guidelines No. 4 of the President of the Civil Aviation Authority of 21 July 2005 on flights in prohibited zones.
H.R.133 - Consolidated Appropriations Act, 2021, Public Law 116–260.
H.R.1319 - American Rescue Plan Act, Public Law 117–2.
Human Factors Training Manual, Doc 9683 iAN/950, ICAO 1998.
Joined Cases T-132/96 and T-143/96 Freistaat Sachsen, Volkswagen AG and Volkswagen Sachsen GmbH v Commission, ECLI:EU:T:1999:326, paragraph 167. Judgment upheld on appeal of 30 September 2003, C:2003:510.
Mechanism for Monitoring Implementation of Safety Systems & Initiatives, AFCAC 2019.
Meeting of the African Union Special Technical Committee in Lome (Togo), from 13 to 17 March 2017.
MIDANPIRG/19 & RASG-MID/9-WP/9, Outcomes of the 2nd MENA RSOO Technical Meeting, Riyadh, Saudi Arabia, 14–17 February 2022.
OECD, *State support to the air transport sector: Monitoring developments related to the Covid-19 crisis*, 21.04.2021.
Part M of Commission Regulation (EU) No 1321/2014 of 26 November 2014 on the continuing airworthiness of aircraft and aeronautical products, parts, and appliances, and on the approval of organisations and personnel involved in such tasks, OJ EU, *L* 362, 17.12.2014.

Plan estratégico 2020–2030 comisión latinoamericana de aviación civil, CLAC, paragraph 6, A.8. Plan approved at the fourth extraordinary session of the Assembly, 12–13 September 2019, Sao Paolo (Brazil).

Protocol on the accession of the European Community to the Eurocontrol International Convention relating to Cooperation for the Safety of Air Navigation of 13 December 1960, as variously amended, and as consolidated by the Protocol of 27 June 1997, *OJ EC, L* 304, 30.09.2004.

Protocol to Suppress Unlawful Acts of Violence at Airports Serving International Civil Aviation, signed in Montreal on 24 December 1988.

PUBLIC LAW 116–136 — MARCH 27, 2020 134 STAT 281.

Raising the Bar: Building "EUROCONTROL 2030", EUROCONTROL 2023.

RASG-MID Annual Safety Report 2016–2020, Ed.10, 2021.

Regulation (EC) No 216/2008 of the European Parliament and of the Council and Council Regulation of 20 February 2008 on common rules in the field of civil aviation and establishing a European Aviation Safety Agency (no longer in force), *OJ EC, L* 79, 19.3.2008.

Regulation (EU) No 376/2014 of the European Parliament and of the Council of 3 April 2014 on the reporting, analysis and follow-up of occurrences in civil aviation, *OJ EU, L* 122, 24.4.2014.

Regulation (EC) No 552/2004 of the European Parliament and of the Council of 10 March 2004 on the interoperability of the European Air Traffic Management network, *OJ EC, L* 96, 31.3.2004.

Regulation (EU) No 996/2010 of the European Parliament and of the Council of 20 October 2010 on investigating and preventing accidents and incidents in civil aviation and repealing Directive 94/56/*EC, OJ EU, L* 295, 12.11.2010.

Regulation (EC) No 1008/2008 of the European Parliament and of the Council of 24 September 2008 on common rules for the operation of air services in the *Community, OJ EC, L* 293, 31.10.2008.

Regulation (EC) No 1592/2002 of the European Parliament and of the Council of 15 July 2002 on common rules in the field of civil aviation and establishing a European Aviation Safety Agency. EC L 240, of 7 September 2002.

Regulation (EU) 2018/1139 of the European Parliament and of the Council of 4 July 2018 on common rules in the field of civil aviation and establishing a European Union Aviation Safety Agency, *OJ EU, L* 212, 22.8.2018.

Regulation (EC) No 2111/2005 of the European Parliament and of the Council of 14 December 2005 on the establishment of a Community list of air carriers subject to an operating ban within the Community and on informing air transport passengers of the identity of the operating air carrier, and repealing Article 9 of Directive 2004/36/EC, OJ EC, *L* 344, 27.12.2005.

Report on the Eighth Meeting of the Steering Committee of the Regional Aviation Safety Group For Africa-Indian Ocean (RASC/8), RASC/8 Report, August 2022, para.5.12.

Report of the First Meeting of the Middle East Regional Aviation Safety Group, Cairo, Egypt, 18–19 September 2011, RASG-MID/1-REPORT.

Report of The Sixth Meeting of the Regional Aviation Safety Group – Middle East, RASG-MID/6, Bahrain, 26–28 September 2017.

Resolution A29-13 adopted at the 29th Ordinary Session of the ICAO Assembly, 22 September to 8 October 1992.

Resolution A32-11 adopted at the 32nd Ordinary Session of the ICAO Assembly, 22 September to 2 October 1998.

Risk Assessment prior to Introduction of COVID-19 Air Travel Requirements, 16 January 2023, Electronic Bulletin, EB 2023/6.

Risk Assessment prior to Introduction of COVID-19 Air Travel Requirements, 16 January 2023, Electronic Bulletin, EB 2023/6.

Safety Management Manual, ICAO, Doc.9858.
Safety Oversight Manual, Part B. Establishment and Management of a Regional Safety Oversight Organisation, ICAO 2011, Doc.9734.
SOM Manual, ICAO 2006, Ed.2, Doc 9734.
Statute of the Civil Aviation Commission of Latin America, signed in Mexico on 14 December 1973, United Nations Treaty Series, Vol. 1241, No. 20170, 1981.
Technical Instructions For The Safe Transport of Dangerous Goods by Air, ICAO, Doc.9284.
The Air Navigation order 2016, 2016, No 765, issued under the Civil Aviation Act 1982. (Civil Aviation Act 1982).
The International Air Transport Treaty, signed at Chicago on 7 December 1944, Doc. 7500.
The International Air Services Transit Treaty, signed at Chicago on 7 December 1944, Doc. 7500.
The Pacific Islands Civil Aviation Safety And Security Treaty, Apia, Western Samoa, 7 August 2004, United Nation Office of Legal Affairs, Treaty Series 2433, No 43780.
Treaty establishing the African Economic Community adopted in Abuja (Nigeria), 3 June 1991.
Treaty on European Union (TEU) in the modified version of the Treaty of Lisbon, *OJ C* 326, 26.10.2012.
Twenty-Fourth Meeting of the Africa-Indian Ocean Planning and Implementation Regional Group (APIRG/24) & Seventh Meeting of the Regional Aviation Safety Group for the AFI Region (RASG-AFI/7), Status of Implementation of the AFI Safety and Air Navigation Targets, AFCAC, 1 and 8 November 2021.
United Nations Convention on the Law of the Sea, done at Montego Bay (Jamaica) on 10 December 1982.
United States Government Accountability Office, COVID19 PANDEMIC Preliminary Observations on Efforts toward and Factors Affecting the Aviation Industry's Recovery, 2.03.2021, GAO-21-412T.
U.S. Code of Federal Regulations (CFR), Title 14 CFR: Aeronautics and Space.
U.S. Department of Transportation, Human Factors Policy, FAA Order 9550.8A.
USOAP Manual, ICAO 2011, Ed.3, Doc 9735.
Vienna Convention on Diplomatic Relations, done in Vienna on 18 April 1961.
Wizzair financial statements: *Annual report and accounts* 2022, Wizzair 2022.
Yamoussoukro Declaration, 7.10.1988. United Nations Economic and Social Council, E/ECA/TRANS/77A, 17.10.1988.

Books and research papers

Akinrinade Samuel Adewuyi, *The Impact of COVID-19 Pandemic on the Global Aviation Industry: Nigeria's Experience*, October 2022, DOI: 10.13140/RG.2.2.20810.44485.
Antonowicz Lech, *Podręcznik prawa międzynarodowego*, Warsaw: PWN, 1998.
Augustyniak Łukasz, *Immunitet jurysdykcyjny organizacji międzynarodowych a immunitet ich funkcjonariuszy*, Ruch prawniczy, ekonomiczny i socjologiczny, Tom LXIX - zeszyt 3 – 2007, pp.43–56.
Balcerowicz B., *Pokój i „nie-pokój" na progu XXI wieku*, Warszawa: Dom Wydawniczy Bellona, 2002.
Bashev. H., *Upravlenie na agrarniya risk.* Ikonomicheska misal. Issue 2, Bulgarian Academy of Science Sofia, 2013, pp. 50–75.
Bertalanffy Ludwig von, *General systems theory: Foundation, development, applications*, New York: George Braziller, 1968.
Bogolasky Jose C., *Air transport in Latin America: The expanding role of the Latin American civil aviation commission*, Journal of Air Law and Commerce, Vol. 44, 1978, pp.75–110.

Burgess Scott, *A systems theory approach for studying safety management systems for operations of small helicopter organizations*, Northcentral University ProQuest Dissertations Publishing, 2016.
Cedro Patrycja, Latynoamerykańska koncepcja bezpieczeństwa, in: Lisińska Magdalena, Beliavska Beata (ed.), *Ameryka Łacińska w stosunkach międzynarodowych*, Kraków, 2015, pp. 43–60.
Ciekanowski Zbigniew, Wyrębek Henryk, *Zarządzanie ryzykiem*, De Securitate: O Bezpieczeństwie i Obronności, Vol. 2, No. 2, 2016, pp. 7–20.
Cieśluk Karol, *How aircraft leasing works & why airlines do it?*, Simple Flying, 12.04.2020. https://simpleflying.com/how-aircraft-leasing-works/, accessed 4.02.2024
Chunli Zhu, Jianping Wu, Mingyu Liu, Linyang Wang, Duowei Li, Anastasios Kouvelas, *Recovery preparedness of global air transport influenced by COVID-19 pandemic: Policy intervention analysis*, Transport Policy, Vol. 106, 2021, pp. 54–63.
Coccia Mario, *COVID-19 pandemic over 2020 (with lockdowns) and 2021 (with vaccinations): similar effects for seasonality and environmental factors*, Environmental Research, Vol. 208, 2022, Article. 112711, pp. 1–11, doi: 10.1016/j.envres.2022.112711. Epub 2022 Jan 13. PMID: 35033552; PMCID: PMC8757643.
Corinne A., Packer A., Rukare D., *The new african union and its constitutive act*, The American Journal of International Law, Vol. 96, No. 2, 2002, pp. 365–379.
Cucinotta D., Vanelli M., *WHO declares COVID-19 a pandemic*, Acta Biomedica, Vol. 91, No. 1, 19 March 2020, pp. 157–160. doi: 10.23750/abm.v91i1.9397. PMID: 32191675; PMCID: PMC7569573.
Czupryński Andrzej, *Bezpieczeństwo w ujęciu teoretycznym*, in: Andrzej Czupryński Wiśniewski Zboina (ed.), *Bezpieczeństwo – badania, teoria, praktyka*, Józefów: CNBOP-PIB, 2015, pp. 9–24.
Diamond Barry, *The Bermuda agreement revisited: A look at the past, present and future of bilateral air transport agreements*, Journal of Air Law and Commerce, Vol. 41, 1975, pp. 419–496.
Don Harris, Neville A. Stanton, *Aviation as a system of systems: Preface to the special issue of human factors in aviation*, Ergonomics, Vol. 53, No 2, 2010, pp. 145–148. doi: 10.1080/00140130903521587.
Dube Kaitano, *Emerging from the COVID-19 Pandemic: Aviation recovery*, Challenges, and Opportunities, Aerospace, 2022, doi:10.20944/preprints202212.0198.v2.
Dubravka Aksamovic, Lidija Simunovic, *The EU scheme for the state aid rules in the air transport sector during the Covid-19 crisis*, Juridical Tribune, Vol. 12, No. 1, March 2022, pp. 51–67.
Eeckelaert Lieven, Annick Starren, Arjella van Scheppingen, David Fox, and Carsten Brück, *Occupational safety and health culture assessment - a review of main approaches and selected tools. Working environment information working paper*, European Agency for Safety and Health at Work, 2011.
Endsley Mica R., *Situation awareness in aviation systems*, in Garland, D. J., Wise, J. A., and Hopkin, V. D., (Eds.), Lawrence Erlbaum Associates, Mahwah, New Jersey: Handbook of Aviation Human Factors, 1999, pp. 257–276.
ESPON STUDY, *Geography of COVID-19 outbreak and first policy answers in European regions and cities*, Luxembourg: EPSON EGTC, 2020.
Etieyibo Edwin, Obvious Katsaura, Mucha Musemwa, *Politics and Decolonization in Africa: Theoretical Pointers and a Preamble*, Africa Today, Vol. 67, No. 4, 2021, pp. 2–9.
Evans G., Newnham J., *The penguin dictionary of international relations*, London: Penguin Books, 1998.
Feller S. Z., *Comment on "criminal jurisdiction over aircraft hijacking"*, Israel Law Review, Vol. 7, 2015, pp. 207–213.

Fiallos Fernando, *LACAC and current challenges of civil aviation in Latin America*, in: Pablo Mendes De Leon, Niall Buissing (eds.), Behind and Beyond the Chicago Convention: The Evolution of Aerial Sovereignty, alphen aan den rijn: Wolters Kluwer, 2019, pp. 83–96.

Gędek Stanisław, *Definiowanie ryzyka*, Prace Naukowe Uniwersytetu Ekonomicznego we Wrocławiu/Research Papers of Wrocław University of Economics, Nr 513, 2018, pp. 119–130.

Gertler Joseph Z., *Bilaterial Air Transport Agreements: Non-Bermuda Reflections*, Journal of Air Law and Commerce, Vol. 42, 1976, pp. 779–824.

Gryz Jerzy, *Współczesny paradygmat bezpieczeństwa międzynarodowego*, Rocznik Bezpieczeństwa Międzynarodowego, Vol. 1, 2019, pp. 11–27.

Grzywna Z., Limański A., Drabik I., *Zarządzanie bezpieczeństwem w portach lotniczych*, Zeszyty Naukowe Politechniki Śląskiej, Vol. 118, 2018, pp. 181–197.

Haig Brian, *Grounded theory as scientific method*, Philosophy of Education, 1995, pp. 1–11.

Haanappel P.P.C., *Bilateral Air Transport Agreements – 1913–1980*, The International Trade Law Journal, Vol. 5, 1980, pp. 241–267.

Haanappel P.P.C., *The law and policy of air space and outer space: A comparative approach*, Alphen aan den Rijn: Wolters Kluwer, 2003.

Hu Buwei, Shen Siqi, *An Overall Analysis of Risk and Risk Mane*, BCP Business & Management, Vol. 38, 2023, pp. 2182–2188.

Hughes Emily, *Meaninglessness and monotony in pandemic boredom*, Phenomenology and the Cognitive Sciences, Springer Nature, 2023, doi.org/10.1007/s11097-023-09888-0.

Jaworski Michał, Raglewski Janusz, *Polityka Just Culture w lotnictwie cywilnym z perspektywy podstaw odpowiedzialności karnej*, Kwartalnik Krajowej Szkoły Sądownictwa i Prokuratury, Zeszyt, Vol. 4, No. 24, Kraków 2016, pp. 5–16.

Kaitano Dube, Godwell Nhamo, David Chikodzi, *COVID-19 pandemic and prospects for recovery of the global aviation industry*, Journal of Air Transport Management, Vol. 92, 2021, pp. 1–12. https://doi.org/10.1016/j.jairtraman.2021.102022;

Kalic Milica, Babic Danica, Dozic Slavica, Kuljanin Jovana, Mijovic Nemanja, *Impact of covid-19 on the aviation industry: an overview of global and some local effects*, Anali Pravnog fakulteta u Beogradu, Vol. 70, No. 4, 2022, pp. 1079–1127, p. 1107. doi:10.51204/Anali_PFBU_22405A.

Kapchangah M. K., *Africa aviation security: Implications for peace and security*, Institute for Security Studies, 2008.

Kilar I., *Geneza funkcjonowanie Organizacji Międzynarodowego Lotnictwa Cywilnego*, p. 32., cited in Zajas S., *Organizacja Międzynarodowego Lotnictwa Cywilnego i jej wpływ na funkcjonowanie i rozwój lotnictwa*, Zeszyty Naukowe AON, Vol. 4, No. 101 2015, pp. 19–43.

Kondrakiewicz D., *System międzynarodowy jako kategoria w nauce o stosunkach międzynarodowych*, Teka Politologii i Stosunków Międzynarodowych, Nr 11, 2016, pp. 75–94.

Kopczewski Marian, Bednarczyk Weronika, Niedźwiecki Sebastian, *Programy prewencyjne elementem bezpieczeństwa na szczeblu lokalnym*, in: Wilk-Woś Zofia (ed.), *Bezpieczeństwo i zarządzanie kryzysowe. Bezpieczeństwo społeczności lokalnych*, Przedsiębiorczość i Zarządzanie, Lodz-Warszawa: Wyd. SAN, 2017, pp. 59–75.

Koziej Stanisław, *Bezpieczeństwo: istota, podstawowe kategorie i historyczna ewolucja*, Bezpieczeństwo narodowe, No. 2/2011, pp. 19–39.

Kraśnicka Izabela, *Standardy żeglugi powietrznej w działalności Organizacji Międzynarodowego Lotnictwa Cywilnego (ICAO)*, Warsaw: CH Beck 2019.

Kraśnicka Izabela, *66 Years of the Chicago convention on international civil aviation - new trends in the international law of the air*, Analele Universităţii "Constantin Brâncuşi" din Târgu Jiu, Seria Ştiinţe Juridice, Nr. 1/2010, pp. 194–212.

Kukułka J., *Problemy teorii stosunków międzynarodowych*, Warsaw: PWN, 1978.
Kukułka J., *Teoria stosunków międzynarodowych*, Warsaw: Scholar, 2000.
Kulikowski R., *Sterowanie w wielkich systemach*, Warsaw: Wydawnictwa Naukowo-Techniczne, 1970.
Lee Shu-Hui, Lee Kuan-Te, *The impact of pandemic-related stress on attentional bias and anxiety in alexithymia during the COVID-19 pandemic*, 2022, doi.org/10.21203/rs.3.rs-2410934/v1.
Maier M. W., *Architecting principles for system of systems*, Systems Engineering, Vol. 1, 1998, pp. 267–284.
Maxmen Amy, *Wuhan market was epicentre of pandemic's start, studies suggest*, Nature Magazine, Vol. 603, 27 February 2022, pp. 15–16. doi.org/10.1038/d41586-022-00584-8.
Mazrui Ali, A., Independent African states and the struggle for southern Africa, in The UNESCO Press: *The decolonization of Africa: southern Africa and the Horn of Africa*, UNESCO, 1981, pp. 13–24.
McKinney, Earl H. Jr., *Systems Theory Implications for Human Factors in Aviation*, Proceedings of the Human Factors and Ergonomics Society Annual Meeting, Vol. 41, No. 1, 1997, pp. 85–89.
Milligan, Jack, *Bet on the field: Why field preemption should apply to the federal aviation act*, Journal of Air Law and Commerce, Vol. 85, No. 3, 2020, pp. 507–535.
Moghtaderi Ali, Zocchi Mark S., Pines Jesse M., Venkat Arvind, Black Bernard, *Estimating the Uncertain Effect of the COVID Pandemic on Drug Overdoses*, 2023, doi.org/10.1101/2023.01.19.23284772.
Mohler Stanley, *Pilot fatigue manageable, but remains insidious threat*, Human Factors and Aviation Medicine, Vol. 45, No. 1, 1998, pp. 1–6.
Moriarty David, *Error management and standard operating procedures for organizations*, Practical Human Factors for Pilots, London: Academic Press, 2015.
Muller Roland, Wittmer Andreas, Drax Christopher, *Aviation risk and safety management: Methods and applications in aviation organizations*, Cham: Springer, 2014.
Muñoz-Marrón Daniel, *Human factors in aviation: CRM (Crew Resource Management)*, Papeles del Psicólogo/Psychologist Papers, Vol. 39, No. 3, 2018, pp. 191–199.
Perkowski Maciej, *Podmiotowość prawa międzynarodowego współczesnego uniwersalizmu w złożonym modelu klasyfikacyjnym*, Białystok: Temida 2, 2008.
Peterson Robert, *Impacts of airline deregulation*, TR NEWS, Vol. 315, 2018, pp. 10–21.
Pietraś Marek, *Bezpieczeństwo ekologiczne w Europie*, Lublin: Wydawnictwo UMCS, 1996.
Reason James, *Human error*, Cambridge University Press, Cambridge, 1990.
Reason James, *Human error: Models and management*, BMJ, Vol. 320, No. 7237, March 18, 2020, pp. 768–770. DOI: 10.1136/bmj.320.7237.768.
Reason James, Safety *paradoxes and safety culture*, Injury Control & Safety Promotion, Vol. 7, No. 1, 2000, pp. 3–14.
Rosicki Remigiusz, *O pojęciu i istocie bezpieczeństwa*, Przegląd Politologiczny, No. 3/2010, pp. 24–32.
Rothengatter Werner, Zhang Junyi, Hayashi Yoshitsugu, Nosach Anastasiia, Wang Kun, Oum Tae Hoon, *Pandemic waves and the time after Covid-19 – Consequences for the transport sector*, Transport Policy, Vol. 110, 2021, ISSN 0967-070X, pp. 225–237, https://doi.org/10.1016/j.tranpol.2021.06.003
Rysińska Irena, *Organizacje międzynarodowe. Zarys problematyki*, in: Parzymies Stanisław, Rysińska Irena (ed.), Polska w organizacja międzynarodowych, Warsaw, 2002, pp. 15–29.
Rysińska Irena, *Uczestnicy stosunków międzynarodowych, ich interesy i oddziaływania*, in: Haliżak Edward, Kuźniar Roman (ed.), Stosunki międzynarodowe: geneza, struktura, dynamika, Warsaw, 2000, pp. 86–106.

Sand P., de Sousa Freitas J., Pratt G.N., *An historical Survey on international Air Law before the Second World War*, McGill Law Journal, Vol. 7, No. 1, 1960–61, pp. 24–42.

Schlumberger Charles E., *Open skies for Africa implementing the yamoussoukro decision*, World Bank, Washington, 2010.

Schlumberger Charles E., Weisskopf Nora, *Is the Arab take-off imminent? Opportunities for the development of the North African air transport sector following the Arab Spring*, Annals of Air and Space Law, Vol. XXXVII, 2012, pp. 245–275.

Sekuła Paweł, *CZARNOBYL. Społeczno-gospodarcze, polityczne i kulturowe konsekwencje katastrofy jądrowej dla Ukrainy*, Kraków: Szwajpolt Fiol, 2014.

Shappel Scott, Wiegamnn Douglas, *The human factors analysis and classification system–HFACS*, Washington: FAA-Office of Aviation Medicine, 2000.

Silva Mario, Cardoso-Junior Moacyr, *Paradigm shift in safety management in the Brazilian army aviation: Proposal and validation of a rag questionnaire*, GEAR 2021, doi: 10.13140/RG.2.2.36039.42405.

Skyttner Lars, *General systems theory: Problems, perspectives, practice,* Singapore: World Scientific Publishing, 2005.

Smith Andrew W.M., Jeppesen Chris (ed.), *Britain, France, and the decolonization of Africa - Britain, France and the decolonization of Africa: Future imperfect?*, London: UCL Press, 2017.

Syahirah Syed Jaafar, *AirAsia, AirAsia X suspend flights, ground most planes; pay cut for top executives*, The Edge Markets, 26.03.2020.

Tikhonov A., Sazonov Andrey, *Major trends in aviation industry during COVID-19*, Journal of Applied Engineering Science, Vol. 20. No. 4, 2022, pp. 1093–1102.

Tiyanjana Maluwa, *Ratification of African union treaties: Law, policy & practice*, Melbourne Journal of International Law, Vol. 13, 2012, pp. 637–655.

Turner Barry A., *The sociology of safety*, in: I Blockley David (ed.), Engineering Safety, London: McGraw Hill, 1992, pp. 186–201.

Uttal B., *The corporate culture vultures*, Fortune Magazine, 17.10.1983, see more: Reason James, *Achieving a safe culture: Theory and practice*, Work and Stress, Vol. 12, No. 3, 1998, pp. 293–306.

Yablokov Alexey V., Nesterenko Vassily B., Nesterenko Alexey V., *Chernobyl: Consequences of the catastrophe for people and the environment*, New York, NY: Annals of the New York Academy of Sciences, Vol. 1181, No. 1, 2009, pp. 1–327; Chernobyl: Looking back to go forward, IAEA, Vienna, 2008.

Zając Grzegorz, *Contemporary political, legal and economic aspects of aviation safety*, International Journal of Social Science and Economic Research, Vol. 5, No. 9, September 2020, pp. 2417–2435.

Zając Grzegorz, *Dwustronne umowy o komunikacji lotniczej zawierane przez Polskę*, [Bilateral agreements on air transport concluded by the republic of Poland], in: „Przegląd Sił Powietrznych", No 4/06. Dowództwo Sił Powietrznych RP, Poznań 2006, pp. 84–94.

Zając Grzegorz, *Kryzys lotniczy w związku z Coronawirusem* [tr: Aviation crisis in connection with Coronavirus], in: Przegląd Komunikacyjny, 11/2020. Stowarzyszenie Inżynierów i Techników Komunikacji RP, Warsaw 2020, pp. 13–18.

Zając Grzegorz, *Podstawy prawne i funkcjonowanie przewoźników lotniczych i lotnisk w Europie*, [Legal basis and functioning of air carriers and airports in Europe]. Rambler, Warszawa, 2016.

Zając Grzegorz, *Rules and procedures of accident investigation in civil aviation,* Science & Military, Vol. 10, No 2, 2015, pp. 36–45.

Zalewska Monika, *The metaphorical aspect of Hans Kelsen's pure theory of law*, Prinicipia, No 65/2018. pp. 185–206.

Zdrodowski Bogdan, *Istota bezpieczeństwa państwa*, Annales Universitatis Paedagogicae Cracoviensis, Studia de Securitate, Vol. 9, No. 3, 2019, pp. 47–71.

Ziarko J., *Paradygmaty i orientacje badawcze w nauce o bezpieczeństwie*, Bezpieczeństwo. Teoria i praktyka, No. 1–2, 2008, pp. 9–21.
Zylicz Marek, *Prawo lotnicze międzynarodowe, europejskie i krajowe*, Warszawa: LexisNexis, 2002.

Internet source:

https://www.iata.org/en/pressroom/2022-releases/2022-03-01-01/, accessed 14.02.2024.
https://www.eurocontrol.int/news/eurocontrol-predicts-growth-aviation-traffic-over-next-8-months, accessed 12.02.2024.
https://www.eurocontrol.int/news/eurocontrol-predicts-growth-aviation-traffic-over-next-8-months, accessed 30.01.2024.
ICAO recommendations on COVID-19 risk management for international air travel, 18.01.2023, https://www.icao.int/Newsroom/Pages/New-ICAO-recommendations-issued-on-COVID-risk-assessment-and-mitigation-for-international-air-travel.aspx, accessed 30.01.2024.
Elliot Robinson, *Survey reveals popularity of train vs plane for business travel*, Global Railway Review, 6.04.2022, https://www.globalrailwayreview.com/news/133334/survey-reveals-popularity-train-plane-business-travel/ accessed 30.01.2024.
Hill, Jeremy, *Express jet airlines goes bankrupt in wake of split from united*, Bloomberg, 23.08.2022, https://www.bloomberg.com/news/articles/2022-08-23/expressjet-airlines-goes-bankrupt-in-wake-of-split-from-united accessed 15.01.2024.
Arthur Nelsen, *Airlines flying near-empty 'ghost flights' to retain EU airport slots*, The Guardian, 26.01.2022, https://www.theguardian.com/environment/2022/jan/26/airlines-flying-near-empty-ghost-flights-to-retain-eu-airport-slots, accessed 30.01.2024.
Charlotte Elton, *Half of all European flights were delayed last summer. Which airports were the worst - and best*? Euronews, 17.01.2023, https://www.euronews.com/travel/2023/01/16/half-of-all-european-flights-were-delayed-last-summer-which-airports-were-the-worst-and-be, accessed 30.01.2024.
Airport nightmares won't end this summer, experts say, CBS, 7.07.2022, https://www.cbc.ca/radio/thecurrent/the-current-for-july-6-2022-1.6511574/airport-nightmares-won-t-end-this-summer-experts-say-1.6512232 accessed 30.01.2024.
Pillar Wolfsteller, *Air Canada to cut 16,500 workers*, Flight Global, 30.03.2020, https://www.flightglobal.com/strategy/air-canada-to-cut-16500-workers/137622.article, accessed 30.01.2024.
Daly, Adam, *Aer Lingus to cut wages by 50% as airline reduces working hours for month of April*, The Journal.ie, 19.03.2020, https://www.thejournal.ie/aer-lingus-coronavirus-staff-wages-forsa-5051915-Mar2020/, accessed 1.02.2024.
2020 Worst Year in History for Air Travel Demand, IATA Press Release, 3.02.2021, https://www.iata.org/en/pressroom/pressroom-archive/2021-releases/2021-02-03-02/, accessed 30.01.2024.
International Aviation Trust Framework (IATF), https://www.icao.int/airnavigation/Pages/IATF.aspx, accessed 5.02.2024.
Morgan Sam, *EU circles around aircraft middle-seat issue in virus travel plans*, 13.05.2020, https://www.euractiv.com/section/aviation/news/eu-circles-around-aircraft-middle-seat-issue-in-virus-travel-plans/, accessed 30.01.2024.
Griff Zach, *How I secure empty middle seats — even if an airline isn't blocking them*, 18.04.2021, https://thepointsguy.com/news/tips-for-empty-middle-seat/, accessed 1.02.2024.
White Alexandra, 63% of U.S. consumers are willing to pay more to have seats blocked—here are the airline policies on this, Select, 2.12.2020, https://www.cnbc.com/select/coronavirus-airline-crowded-flight-policies/, accessed 20.01.2024.

FAA, Airport Rescue Grants, https://www.faa.gov/airports/airport_rescue_grants, accessed 30.01.2024.

U.S. Airlines, Aviation contractors to receive additional $15 billion under American rescue plan act, 3/16/2021, https://www.jdsupra.com/legalnews/u-s-airlines-aviation-contractors-to-2900824/, accessed 1/30/2024.

FAA, *Airport Improvement Program (AIP) 2021–2023 supplemental appropriation*, https://www.faa.gov/airports/aip/aip_supplemental_appropriation/2021, accessed 29.01.2024.

NBAA, *Provisions of interest to business aviation in the consolidated appropriations act of 2021*, 11.01.2021, https://nbaa.org/aircraft-operations/safety/coronavirus/provisions-of-interest-to-business-aviation-in-the-consolidated-appropriations-act-of-2021/, accessed 30.01.2024.

Petrauskaite Gabriele, *Berlin Brandenburg airport to receive €1.7 billion state aid*, 2.02.2022, https://www.aerotime.aero/articles/30122-eu-commission-approves-aid-to-brandenburg-airport, accessed 27.01.2024.

LOT Polish Airlines, https://www.lot.com/pl/en/corporate/state-aid, accessed 27.01.2024.

Report of the First Meeting of the Middle East Regional Aviation Safety Group, Cairo, Egypt, 18–19 September 2011, RASG-MID/1-REPORT. See, https://www.icao.int/MID/Documents/2011/RASG_MID_1/Docs/rasg_mid_1_Final_Report_EN.pdf, accessed 25.01.2024.

https://aviationbenefits.org/environmental-efficiency/climate-action/offsetting-emissions-corsia/corsia/corsia-explained/, accesse 29.01.2024.

http://icscc.org.cn/upload/file/20221215/20221215160026_47549.pdf, accessed 25.01.2023.

https://docplayer.net/84035733-International-civil-aviation-organization-aviation-security-and-facilitation-plan-development-group.html, accessed 25.01.2024.

https://uia.org/s/or/en/1100052983, accessed 18.01.2024.

https://acao.org.ma/site/en/page10.php?idem=2&pgi=12&cat=1, accessed 18.01.2024.

https://acao.org.ma/site/en/page10.php?idem=20&pgi=24&cat=333, accessed 18.01.2024.

https://acao.org.ma/site/en/page10.php?idem=2&pgi=26&cat=2, accessed 18.01.2024.

https://acao.org.ma/site/en/page10.php?idem=2&pgi=12&cat=1, accessed 18.01.2024.

Declaration of Riyadh, https://docplayer.net/84035733-International-civil-aviation-organization-aviation-security-and-facilitation-plan-development-group.html, accessed 25.01.2024.

Pacific aviation safety reports can be viewed: https://paso.aero/publications/#annualreports, accessed 27.01.2024.

Declaration of Riyadh on Aviation Safety and Facilitation, adopted by the Arab Civil Aviation Commission on 31 August 2016 in Riyadh, Saudi Arabia, https://docplayer.net/84035733-International-civil-aviation-organization-aviation-security-and-facilitation-plan-development-group.html, accessed 15.01.2024.

Stefan Ellerbeck, *The aviation sector wants to reach net zero by 2050. How will it do it?*, World Economic Forum, 9.12.2022, https://www.weforum.org/agenda/2022/12/aviation-net-zero-emissions/, accessed 31.01.2024.

STPO constitution, http://www.paclii.org/pits/en/treaty_database/1999/1.html, accessed 30.01.2024.

https://www.forumsec.org/who-we-arepacific-islands-forum/, accessed 30.01.2024.

RASG-APAC Regional Aviation Safety Priorities and Targets, https://www.icao.int/APAC/RASG/RASG%20eDocs/APAC%20Aviation%20Safety%20Priorities%20and%20Targets.pdf, accessed 10.01.2024.

https://paso.aero/about/paso/, accessed 20.01.2024.

https://www.atc-network.com/atc-organisations/paso-pacific-aviation-safety-office-vanuatu, accessed 28.01.2024.

https://paso.aero/our-work/audits-and-inspections/, accessed 28.01.2024.

https://paso.aero/about/paso/, accessed 20.01.2024.

Acuerdo Multilateral de Cielos Abiertos para Los Estados Miembros de La Comision Latinoamericana De Aviacion Civil, https://clac-lacac.org/multilateral-open-skies-agreement-2/?lang=en#eng-am_ta, accessed 4.01.2024.

https://www.srvsop.aero/site/wp-content/uploads/2017/02/AmmendReglSRVSOPJun2013.pdf, accessed 20.02.2024.

https://www.gov.br/anac/en/topics/international-activities/international-organizations/regional-aviation-safety-group-pan-america-rasg-pa, accessed 5.01.2024

https://www.icao.int/RASGPA/Pages/About.aspx, accessed 4.01.2024

https://clac-lacac.org/meetings/categories/asembly/?lang=en, accessed 31.01.2024.

https://clac-lacac.org/us/?lang=en#res-his_eng, accessed 22.01.2024.

http://news.bbc.co.uk/onthisday/hi/dates/stories/april/6/newsid_2472000/2472195.stm, accessed 3.02.2024.

https://www.icao.int/safety/Implementation/Pages/COSCAPs-RSOOs-RAIOs.aspx, accessed 20.01.2024.

https://ncaa.gov.ng/media/it3gdrxe/afi-min-ezulwini-declaration-rsoo_eng.pdf, accessed 10.01.2024.

https://www.lawinsider.com/dictionary/airprox, accessed 15.01.2024.

https://repository.uneca.org/ds2/stream/?#/documents/2288a96a-b678-507f-bd22-cd8e539b1baa/page/5, accessed 10.01.2024.

https://ncaa.gov.ng/media/it3gdrxe/afi-min-ezulwini-declaration-rsoo_eng.pdf, accessed 10.01.2024.

https://www.icao.int/MID/Documents/2011/RASG_MID_1/Docs/rasg_mid_1_Final_Report_EN.pdf, accessed 25.01.2024.

https://unitingaviation.com/regions/eurnat/european-regional-aviation-safety-group-rasg-eur/, accessed 17.01.2024.

https://www.icao.int/EURNAT/Pages/news_articles/20130127-rasg-eu.aspx, accessed 17.01.2024.

https://www.ecac-ceac.org/index.php/activities/safety/european-safety-and-air-navigation-coordination-group-esancg accessed 27.02.2024.

Code of Conduct on Cooperation in the Field of Accident/Incident Investigation. https://www.ecac-ceac.org/activities/safety/air-accident-and-incident-investigations, tostep, 27.02.2024.

https://www.ecac-ceac.org/about-ecac/member-states, accessed 2.02.2024.

https://www.easa.europa.eu/en/newsroom-and-events/press-releases/easaicao-forum-results-new-global-framework-regional-aviation, accessed 17.02.2024.

What Prompted Airline Deregulation 20 Years Ago? What were the objectives of that deregulation and how were they achieved?, 15.09.1998, Vancouver, http://corporate.findlaw.com/law-library/what-prompted-airline-deregulation-20-years-ago-what-were-the.html#sthash.I5IhRBGb.dpuf, accessed 23.02.2024.

https://www.icao.int/secretariat/legal/list%20of%20parties/2009_uicc_en.pdf, accessed 20.02.2024.

https://www.icao.int/secretariat/legal/List%20of%20Parties/Rome1952_EN.pdf, accessed 20.02.2024.

https://www.icao.int/secretariat/legal/List%20of%20Parties/Mtl99_EN.pdf, accessed 20.02.2024.

https://www.icao.int/secretariat/legal/List%20of%20Parties/Mtl71_EN.pdf, accessed 20.02.2024.

https://www.icao.int/secretariat/legal/List%20of%20Parties/Mtl71_EN.pdf, accessed 20.02.2024.

https://www.icao.int/secretariat/legal/List%20of%20Parties/Hague_EN.pdf, accessed 20.02.2024.

https://www.icao.int/secretariat/legal/List%20of%20Parties/Tokyo_EN.pdf, accessed 20.02.2024.

https://applications.icao.int/postalhistory/the_air_navigation_commission.htm, accessed 20.02.2024.

Campbell S., *Germanwings A320 crash: Rescuers continue search amid reports plane's black box is damaged*, Express, 25.03.2015, http://www.express.co.uk/news/world/566001/Plane-crash-horror-two-babies-among-150-dead-in-Germanwings-Alps-crash?_ga=1.63829675.581465833.1438252774, accessed: 11.01.2024.

Eric Marsden, *Safety culture. A contentious and confused notion*, https://risk-engineering.org/concept/safety-culture#ref-Turner1992, accessed 18.02.2024.

https://www.airsafety.aero/safety-information-and-reporting/safety-management-systems/safety-culture, accessed 27.02.2024.

Typical Systems in the Aviation Domain, https://ebrary.net/199963/engineering/typical_systems_aviation_domain, accessed 25.02.2024.

Reason James, *Human error*, op.cit., cited in https://www.airsafety.aero/safety-information-and-reporting/safety-management-systems/safety-culture, accessed: 27.02.2024.

The Compliance Program was modified in 2018 and in 2022. FAA's Compliance Program, 7.07.2022, https://www.faa.gov/about/initiatives/cp/compliance-program-and-airman-rights-brochure-e-mail-version, accessed 16.02.2024.

European Parliament, https://www.europarl.europa.eu/factsheets/pl/sheet/134/bezpieczenstwo-lotnicze, accessed 5.03.2024.

The Pure Theory of Law, Stanford Encyclopedia of Philosophy, 2002, https://plato.stanford.edu/entries/lawphil-theory/, accessed 15.03.2024.

ICCT, *Polishing my crystal ball: Airline traffic in 2050, https://theicct.org/global-aviation-airline-traffic-jan22/,* accessed 28.02.2024.

ACI, *What to expect: Latest air travel outlook reveals short- and long-term demand*, 22.02.2023, https://aci.aero/2023/02/22/what-to-expect-latest-air-travel-outlook-reveals-short-and-long-term-demand/, accessed 28.02.2024.

Index

Abuja: Safety Targets 119, 121, 123–126; Treaty 128
ACAO 156–159, 161, 163
AFCAC 82, 106, 116, 121, 123–131, 134–135, 147, 158
African Civil Aviation Commission *see* AFCAC
African Union *see* AU
air navigation: services 39, 85–86, 118, 122, 131, 144, 160; safety 48, 62, 77; and Commission 52–53, 55, 78, 114, 129, 158
air traffic management *see* ATM
airlines 96, 101, 120, 131, 147, 151, 160, 162, 168–172, 174–176, 179, 181, 182, 184
airports 2, 9, 13, 18, 24, 34, 39, 42, 45, 47, 49, 55, 61, 64–65, 70, 73, 77, 80, 86, 96–97, 100, 103, 113, 118, 122, 139–140, 144, 159–160, 167–171, 173, 175, 177–178, 183, 185, 190
air traffic management *see* ATM
Altmark judgment 177–178
American Rescue Plan Act *see* ARPA
annexes to the Chicago Convention 5, 15–16, 20, 31, 34, 42, 44–45, 50–52, 54–66, 70, 80–81, 87–88, 104, 117, 120, 126, 139, 141, 144–145, 150, 155
Apia Treaty 150–154
Arab Civil Aviation Organization *see* ACAO
ARPA 168, 170
ATM 2, 12, 18, 24, 34, 38, 55–56, 100, 103, 107, 112–113, 122
AU 119, 121, 127–129
aviation: codification 3, 5–6, 16–17, 36, 38–40, 42–43, 51, 56–57, 86, 91, 97–101, 111–112, 116, 118–120, 128, 133, 142, 147, 154, 156, 189–191; incidents 10, 16–22, 25–32, 39, 41, 57, 63, 65–66, 71, 79, 82, 86, 96–97, 102, 104, 111, 115, 191; and investigation 63, 86, 102, 104, 110–112, 127, 129, 134, 140

Beijing: Convection 45, 66; Protocol 69
bilateral air agreements 6, 14, 35, 37, 41, 43, 46–47, 55, 91–98, 101, 104–106, 112, 120, 133, 143–145, 158–159

CARES Act 168–169
Chicago Convention 14–16, 20, 31, 34, 37, 38, 42, 44–62, 65, 70, 80–81, 83–85, 87, 92–93, 96, 104, 117, 120, 126, 128, 131, 133, 136, 139, 141, 143–145, 150–151, 155
compensation system 6, 10, 42, 45, 71–77, 177–178
Consolidated Appropriations Act 168–170
coronavirus *see* COVID-19
COSCAP NA 90, 149–150
COSCAP SA 90, 149–150
COSCAP SEA 88, 90, 149–150
COVID-19 1–3, 6–7, 81, 84, 113–114, 124–126, 135, 149, 161–162, 164–176, 178–187, 190

Damascus Agreement 159
de minimis aid 176, 178

EASA 38, 49, 83, 88, 90–91, 100, 102–110, 113–116, 123, 127, 134, 147, 166, 174
ECAC 105, 107, 112, 135, 158, 166
EUROCONTROL 32, 80, 100, 105, 107, 110, 112, 158, 166, 187
European Civil Aviation Conference *see* ECAC
European Organization for the Safety of Air Navigation *see* EUROCONTROL
European Union Aviation Safety Agency *see* EASA

Ezulwini Declaration 106, 117, 119, 122–123

GANP 77, 148, 161
GASP 57, 77–78, 80–82, 115
Global Air Navigation Plan *see* GANP
Global Aviation Safety Plan *see* GASP

Hague Convention 6, 16, 45, 66–70, 96, 126, 144
human factors 5, 18, 21–23, 25–28, 30

IATA 38, 80, 105, 122–123, 140, 179–182, 187
ICAO: Council 45, 49, 51, 58, 78, 82, 129, 131, 147; Assembly 48, 77–78, 85; regional office 54, 79, 114–115, 139
incident reporting 20, 31–32, 61, 81
International Air Transport Association *see* IATA
International Civil Aviation Organization *see* ICAO

Just Culture 18, 20–21, 29

LACAC 91, 132, 134–139, 141–142, 145–147, 158
Latin American Civil Aviation Commission *see* LACAC
liberalization 36, 42, 92–95, 97–98, 102, 119–120, 126, 132, 142, 146, 158–159
lockdown 166, 172

Milligan, J. 19, 39
Montreal Convention 6, 16, 45, 66, 69–77

open skies: regulations 93, 98; in Latin America 142–146, in the Middle East 158–159
oversight *see* safety oversight; safety oversight system

Pacific Aviation Safety Office *see* PASO
Pacific Islands Civil Aviation Safety and Security Treaty *see* PICASST
pandemic restrictions 173, 176
pandemic *see* COVID-19
paradigms: of international security 5, 12–14, 189realistic 5, 13, 189liberal 5, 13–14, 189; constructivist 5, 13–14, 189; liberal 5, 13–14, 189; realistic 5, 13, 189
PASO 88, 90, 149–150, 152–154
PICASST 151
preemptive safety 18
PSO 176–178
public service obligations *see* PSO

quarantine 172–173

RAIO 127, 140
RASG 79–80, 82–83
RASG-AFI 83, 125, 131–132
RASG-APAC 83, 147–148
RASG-EUR 114–115
RASG-MID 83, 114, 156, 161–163
RASG-PA 83, 137, 139–140
Reason, J. 21, 27, 29–30
Reason's Model 26
Regional Accident and Incident Investigation Organization *see* RAIO
Regional Aviation Safety Group for Africa and the Indian Ocean *see* RASG-AFI
Regional Aviation Safety Group for Europe *see* RASG-EUR
Regional Aviation Safety Group *see* RASG
Regional Aviation Safety Group–Asia & Pacific *see* RASG-APAC
Regional Aviation Safety Group–Middle East *see* RASG-MID
Regional Aviation Safety Group–Pan America *see* RASG-PA
Regional Safety Oversight Organization *see* RSOO
risk: identification 31; assessment 32, 138, 186mitigation 32; monitoring 32management 5, 23, 27–28, 30–34, 44, 66, 81, 104, 113, 148, 161–162, 186; mitigation 32; monitoring 32
Riyadh Declaration 154–155
RSOO 54, 78–79, 83, 88–89, 91, 111, 117, 122–123, 127, 137, 140–141, 150, 156, 160–161

safety culture 5, 19–21, 23, 28–30, 33, 39, 117, 138
safety: management 12, 15, 20, 31, 38, 57, 60–61, 65–66, 80–82, 88, 104, 107, 140, 150; oversight 2, 6, 10, 15, 31, 33, 54, 57, 64, 66, 78–80, 82–91, 97–98, 100, 102–103, 105–108, 110–111, 113–114, 117, 121, 123, 127, 131, 137–141, 148–152, 154–156, 160, 162–164, 185; oversight system 33, 84–87, 113, 117, 123, 131, 155, 160, 162; performance 15, 18, 21, 28, 105; risk 15, 18, 32, 34, 44, 66, 78–79, 87, 105, 161

Safety Management System *see* SMS
SARPs 10, 54, 57–58, 85, 89, 129, 134, 141, 145, 148, 150
SES 107
Single European Sky *see* SES
SES 107
SMS 15, 18, 28, 34, 65–66, 79–80, 122, 148
standards and recommended practices *see* SARPs
system theory 5, 23–24

terrorist attacks 16–17, 33–34, 67, 94, 96, 155
theories of aviation safety *see* system theory; human factors; risk management; and safety culture
Tokyo Convention 45, 66–67
Tokyo-Hague-Montreal system 16, 96, 126, 144
Tokyo-Hague-Montreal-Beijing system 6, 45, 66, 70
Tokyo-Hague-Montreal system 16, 96, 126, 144

Universal Safety Oversight Audit Program *see* USOAP
use it or lose it slot rule 183
USOAP 57, 79, 85–86, 121

Vaccination 166, 173, 185, 187

Warsaw-Montreal system 6, 45, 71

Yamoussoukro Decision 119–121, 128, 159
Yamoussoukro Declaration 119–120, 127

For Product Safety Concerns and Information please contact our EU representative GPSR@taylorandfrancis.com
Taylor & Francis Verlag GmbH, Kaufingerstraße 24, 80331 München, Germany

www.ingramcontent.com/pod-product-compliance
Ingram Content Group UK Ltd.
Pitfield, Milton Keynes, MK11 3LW, UK
UKHW022042061126
477531UK00009B/498
* 9 7 8 1 0 3 2 9 0 4 1 3 9 *